Artificial Brilliance: Crafting Jewelry Inspired by the Masters

by Aleksandr Makarov

From Inspiration to Creation: How AI is Transforming Jewelry Design

Artificial Brilliance Crafting Jewelry Inspired by the Masters

Aleksandr Makarov

Published by Aleksandr Makarov, 2024.

While every precaution has been taken in the preparation of this book, the publisher assumes no responsibility for errors or omissions, or for damages resulting from the use of the information contained herein.

ARTIFICIAL BRILLIANCE CRAFTING JEWELRY INSPIRED BY THE MASTERS

First edition. April 27, 2024.

Copyright © 2024 Aleksandr Makarov.

ISBN: 979-8224878918

Written by Aleksandr Makarov.

Unlocking the Mysteries of Neural Networks: My First Step on a Journey of Creativity

I have always been a huge fan of Freywille jewelry. These Austrian pieces are true works of art! Their unique style, inspired by art and culture from different eras and traditions, is simply captivating. But who would have thought that I could create something similar with the help of a neural network, since drawing is not my strong suit!

But I finally took the plunge and gave it a try. I fired up the neural network and began to experiment. In the process of creating images of Freywille jewelry, I felt like I was traveling through time and space. And then, by choosing the right description for the Lexica neural network, I got images of a bracelet in the style of Gustav Klimt, very similar to those produced by Freywille.

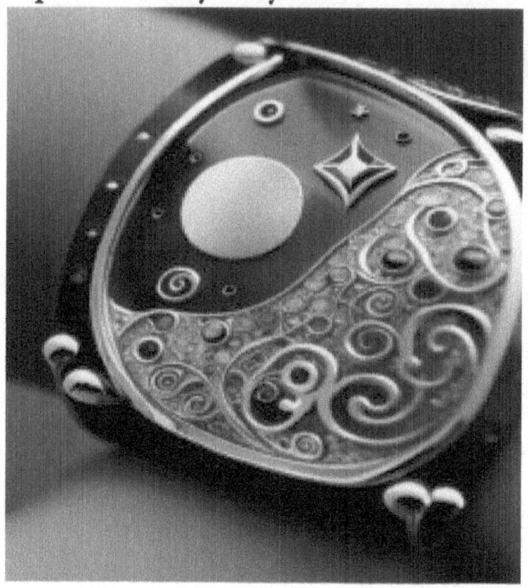

So, dear friends, if you also dream of jewelry masterpieces but don't consider yourself an artist, don't give up! A neural network will always help you, capable of turning your creative experiments into a real adventure. And who knows, maybe your neural network creation will become the next hit in the fashion world!

Bold Traditions

Are you a jewelry lover with a passion for art? Have you ever wondered how you can combine the two and create stunning pieces that are truly unique? Look no further than the world of neural networks!

With the help of neural networks, you can create jewelry inspired by the works of famous artists like Picasso and Kandinsky. Imagine wearing earrings that capture the essence of a Picasso painting, or a necklace that embodies the vibrant colors of a Kandinsky masterpiece.

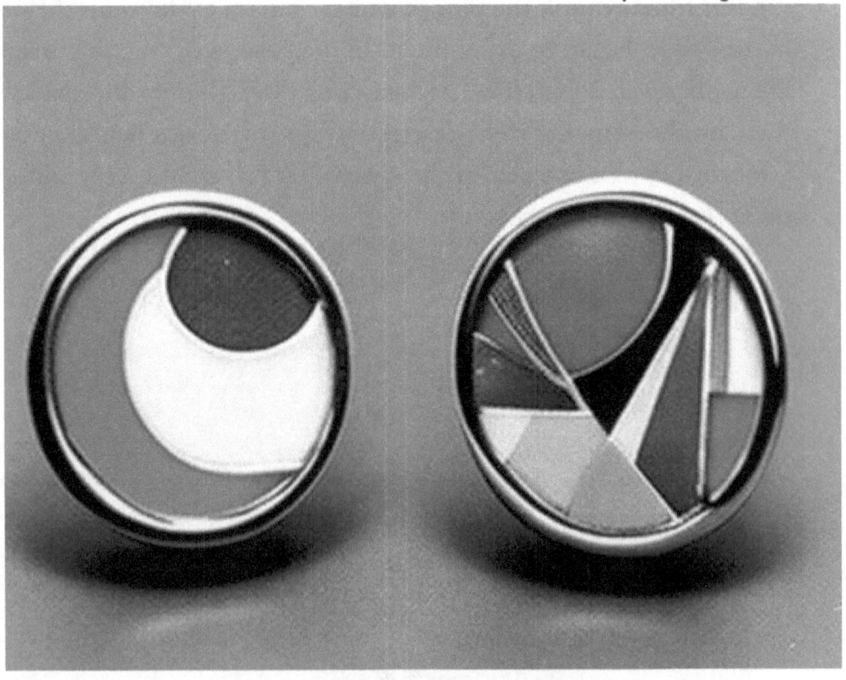

In our book, "Artificial Brilliance: Crafting Jewelry Inspired by the Masters," we'll show you how to use these cutting-edge technologies to create stunning jewelry that reflects your favorite artist's style. We'll take you through the process step-by-step, to bring your designs to life.

But this book isn't just about teaching you how to use neural networks. We want to inspire you to create your own unique designs and to explore the creative possibilities that these technologies offer. We'll share our experiences and insights so you can develop your skills and unleash your own creativity.

Don't miss out on this opportunity to learn how to create beautiful jewelry that reflects your love of art. "Artificial Brilliance: Crafting Jewelry Inspired by the Masters" is your ultimate guide to exploring the intersection of art, technology, and creativity. Get ready to embark on an exciting journey of discovery and innovation!

First, we'll need to study the works of these artists to gain a deeper understanding of their styles and creative processes. Neural networks can still be a helpful tool in analyzing these works, but we'll also need to explore traditional techniques like sketching, painting, and sculpting to fully capture their essence.

Once we have a strong understanding of the artists' styles, we can use these elements to create jewelry pieces using a range of handmade techniques, such as metalsmithing, wire wrapping, and beadwork. We can create earrings in the style of Van Gogh or a necklace inspired by Matisse, all with the unique touch of handmade craftsmanship.

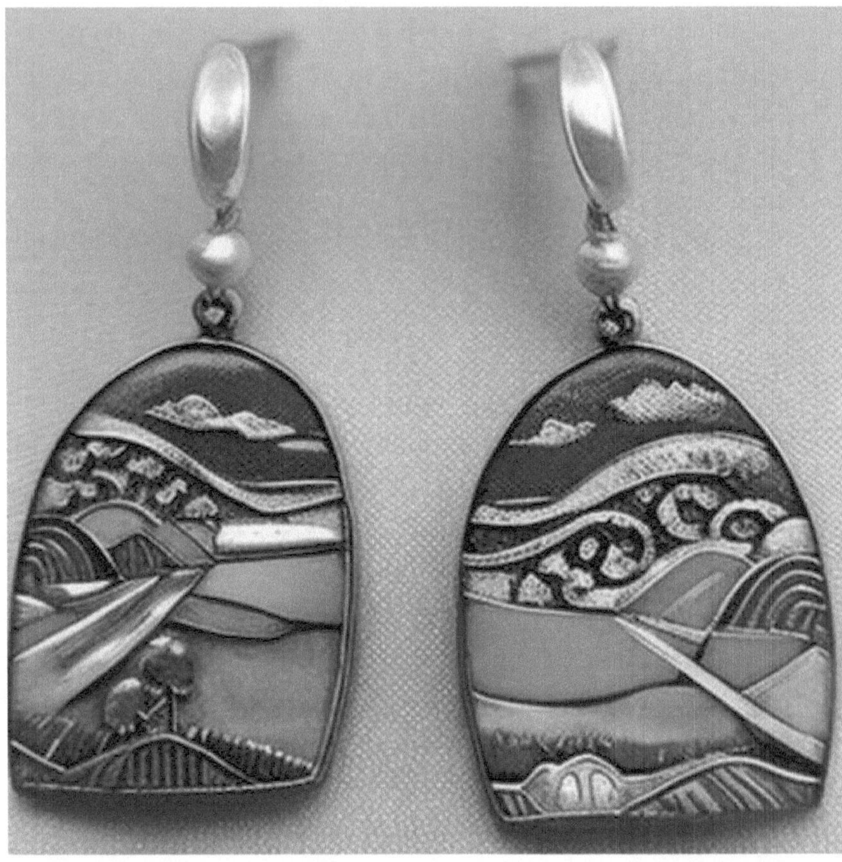

Our book will showcase several jewelry-making projects, detailing each step of the process and incorporating both the use of neural networks and handmade techniques. We'll share our insights and experiences to help readers create their own stunning jewelry pieces.

It's important to remember that handmade techniques are not just a nostalgic throwback to the past, but a powerful and creative way to bring the unique style of an artist to life in a one-of-a-kind piece of jewelry.

The book "Artificial Brilliance: Crafting Jewelry Inspired by the Masters" will serve as a valuable resource for anyone looking to explore the intersection of technology and traditional craftsmanship in their creative endeavors.

Here's a guide on how to use Bing Image Creator to make beautiful images:

1. Open the Bing chatbot in any messenger or on the websitehttps://www.bing.com/chat.

2. Select the "Creative" mode in the chatbot settings. This will allow you to use the Bing Image Creator feature, which can create images based on your requests.

3. Write to the chatbot what image you want to receive. You can use helper words that will prompt the neural network about the style, quality, or theme you want. For example, you can write "Create an image of a dog in a pirate costume" or "Create an image of a city of the future in a cyberpunk style."

4. Wait a few seconds while the chatbot processes your request and creates an image. You will see it in the chat and be able to save it to your device or share it with friends.

5. If you don't like the image or want to change something on it, you can write your wishes to the chatbot. For example, you can write "Make the dog bigger" or "Change the background color to green." The chatbot will try to take your wishes into account and create a new image.

6. Repeat steps 3-5 until you get the desired image. You can create as many images as you want and experiment with different requests and helper words.

Using Bing Image Creator is a fun and exciting way to unleash your creativity and bring your imagination to life. With just a few clicks, you can turn your ideas into stunning images that you can share with the world. So go ahead, give it a try, and let your creativity soar!

Get Started with AI: Best Free Neural Networks to Try

Let me introduce you to some incredible neural networks that offer free usage plans! Are you ready to unleash your creativity and produce amazing images? Then check out Lexica.art, where you can generate up to 100 high-quality images for free each month. And if you need more, don't worry, they also offer paid plans that provide even better results with their upgraded model, Aperture.

Creating images with Lexica.art is as easy as pie! Just enter a prompt in English, specify any features you don't want to appear in the image, adjust the image size, and then hit create. That's it! You'll be amazed at the stunning images it generates. And if you want to enhance or modify your image further, you can experiment with various tools to make it even better.

Prompt: Faberge style brooch with blue enamel background and gold floral design. The brooch has a large oval ruby in the center and four smaller diamonds around it. The brooch is made of 18 carat gold.

Got four great pictures.

But that's not all, folks! Another amazing neural network you should check out is nightcafe.studio[1]. It offers a variety of tools for unleashing your creativity, from using the Stable Diffusion and

---

1.   https://nightcafe.studio/

DALLE-2 neural networks to creating unique works of art based on your own uploaded images.

But that's not all - nightcafe.studio goes even further by allowing you to upload your own images and transform them into unique works of art. Want to see your pet transformed into a surreal masterpiece, or turn a landscape into an otherworldly dreamscape? With nightcafe.studio, the possibilities are endless.

We insert the same prompt.

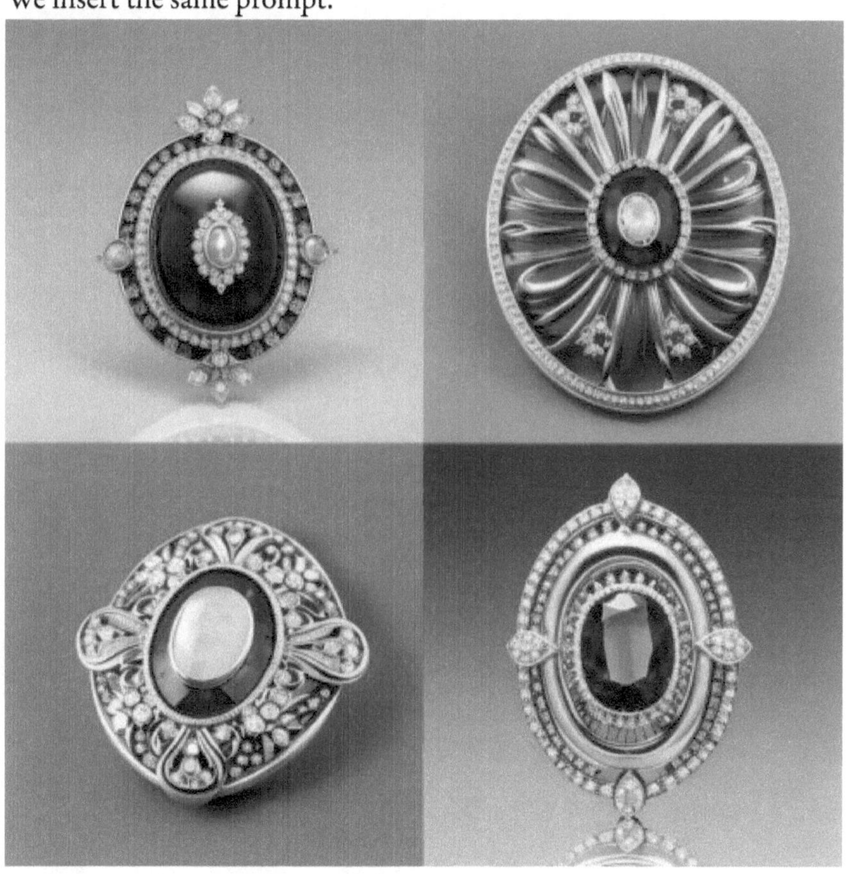

And let's not forget about DREAM AI https://dream.ai/, which offers up to four image generations with their paid plan, all with various styles to choose from. You can create the most amazing works of art with just one prompt!

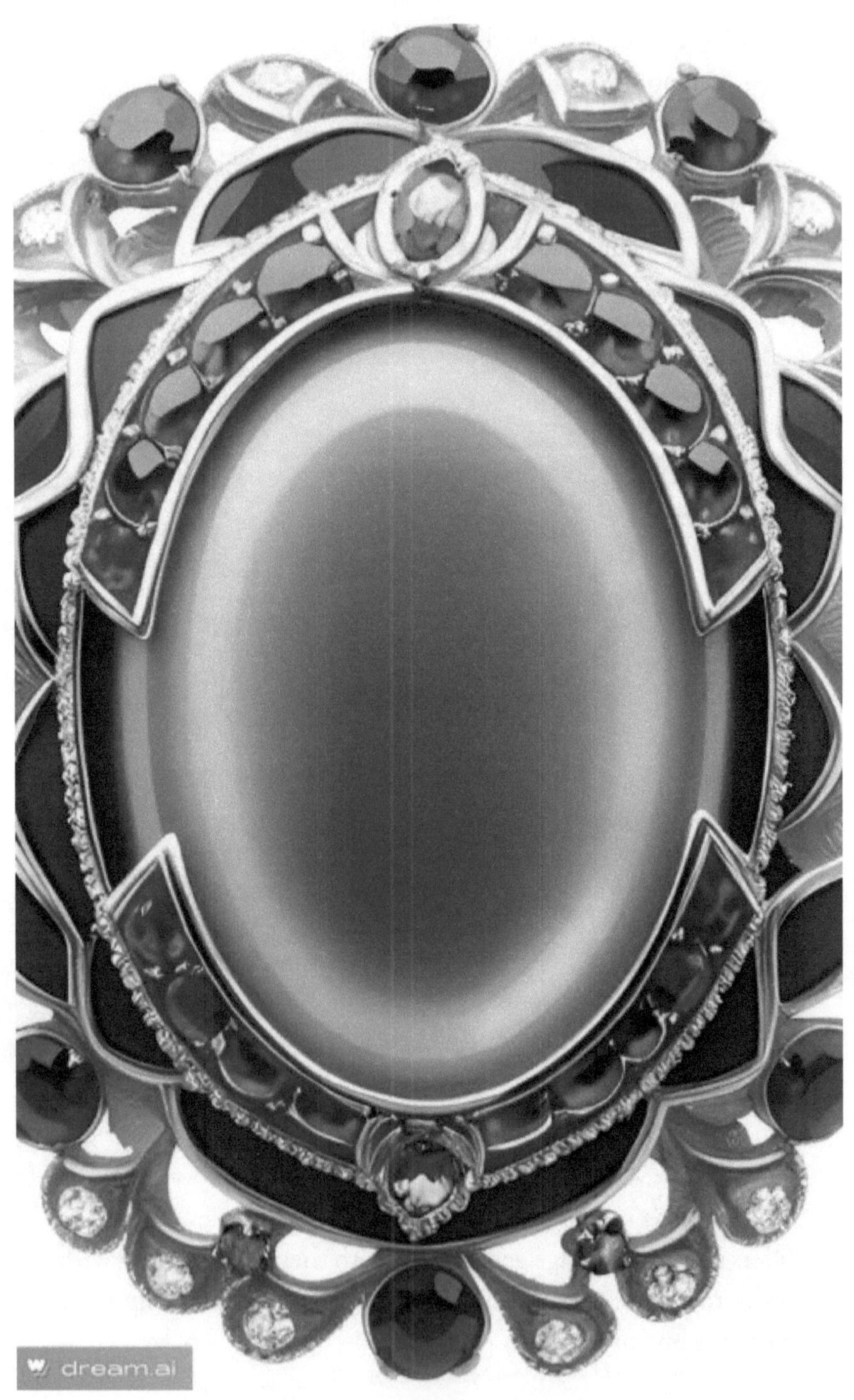

Are you ready to unleash your imagination and create something truly unique and breathtaking? Look no further than Playgroundai https://playgroundai.com/! This incredible platform is taking the world by storm with its state-of-the-art neural networks and innovative tools.

To get started, simply visit the Playgroundai website and click on the "Create" button in the top right corner. Then, in the "Prompt" field located in the upper left corner, enter the text you want to use as your inspiration. Maybe you're dreaming of a brooch in the style of Fabergé, or perhaps you have something entirely different in mind. Whatever your vision, Playgroundai is here to help you bring it to life.

Once you've entered your prompt, click "Generate" in the bottom left corner to start the magic. In just seconds, you'll be amazed at the incredible results that the neural network produces. Whether you're a professional artist or just starting out, Playgroundai offers endless possibilities for exploring your creativity and creating something truly remarkable.

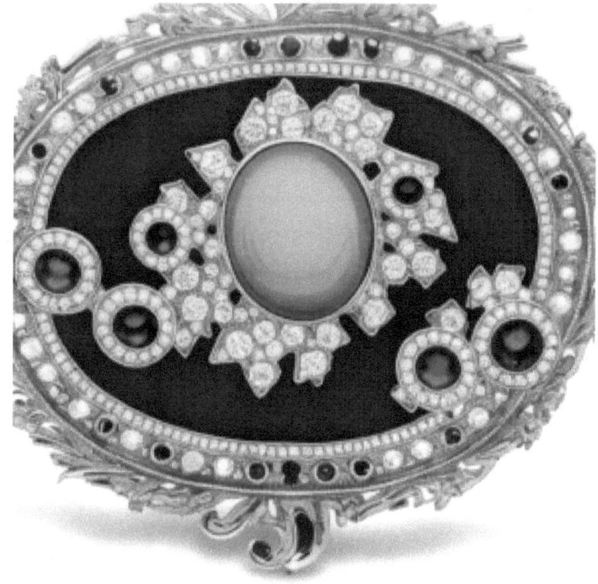

So what are you waiting for? Let your imagination run wild with these incredible neural networks and see what you can create. And don't forget to share your masterpieces with your friends and colleagues. Get started now and watch as your creativity flourishes like never before!

Alright, let's get down to business and create some stunning images! Have you heard of Deep Dream Generator https://deepdreamgenerator.com/? It's a powerful tool that can turn your wildest imaginations into reality.

First things first, registration is a breeze. Just enter your email address and confirm it through the email they send you. Easy peasy.

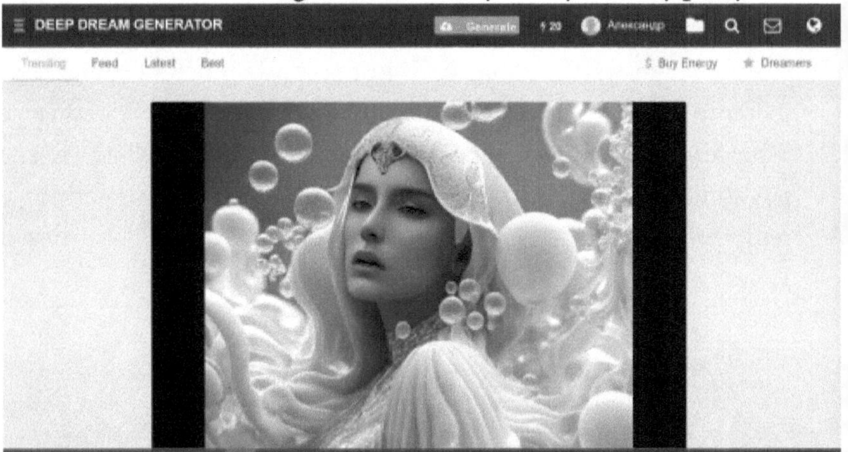

Now, let's dive into the fun part. Click on the orange button that says "Generate" on the top right corner of the main page, and you'll be taken to the image creation section, Text 2 Dream.

At the top of the page, you'll see the Text Prompt field, where you can enter a text query in English. Get ready to let your imagination run wild because this is where the magic happens.

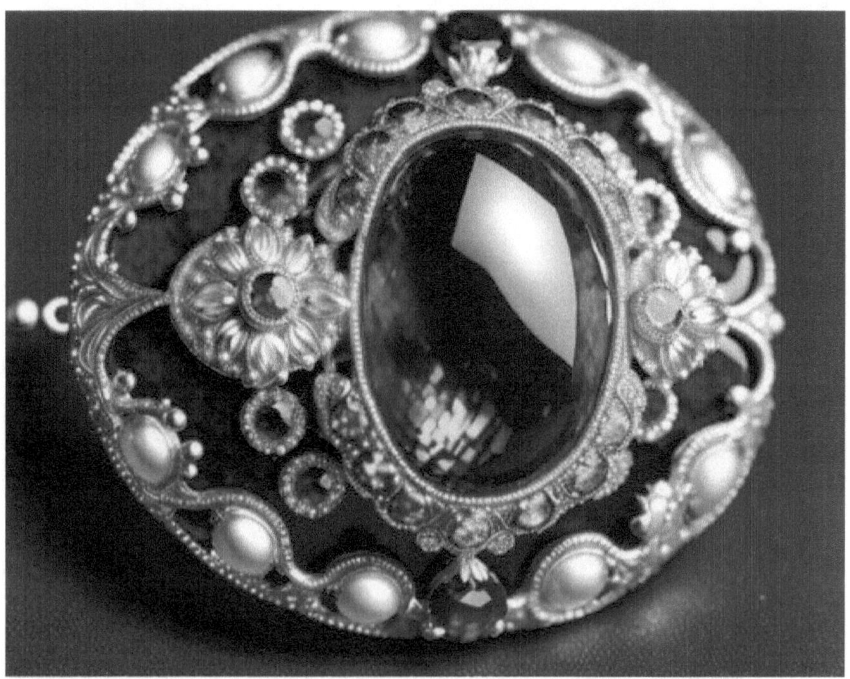

With Deep Dream Generator, you can create images that are beyond your wildest dreams. Just type in a phrase or word, and watch as it's transformed into a stunning work of art.

You can also adjust the Style and Model parameters to fine-tune your image to your liking. Want a dreamy watercolor effect? No problem. How about a futuristic neon look? Done.

And the best part? You can download your creations in high-resolution quality, perfect for sharing on social media or printing out and displaying in your home.

So, what are you waiting for? Let your creativity soar and start generating some amazing images with Deep Dream Generator today!

Discovering the World of Popular Jewelry Styles

Jewelry has been a part of human culture for thousands of years, and it has evolved alongside the changing trends, cultures, and aesthetics.

Today, there are countless jewelry styles, each with its unique history, symbolism, and design.

Let's explore some of the most popular jewelry styles that are used today to create stunning and exquisite pieces.

Baroque Style:

The Baroque style emerged in the 17th century in Europe, and it's characterized by its opulent, dramatic, and ornate designs. Baroque jewelry often features elaborate details, such as intricate metalwork, gemstones, and pearls, and it's perfect for those who want to make a bold and luxurious statement.

Victorian Style:

The Victorian style spans the reign of Queen Victoria from 1837 to 1901, and it's characterized by its romantic, sentimental, and ornate designs. Victorian jewelry often features intricate metalwork, filigree, and gemstones, and it's known for its symbolism and sentimentality.

Romanticism Era:

The Romanticism era flourished in the 18th and 19th centuries, and it's characterized by its emotional, mystical, and imaginative designs. Romanticism jewelry often features nature-inspired motifs, such as flowers, leaves, and animals, and it's perfect for those who seek a poetic and dreamy aesthetic.

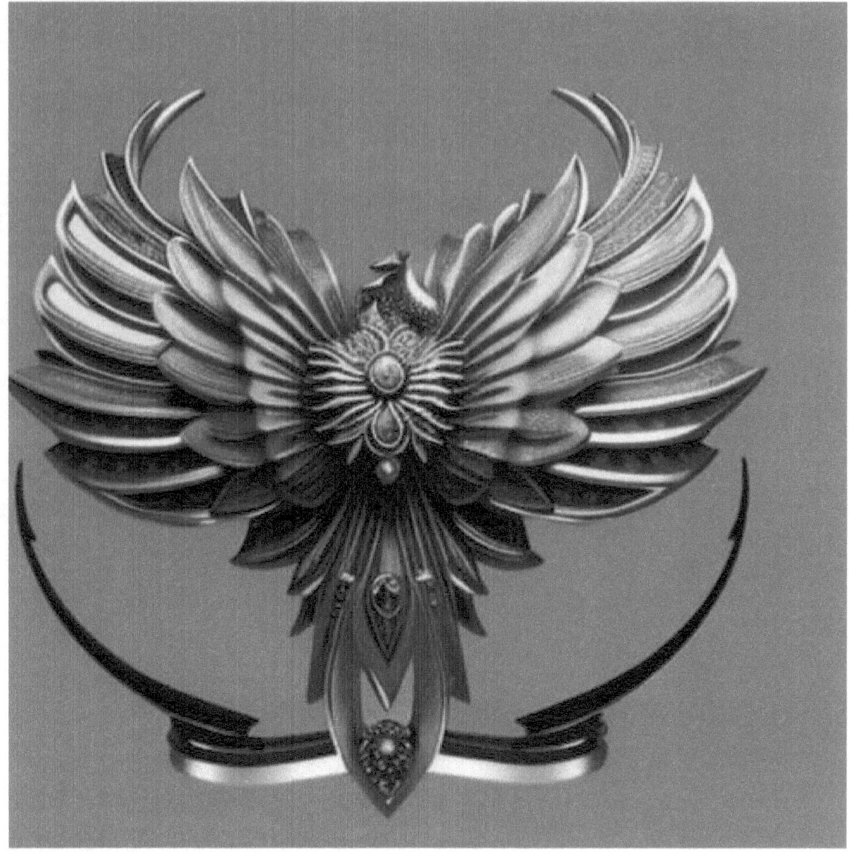

Neo-Gothic Style:

The Neo-Gothic style emerged in the 19th century as a revival of the medieval Gothic style, and it's characterized by its dark, ornate, and mysterious designs. Neo-Gothic jewelry often features symbols and motifs inspired by Gothic architecture, such as arches, spires, and gargoyles, and it's perfect for those who appreciate the eerie and macabre.

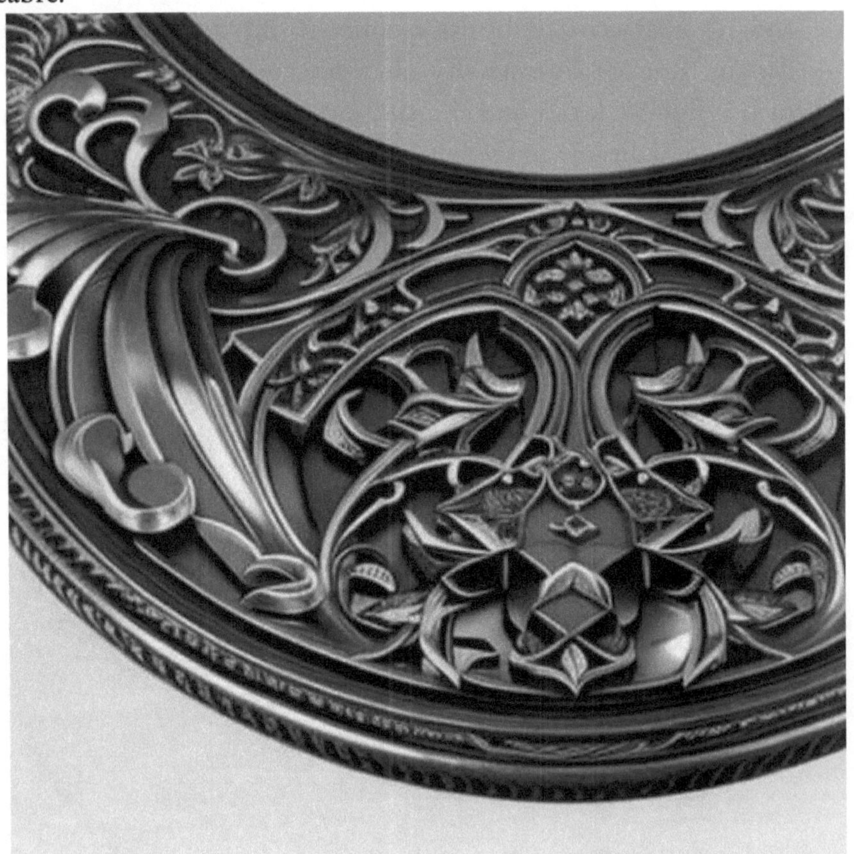

Neo-Renaissance Style:

The Neo-Renaissance style emerged in the 19th century as a revival of the Renaissance style, and it's characterized by its opulent, detailed, and classical designs. Neo-Renaissance jewelry often features elements of classical architecture, such as columns, friezes, and pediments, and it's perfect for those who appreciate the grandeur and elegance of classical art.

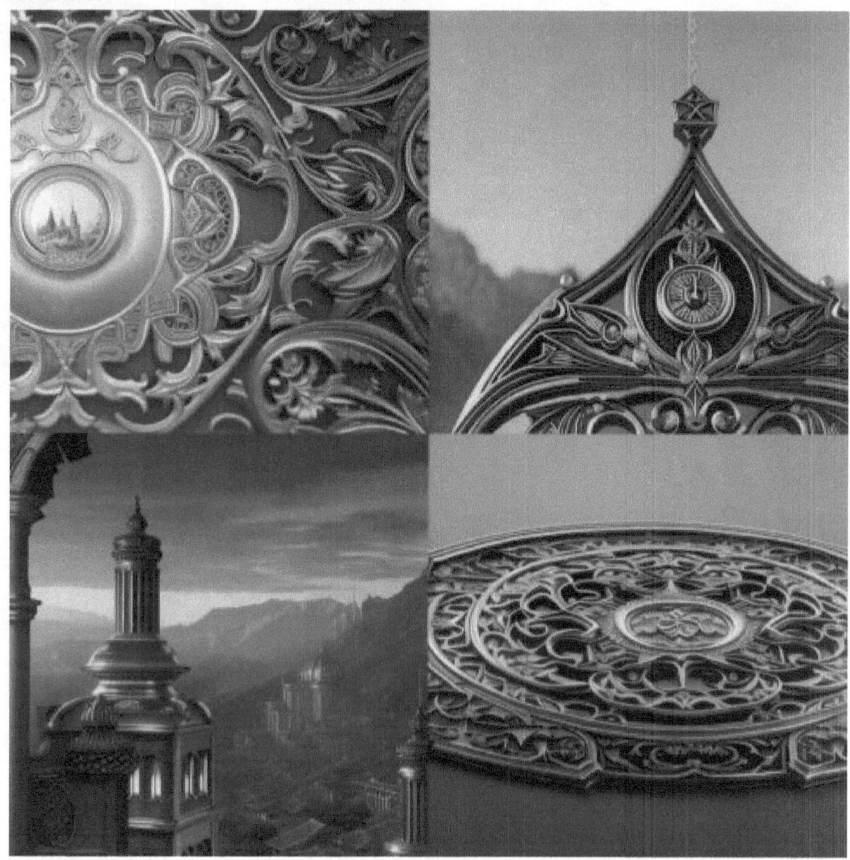

Egyptian Style:

The Egyptian style emerged in the early 20th century, and it's characterized by its exotic, mystical, and symbolic designs. Egyptian jewelry often features motifs inspired by ancient Egyptian art, such as hieroglyphs, scarabs, and sphinxes, and it's perfect for those who seek   a   mystical   and   exotic   aesthetic.

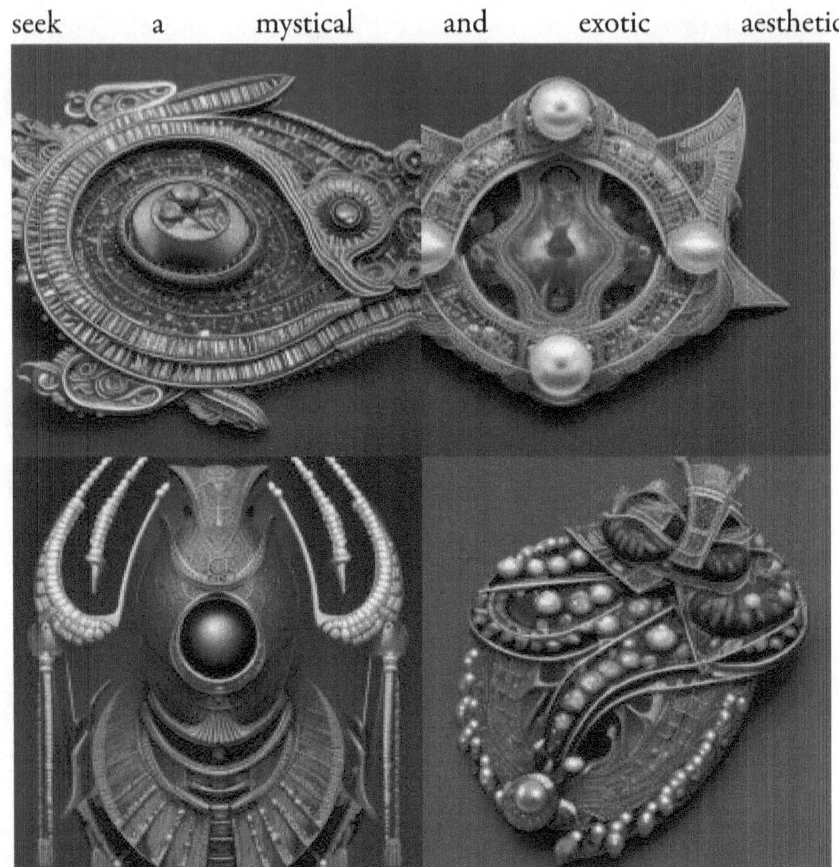

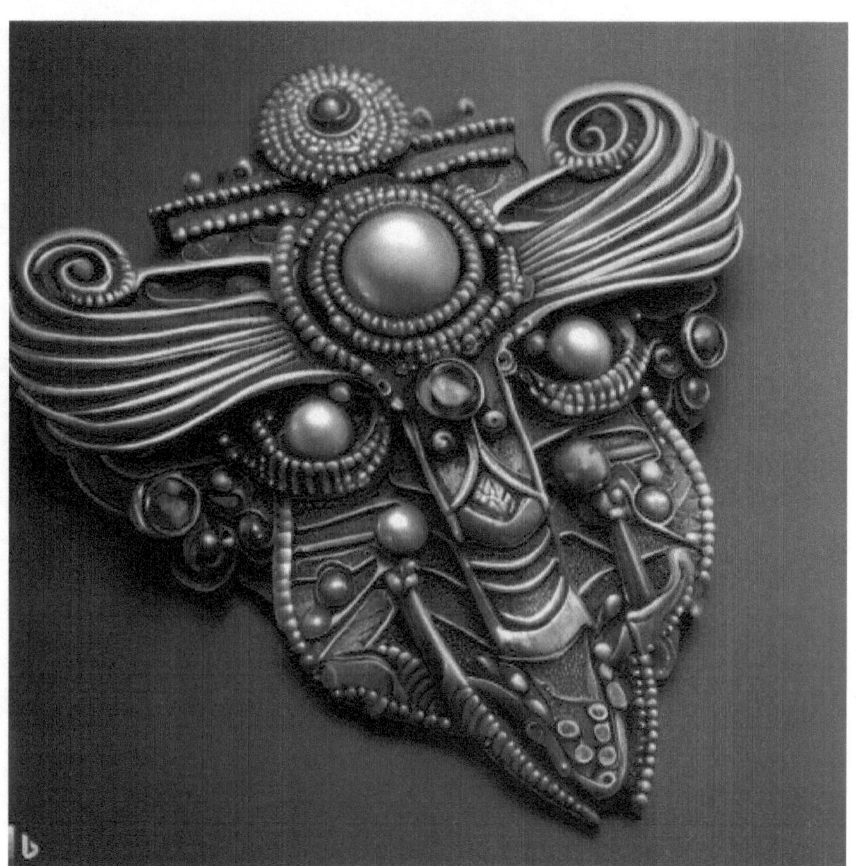

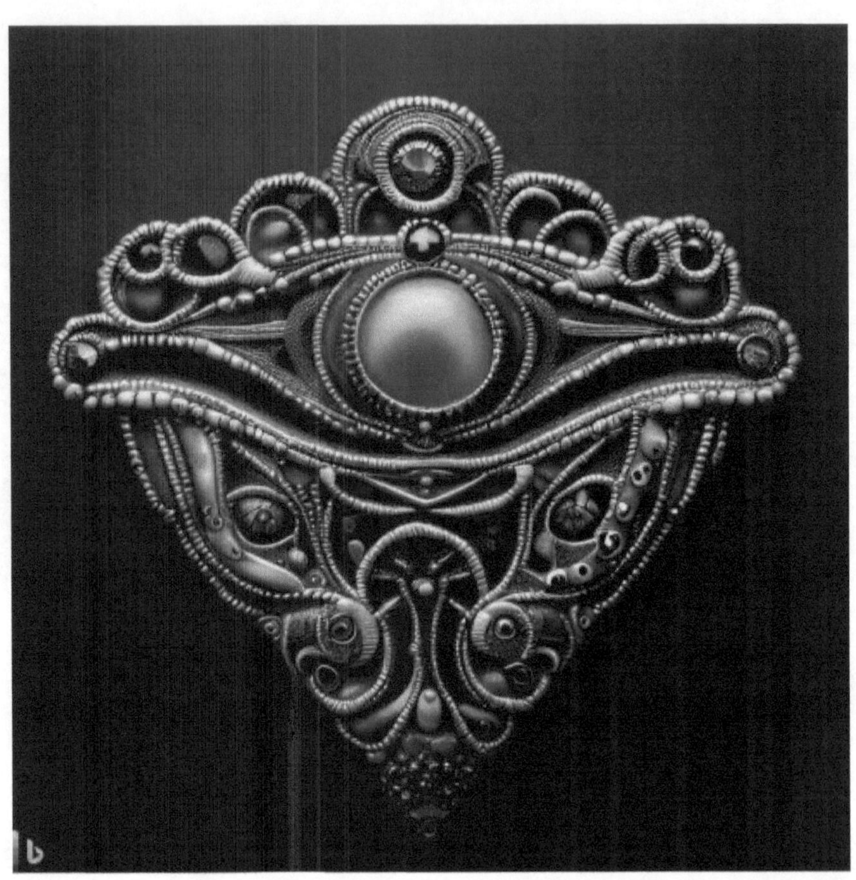

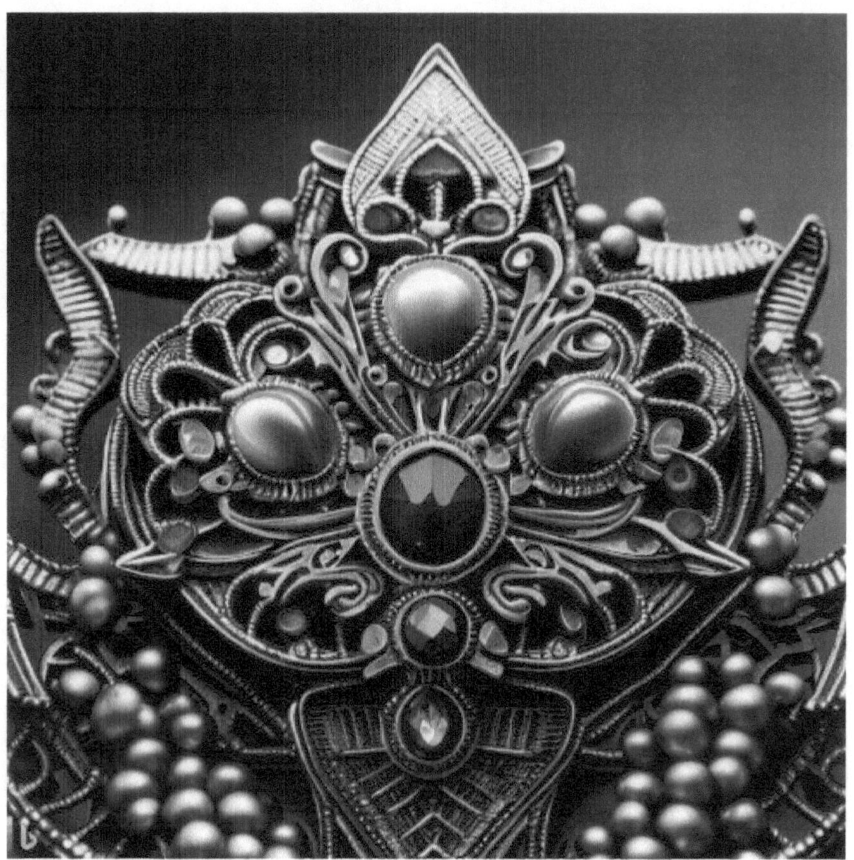

Greek Style:

The Greek style emerged in the ancient Greek civilization, and it's characterized by its simple, elegant, and timeless designs. Greek jewelry often features geometric shapes, such as circles, triangles, and squares, and it's known for its purity, symmetry, and balance.

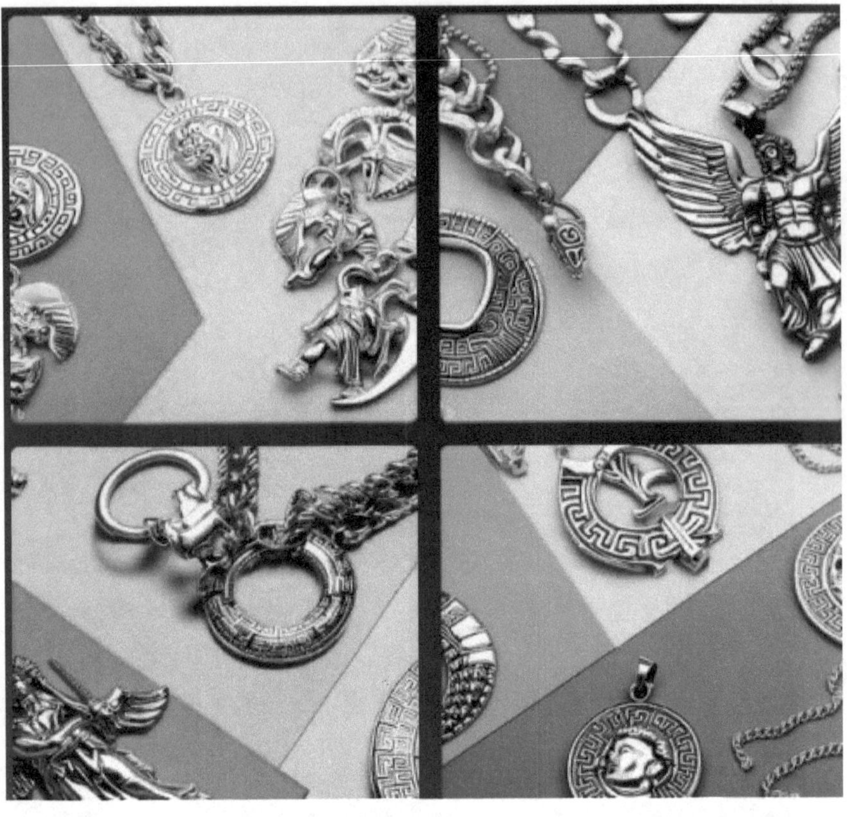

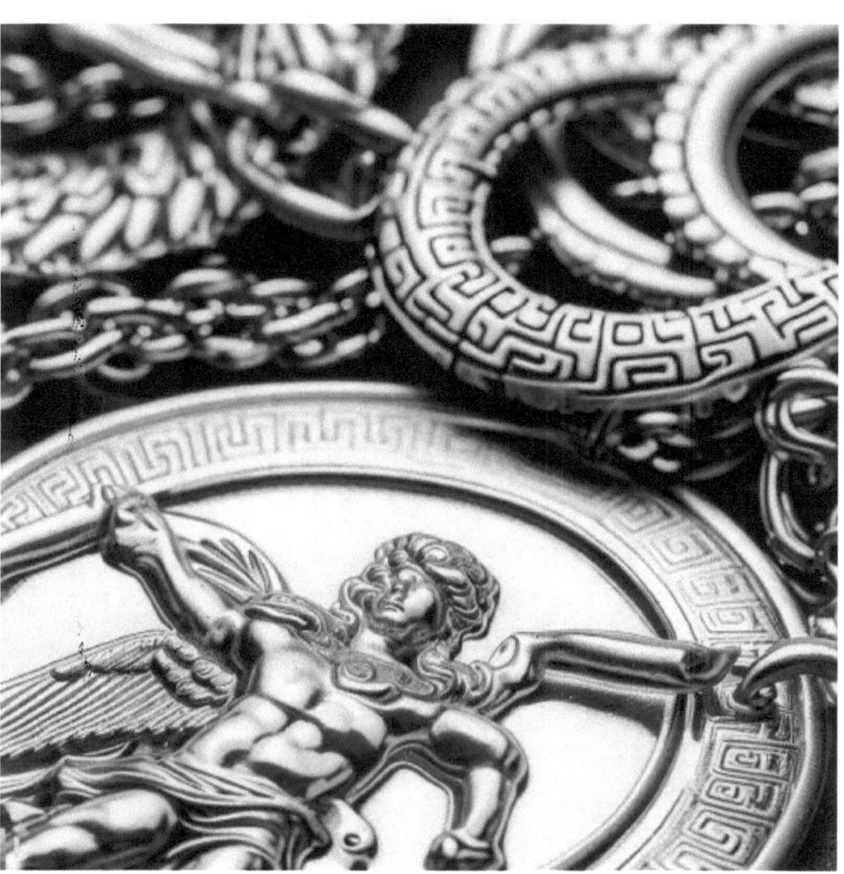

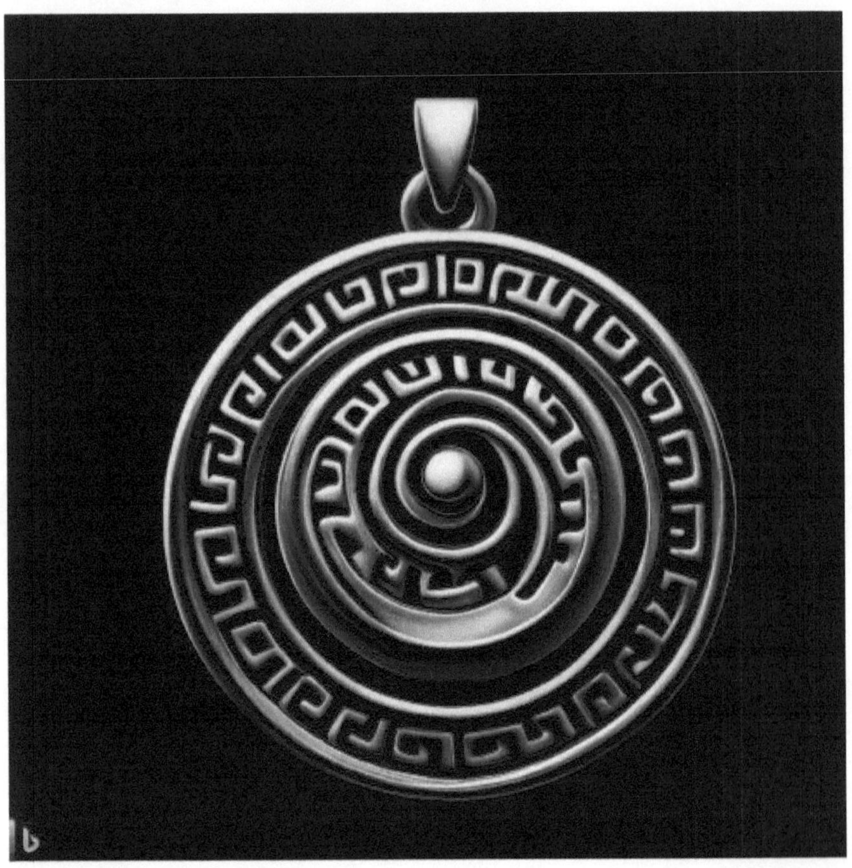

Steampunk Style:

The Steampunk style emerged in the 1980s as a subgenre of science fiction, and it's characterized by its industrial, mechanical, and Victorian-inspired designs. Steampunk jewelry often features gears, cogs, and other mechanical elements, and it's perfect for those who appreciate the beauty of the industrial age.

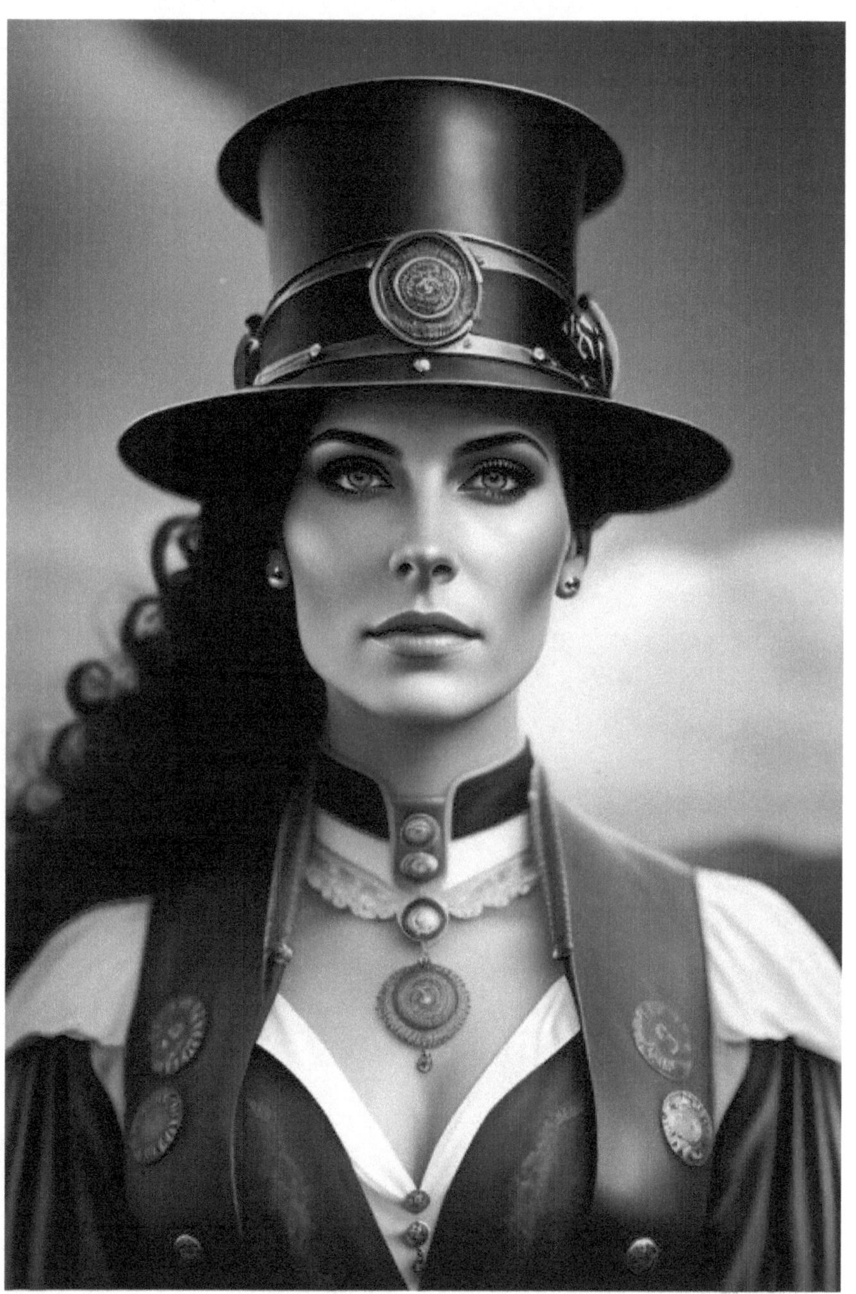

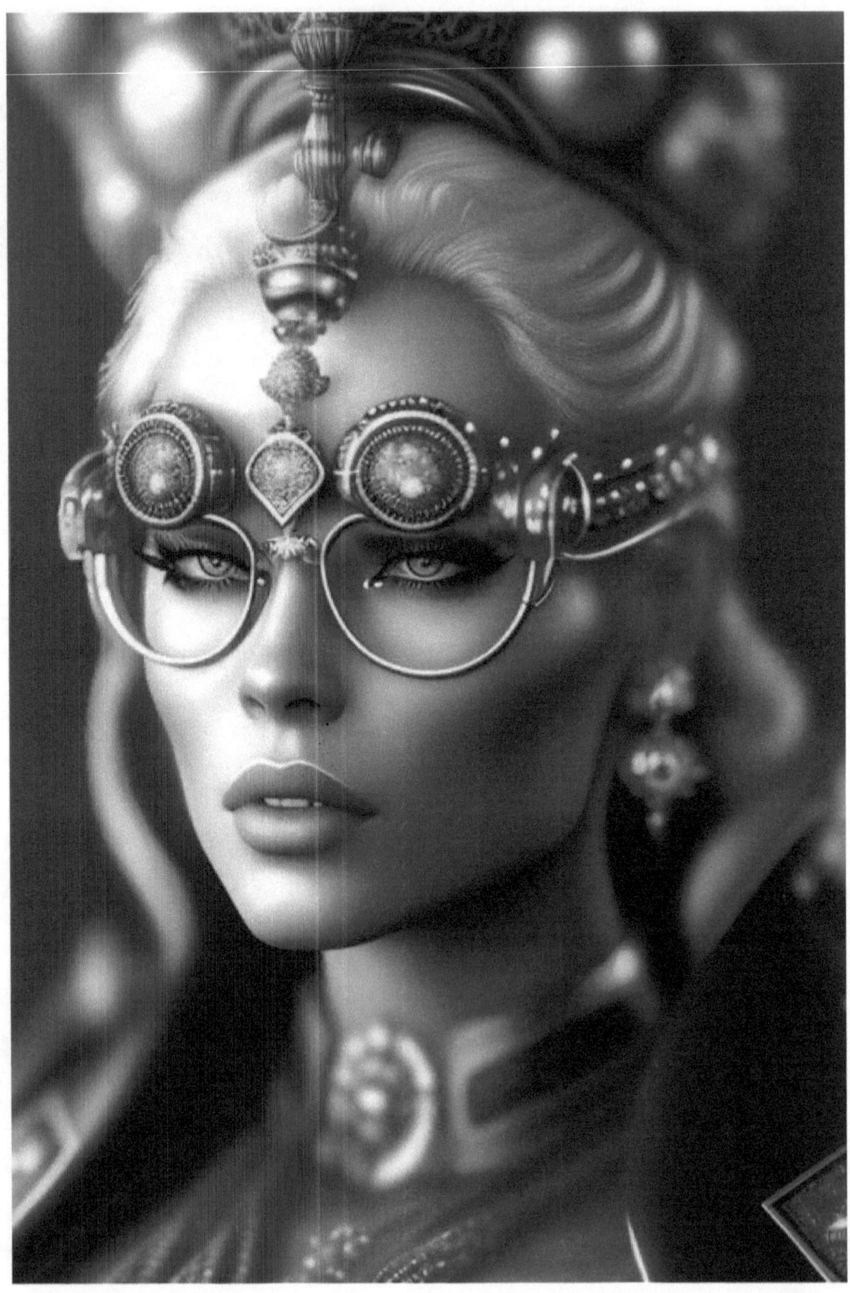

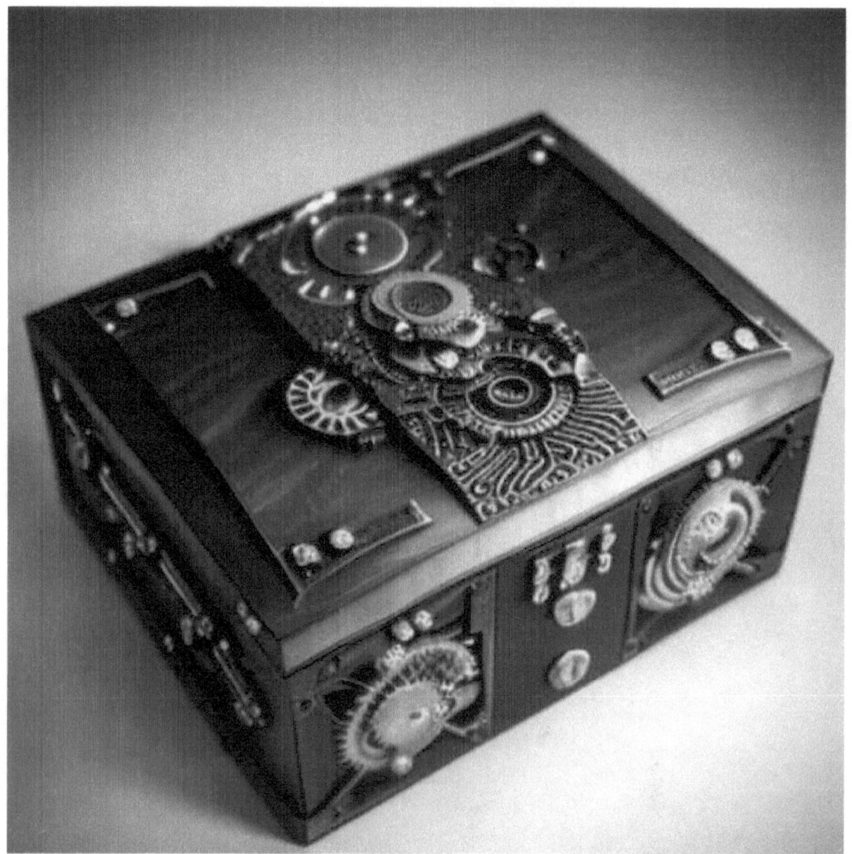

Vintage Retro Style:

The Vintage Retro style emerged in the 1940s and 1950s, and it's characterized by its bold, colorful, and playful designs. Vintage Retro jewelry often features large, chunky pieces, and it's known for its Hollywood glamour, fun, and optimism.

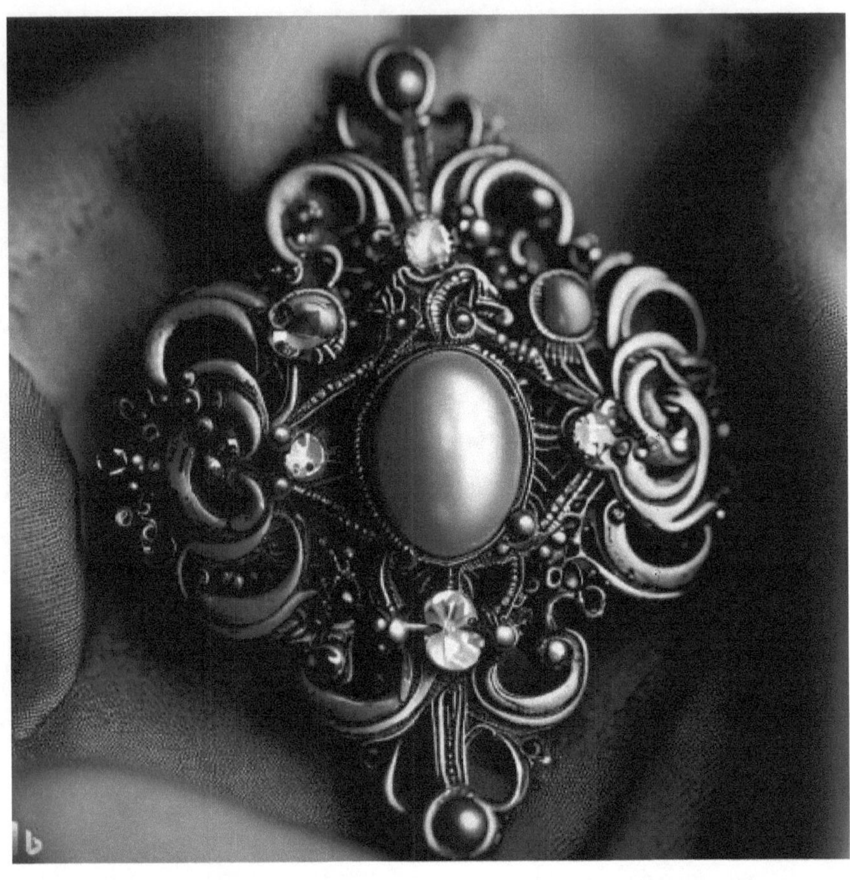

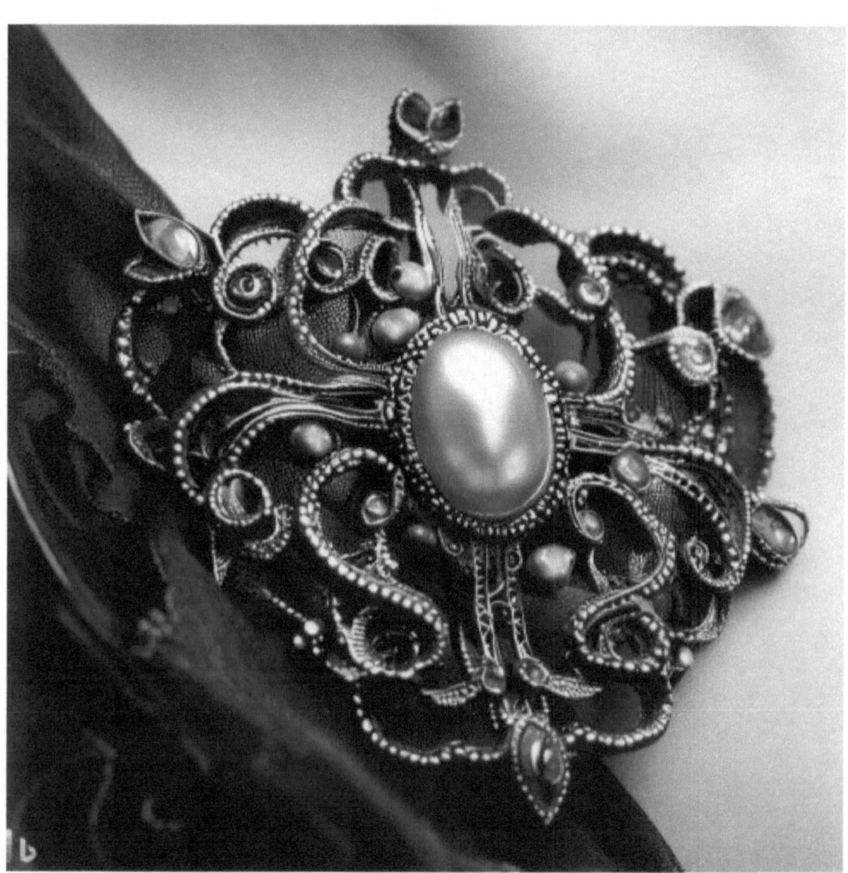

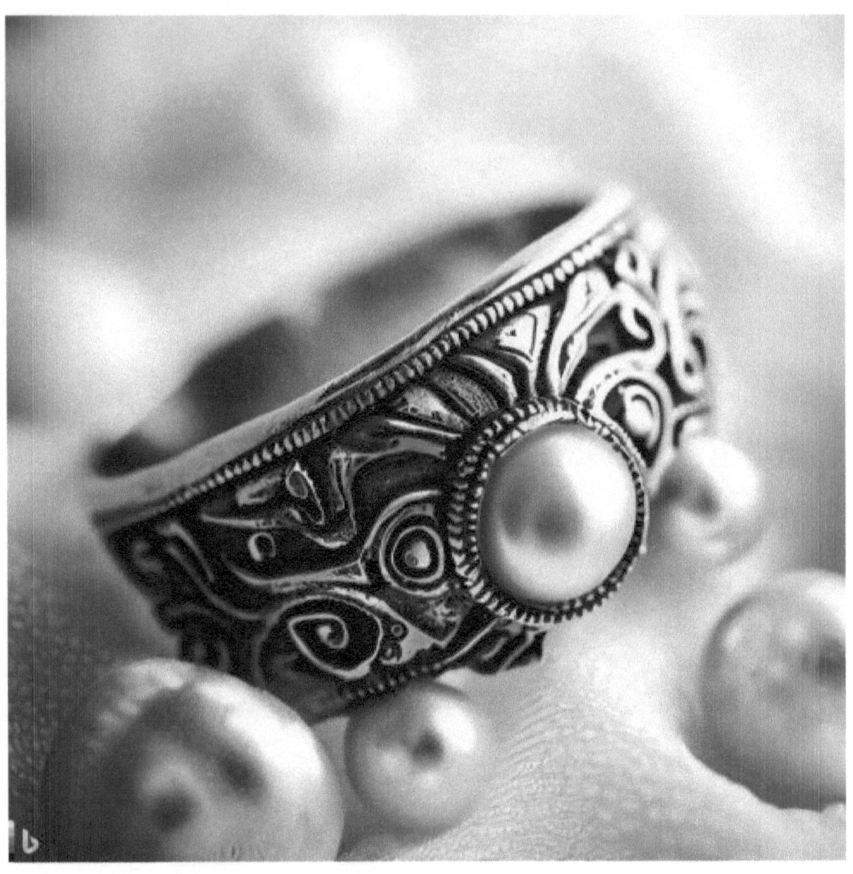

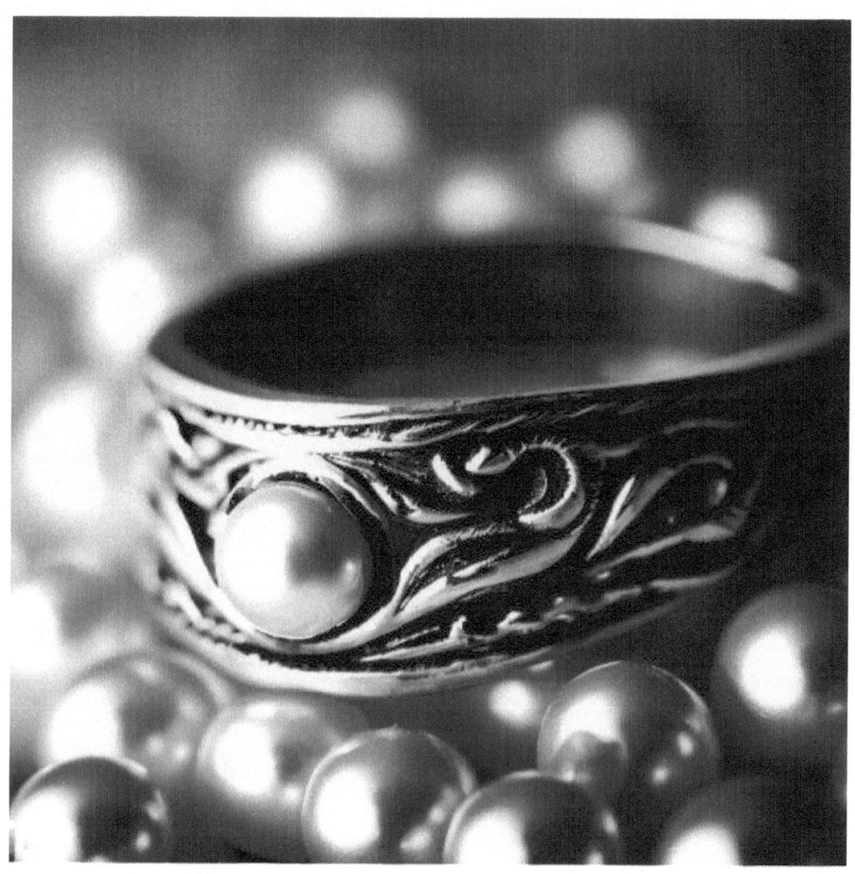

Art Nouveau Style:

The Art Nouveau style emerged in the late 19th and early 20th century, and it's a style that continues to captivate people today. There's something about the fluid, organic lines and the whimsical shapes that draws us in and speaks to our sense of beauty.

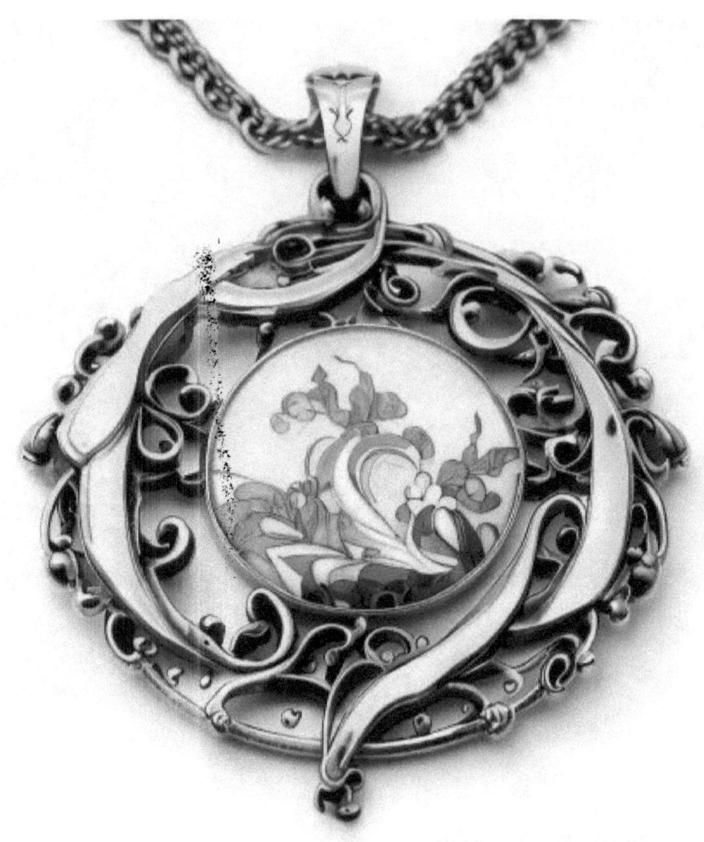

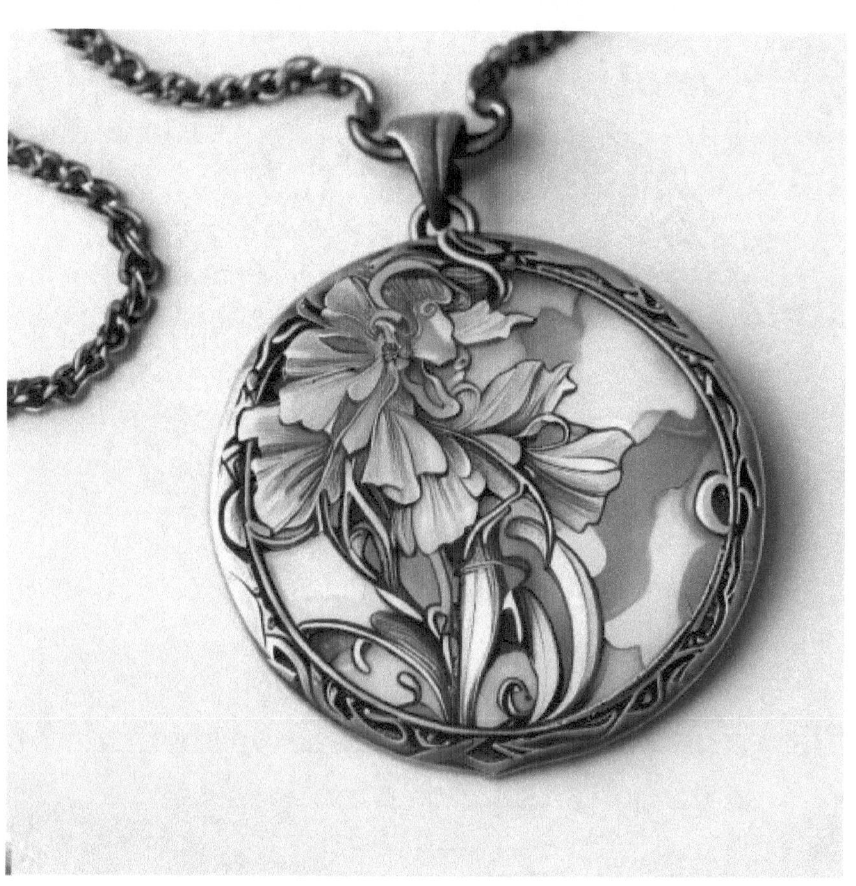

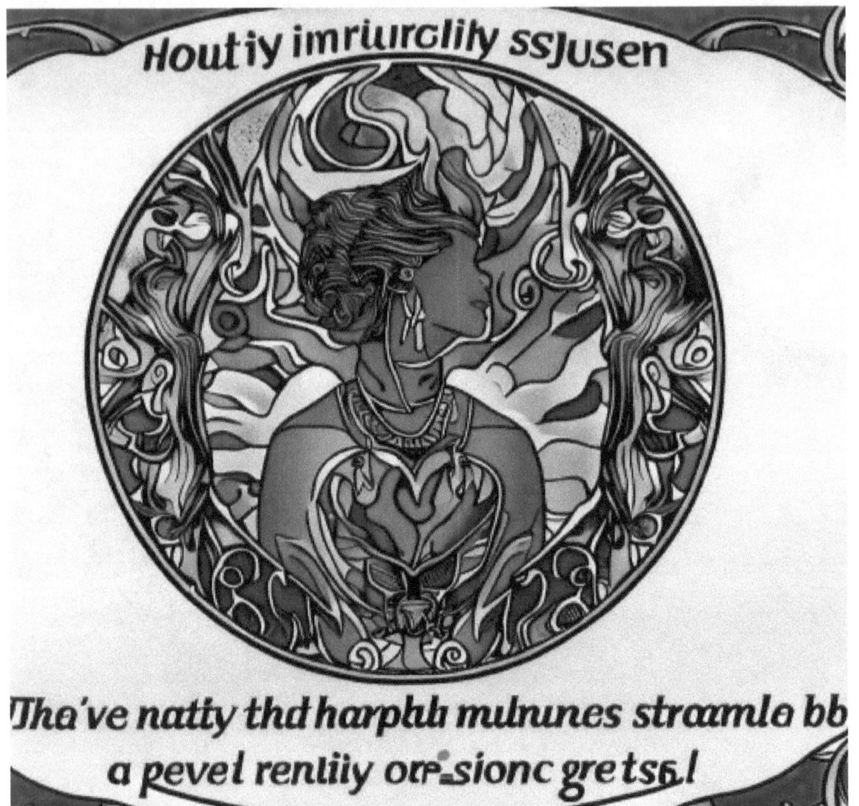
Houtiy imriurclily ssjusen
Tha've natiy thd harphli mulnunes straamlo bb
a pevel rentiy orr sionc gre ts&l

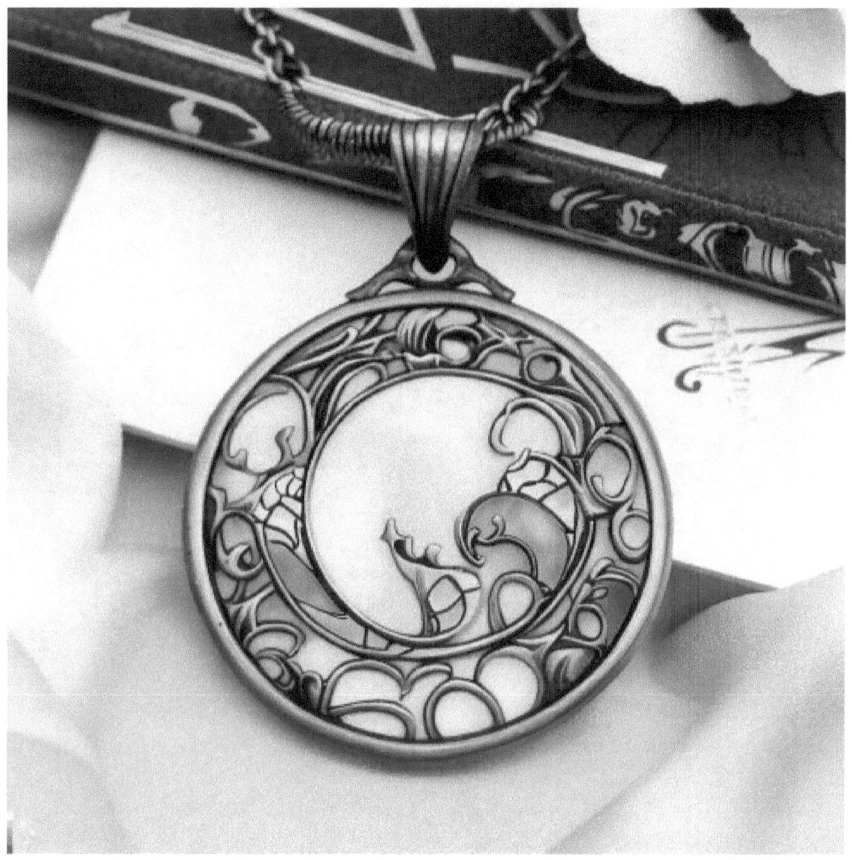

In Art Nouveau jewelry, you'll find an abundance of flowing, sinuous lines, often inspired by nature. The motifs can include flowers, vines, leaves, and even insects, all rendered in a style that is simultaneously realistic and stylized. There's a sense of harmony and unity to the designs, as if the pieces were grown rather than crafted.

Art Deco:

The Art Deco movement emerged in the 1920s and 1930s and is characterized by its sleek lines, geometric shapes, and bold colors. Jewelry from this period often features platinum, diamonds, and colored gemstones in a variety of geometric shapes such as rectangles, triangles, and circles. The Art Deco style is luxurious, glamorous, and exudes a sense of opulence that is unmistakable.

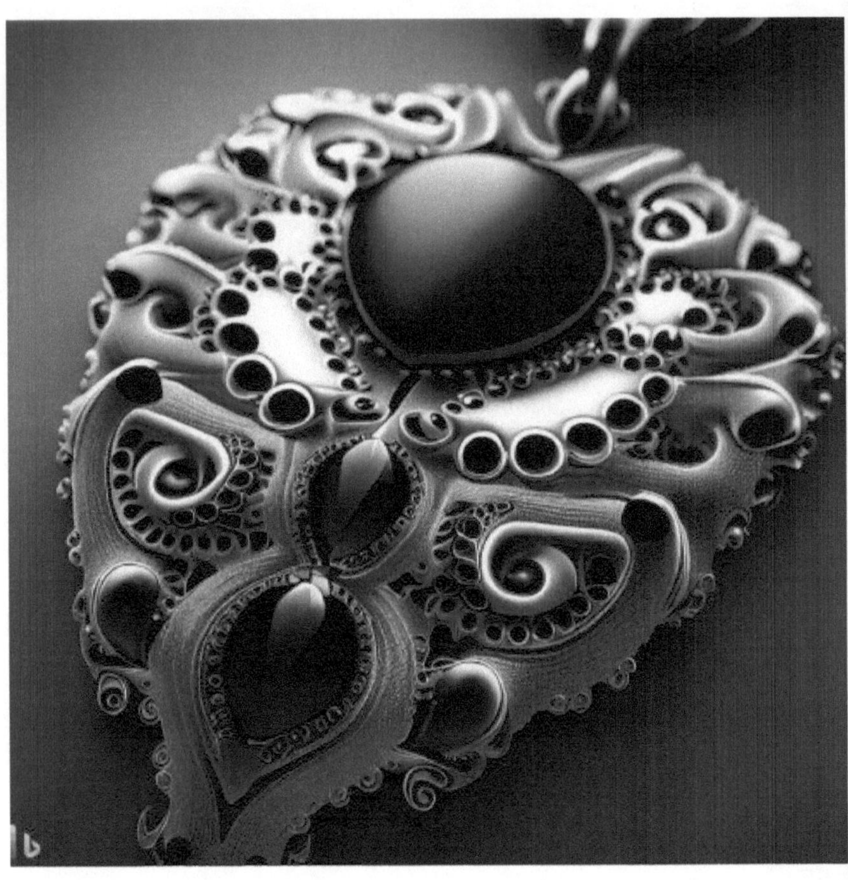

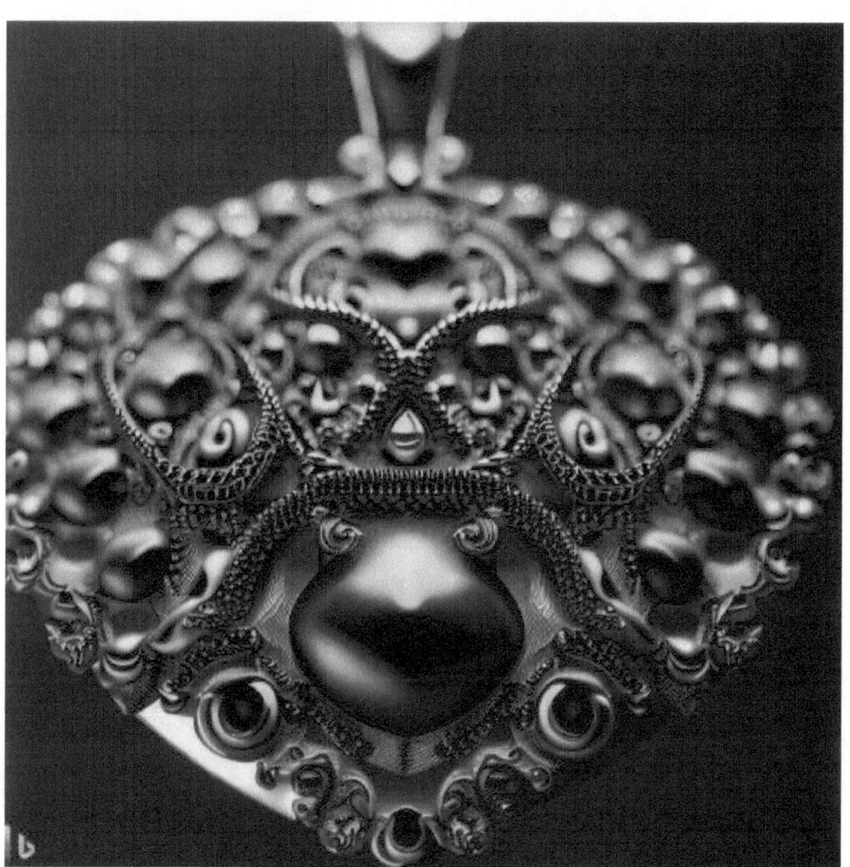

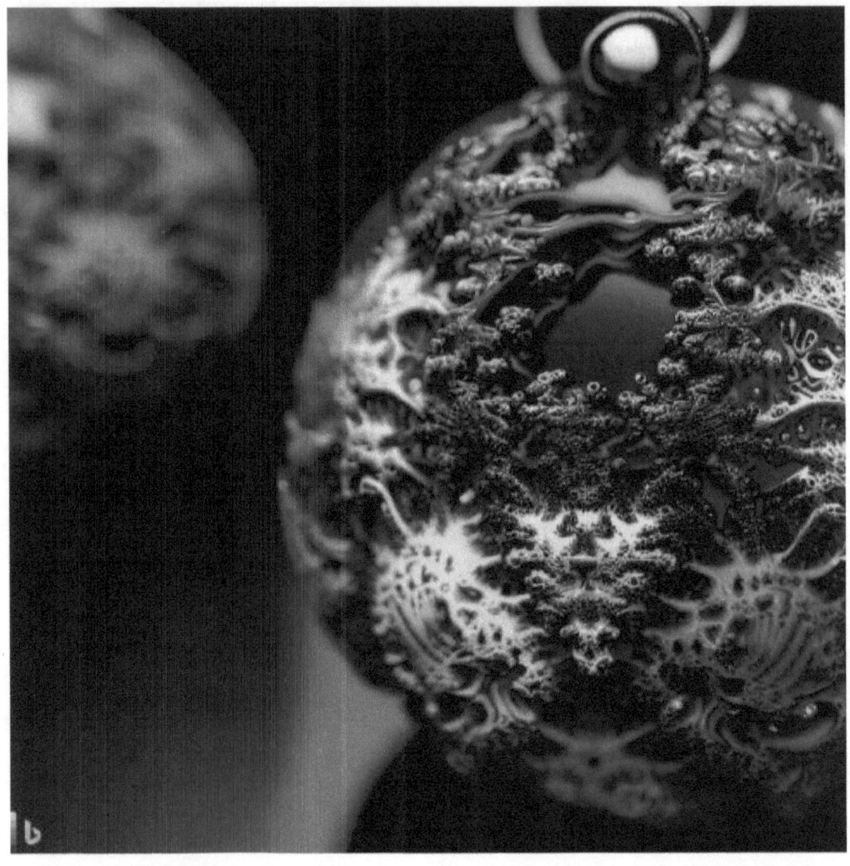

Gothic Style:

The Gothic style is dark, dramatic, and steeped in history. Jewelry in this style often features intricate patterns, heavy metalwork, and dark stones such as onyx and hematite. Gothic jewelry is often inspired by medieval art and architecture, and it has a unique sense of mystery and enchantment that draws people in.

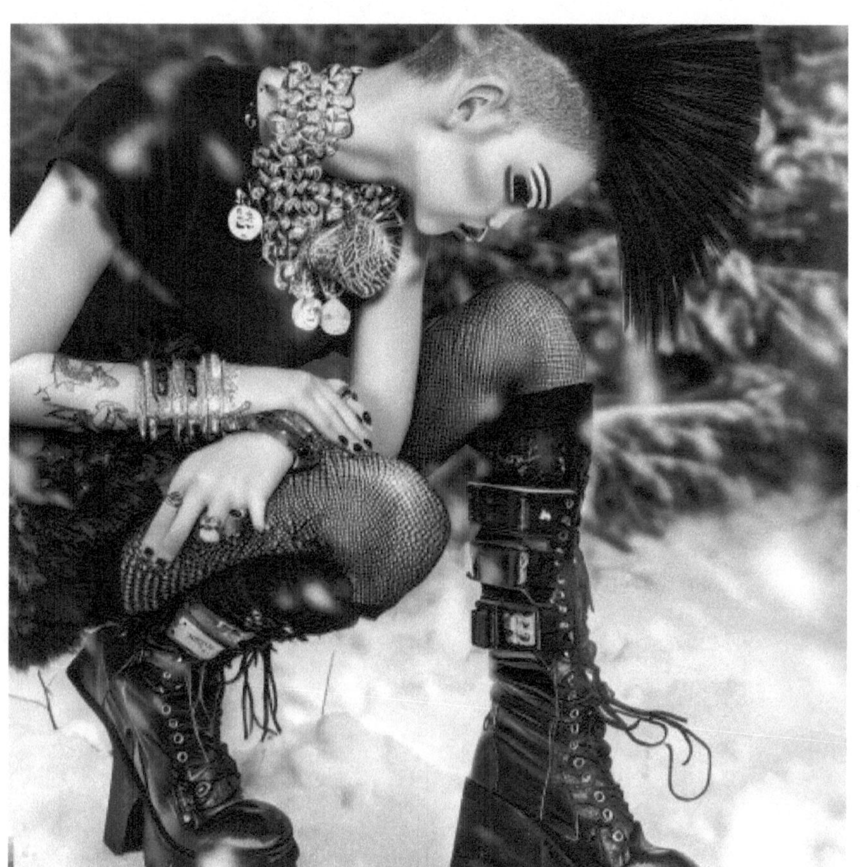

Ethnic Style:

Ethnic jewelry is diverse and encompasses a wide range of styles from around the world. These styles can be inspired by traditional clothing, symbols, and motifs from different cultures. Ethnic jewelry often incorporates natural materials such as shells, beads, and feathers, and it can have a rustic, earthy, and handmade feel to it.

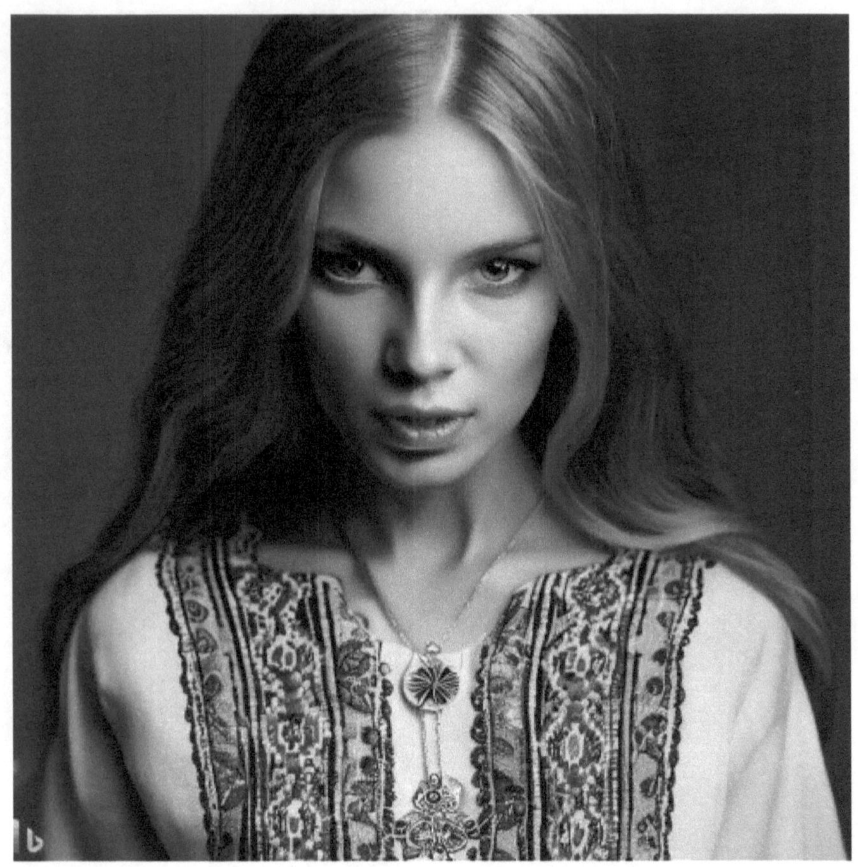

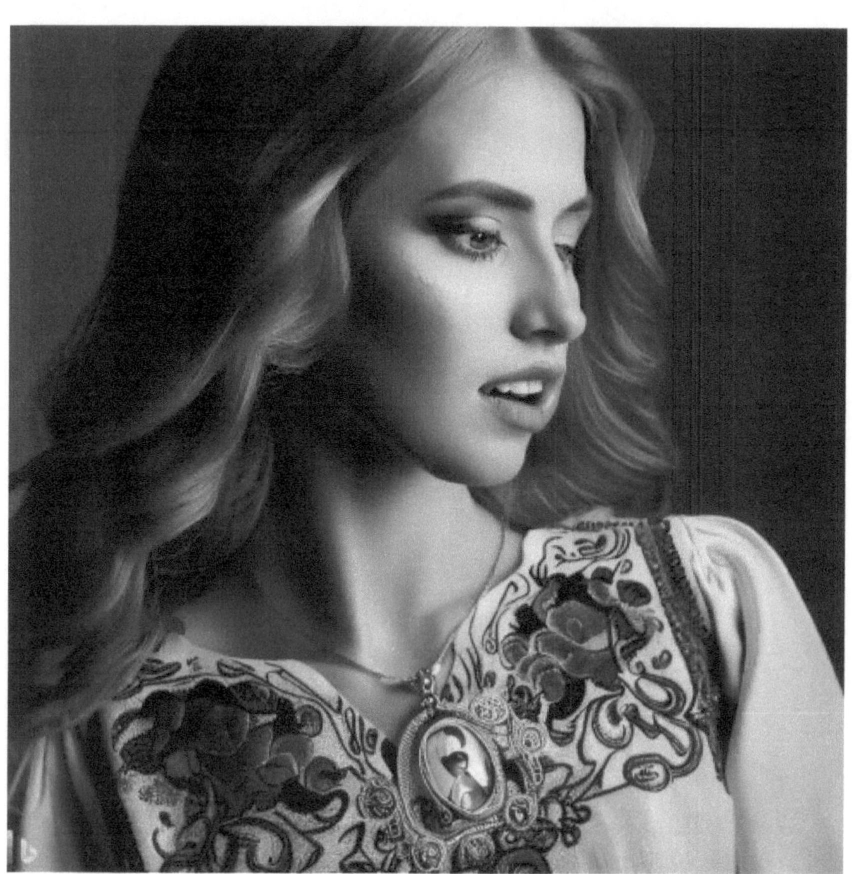

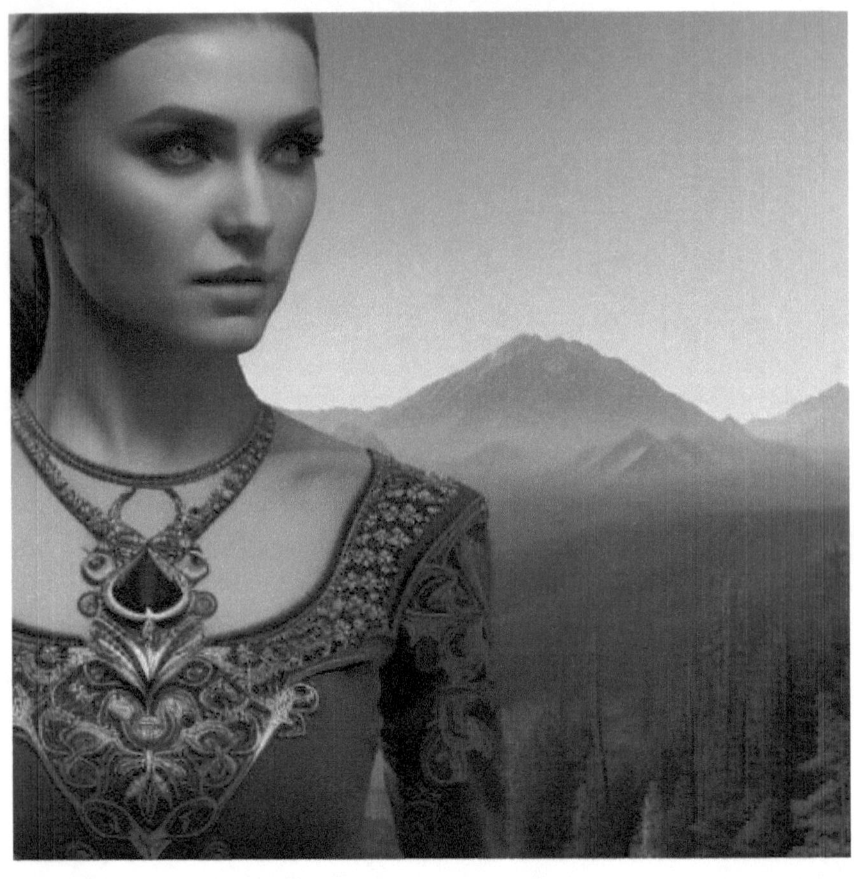

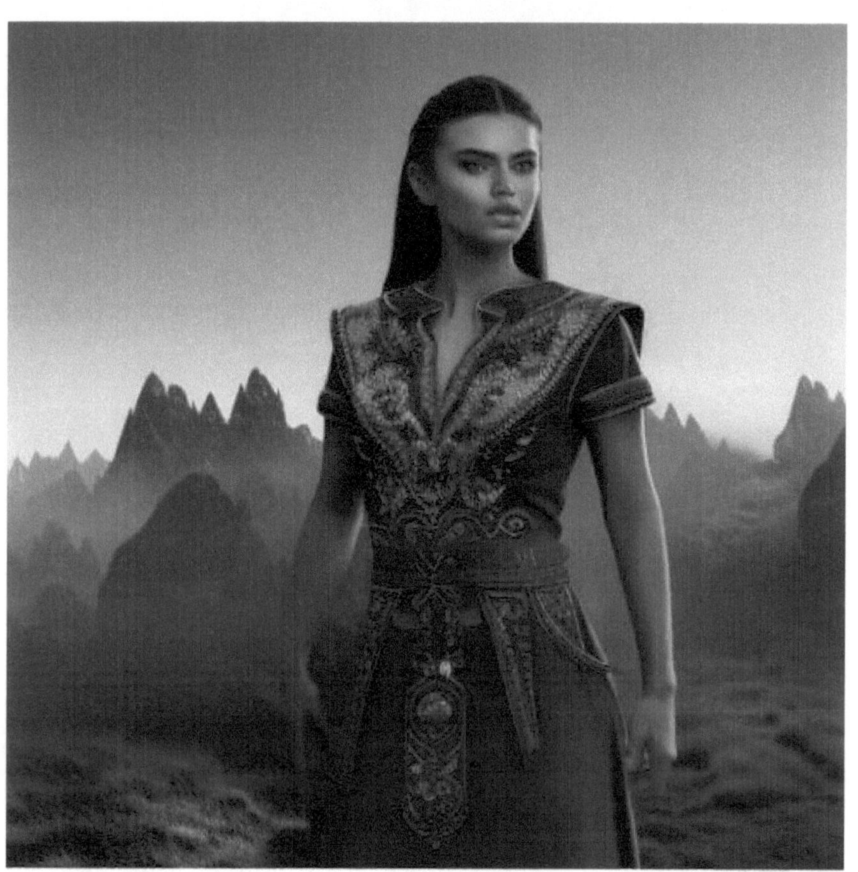

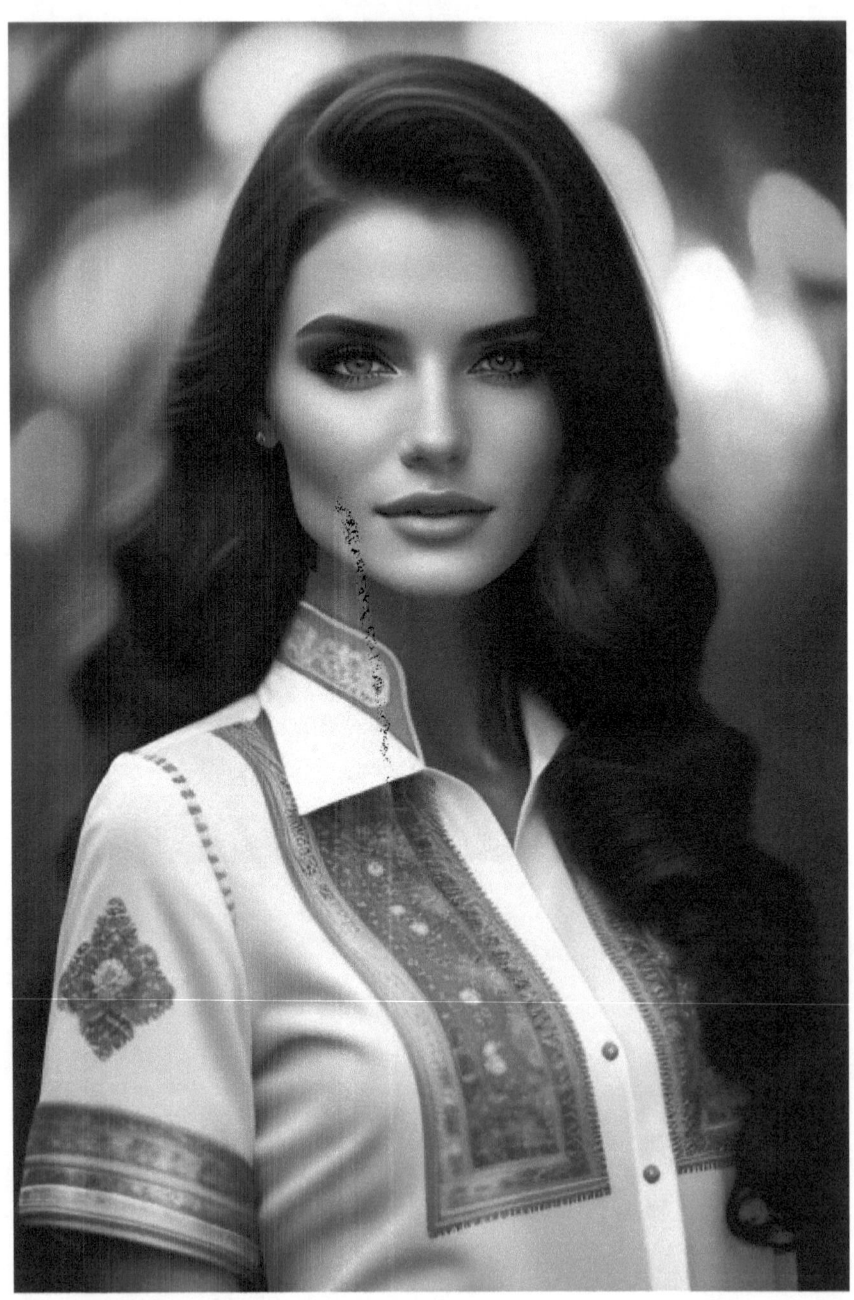

Minimalism:

Minimalist jewelry is simple, elegant, and understated. The focus is on clean lines, geometric shapes, and a lack of excess ornamentation. Minimalist jewelry is perfect for those who prefer a more subtle look or who want to emphasize the natural beauty of the materials used.

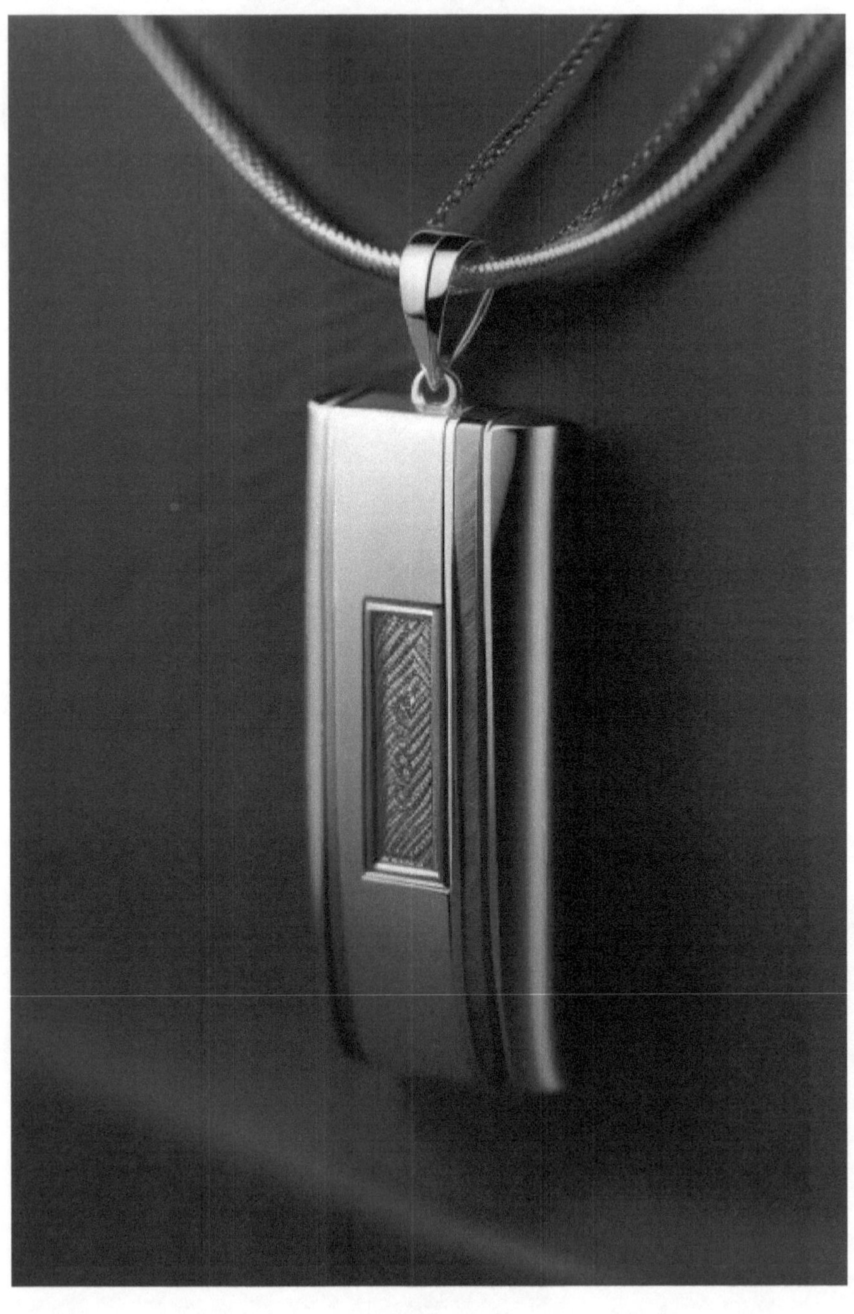

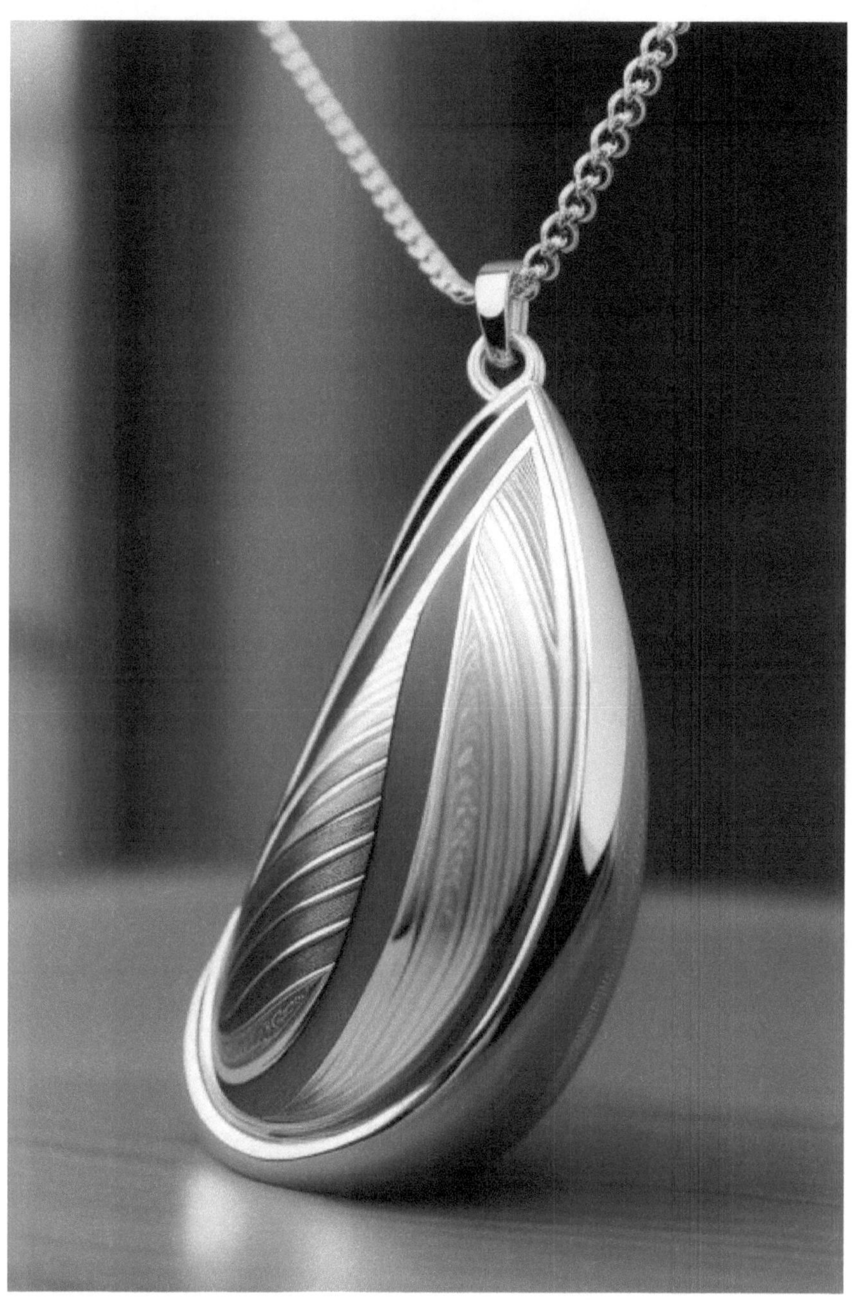

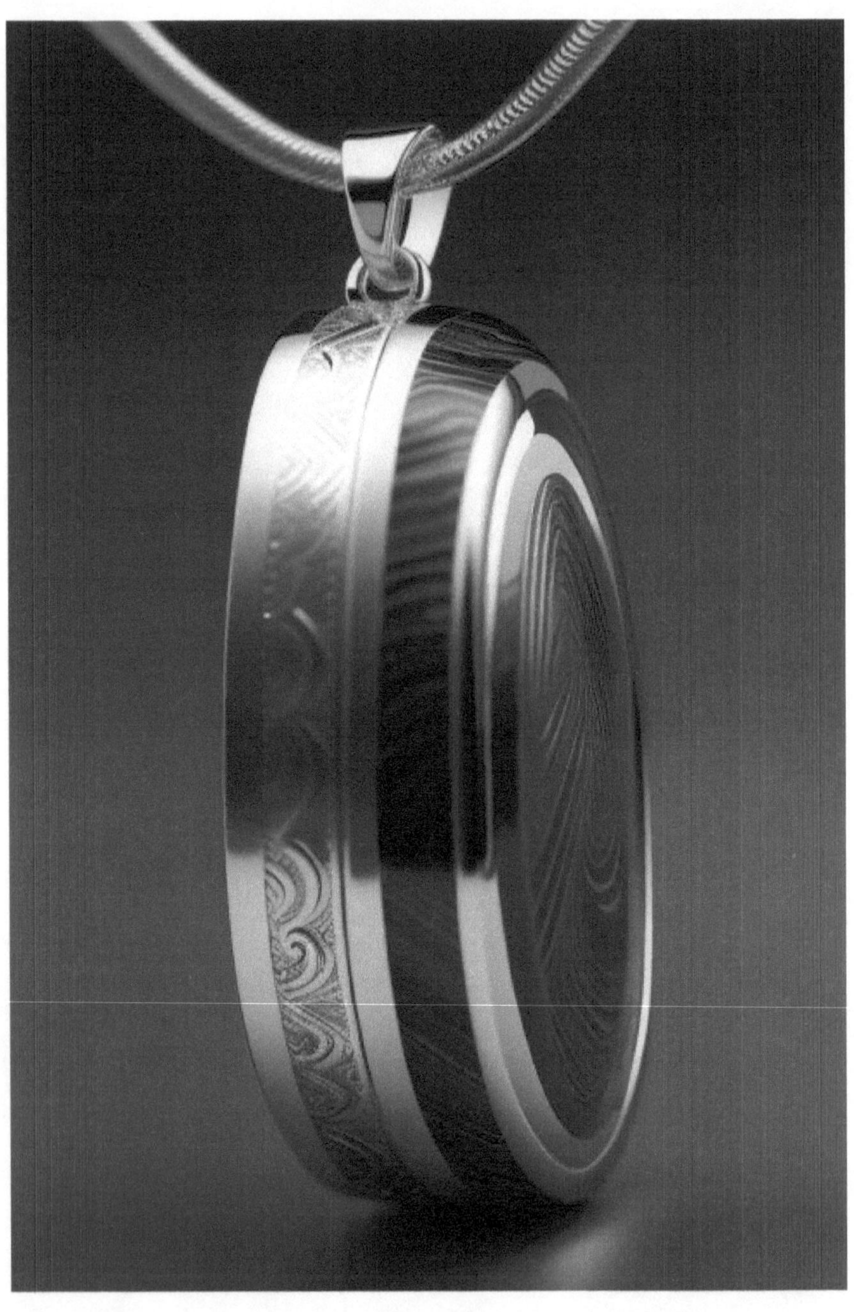

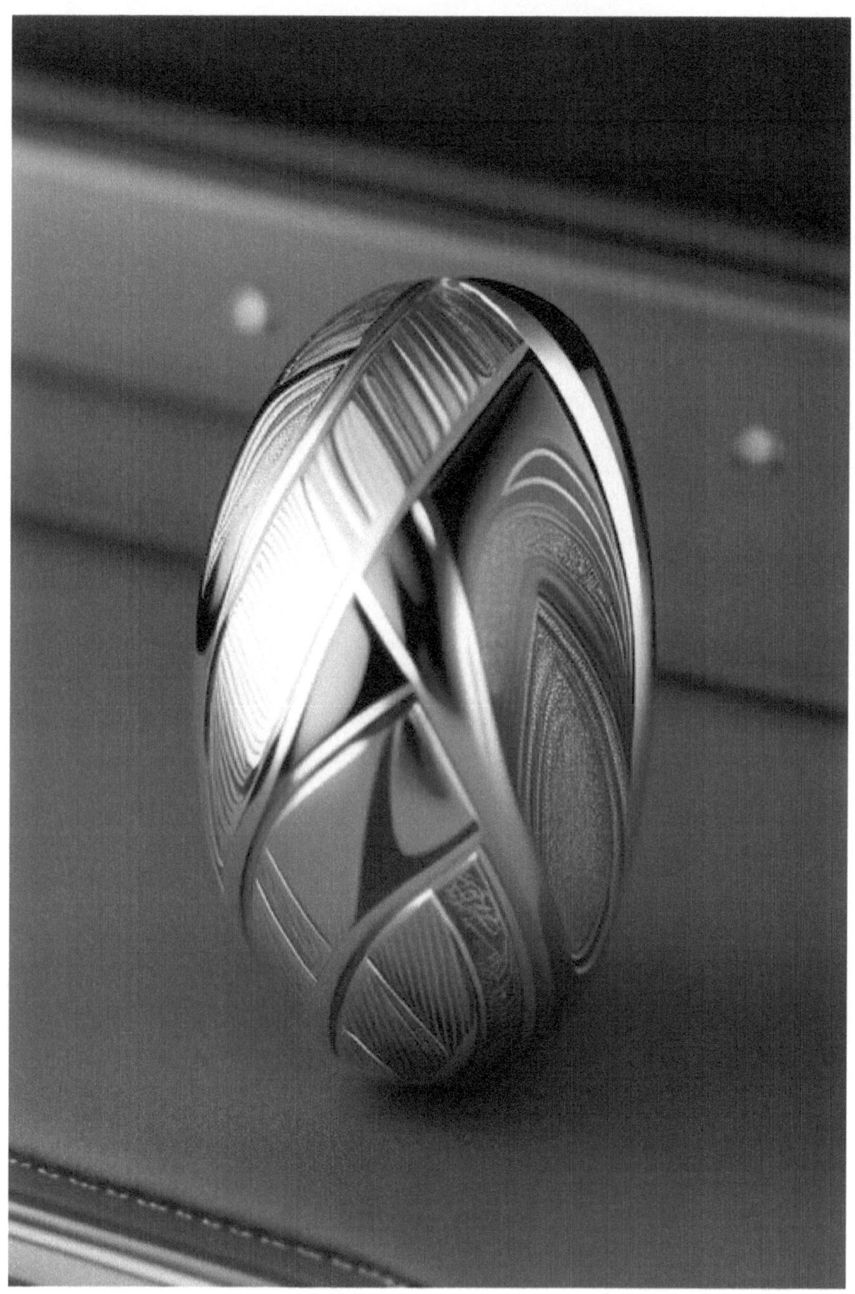

Indian Style:

Indian jewelry is rich, vibrant, and ornate. It often features intricate patterns and designs, including floral and paisley motifs. Indian jewelry is typically made from gold and silver and adorned with colorful gemstones such as rubies, sapphires, and emeralds.

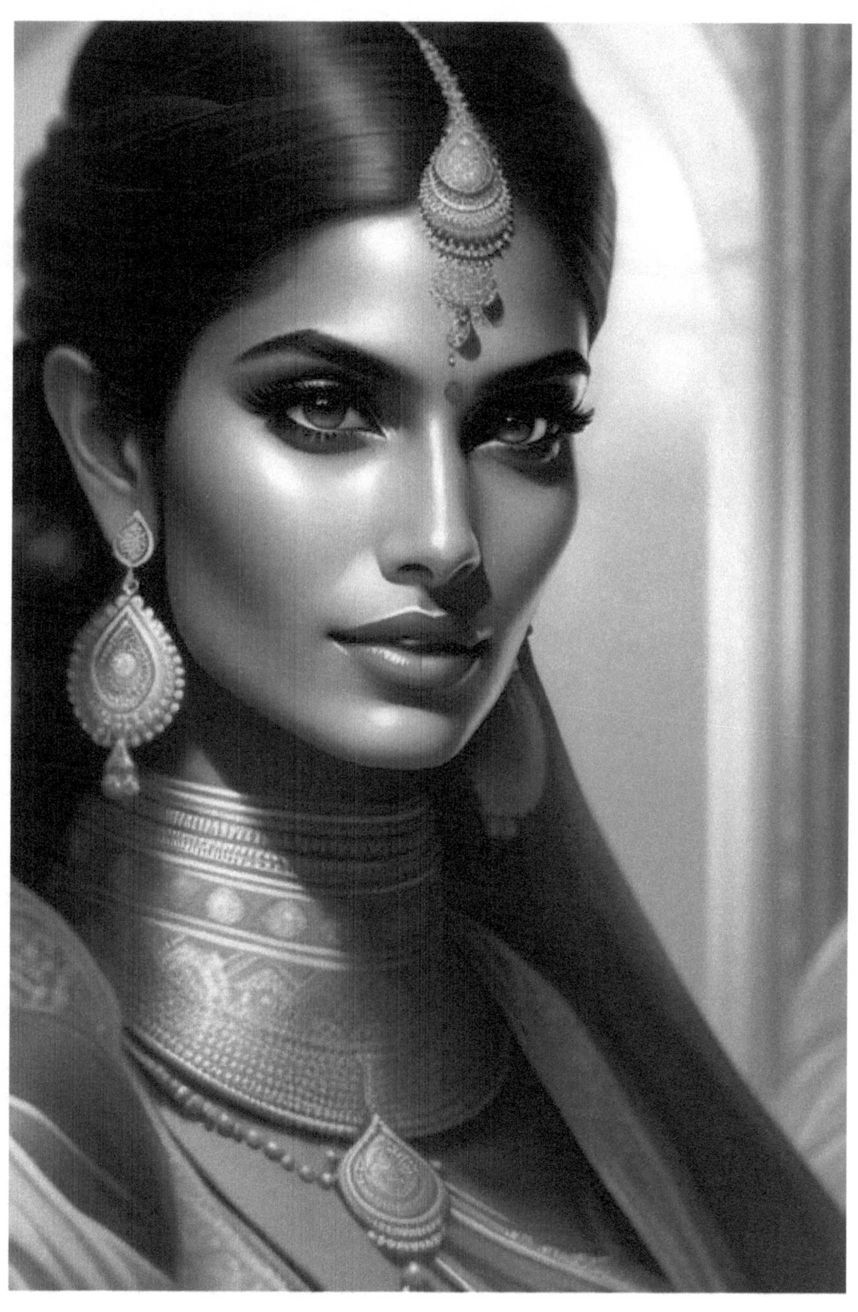

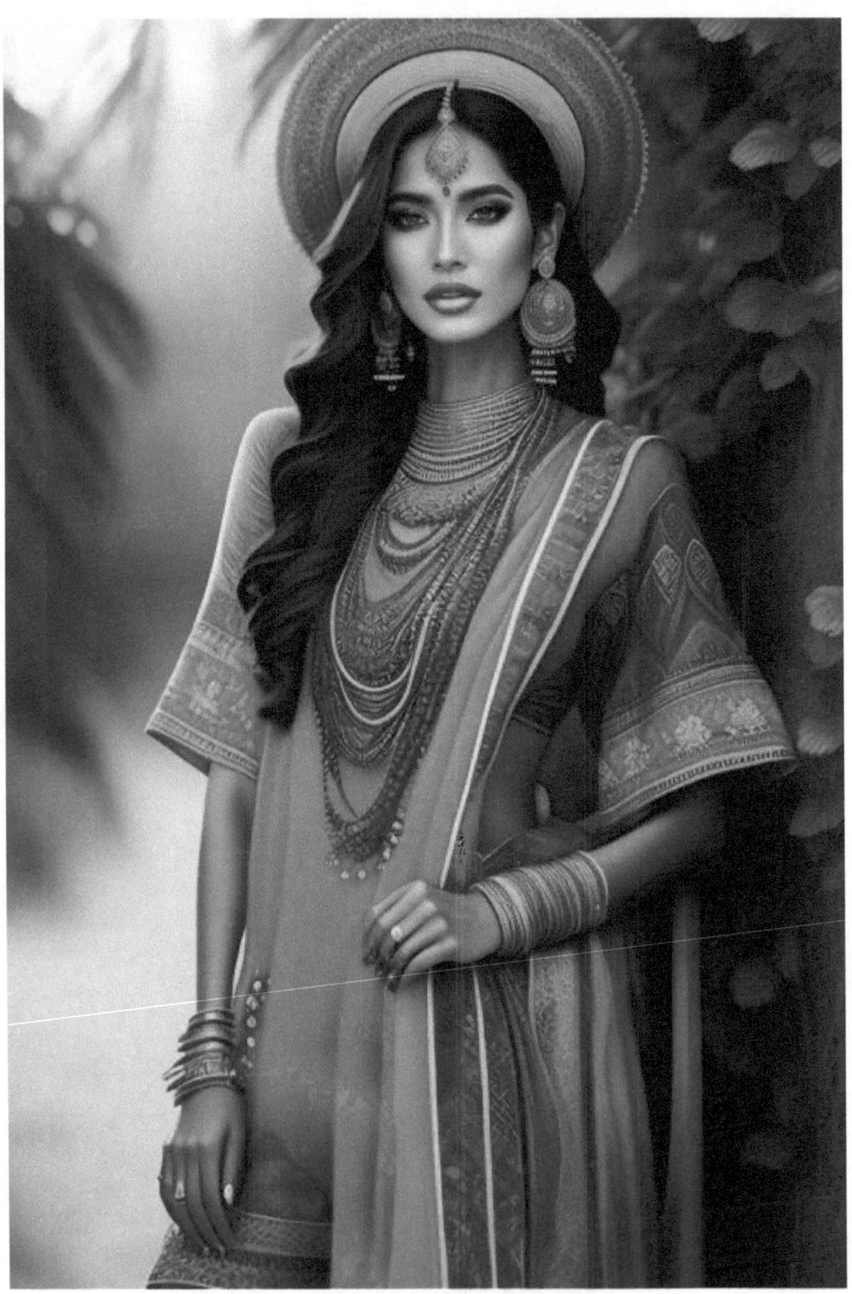

Japanese Style:

Japanese jewelry is influenced by the country's unique culture and history. Jewelry in this style is often minimalist and features natural materials such as bamboo, wood, and pearls. Japanese jewelry is known for its delicate designs and attention to detail, and it is often inspired by nature.

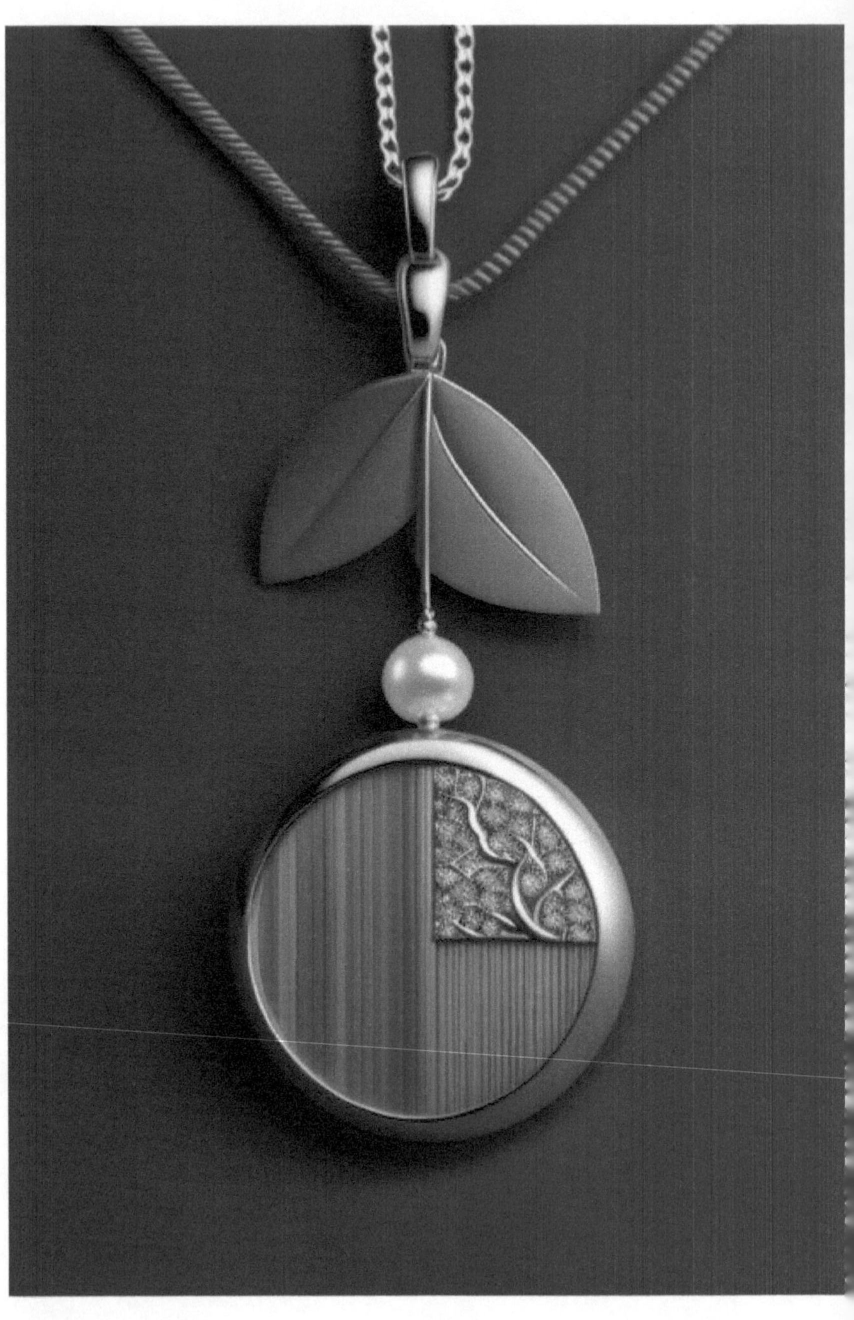

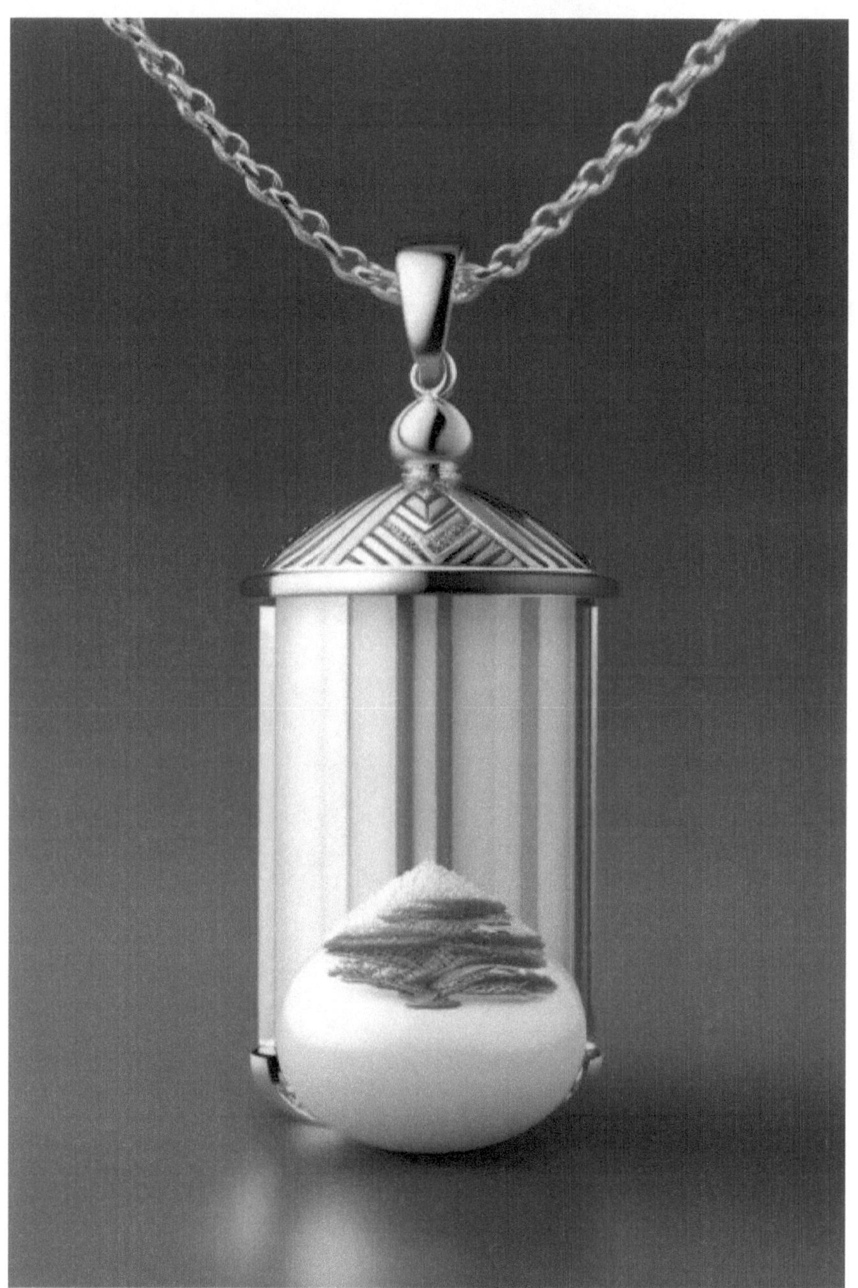

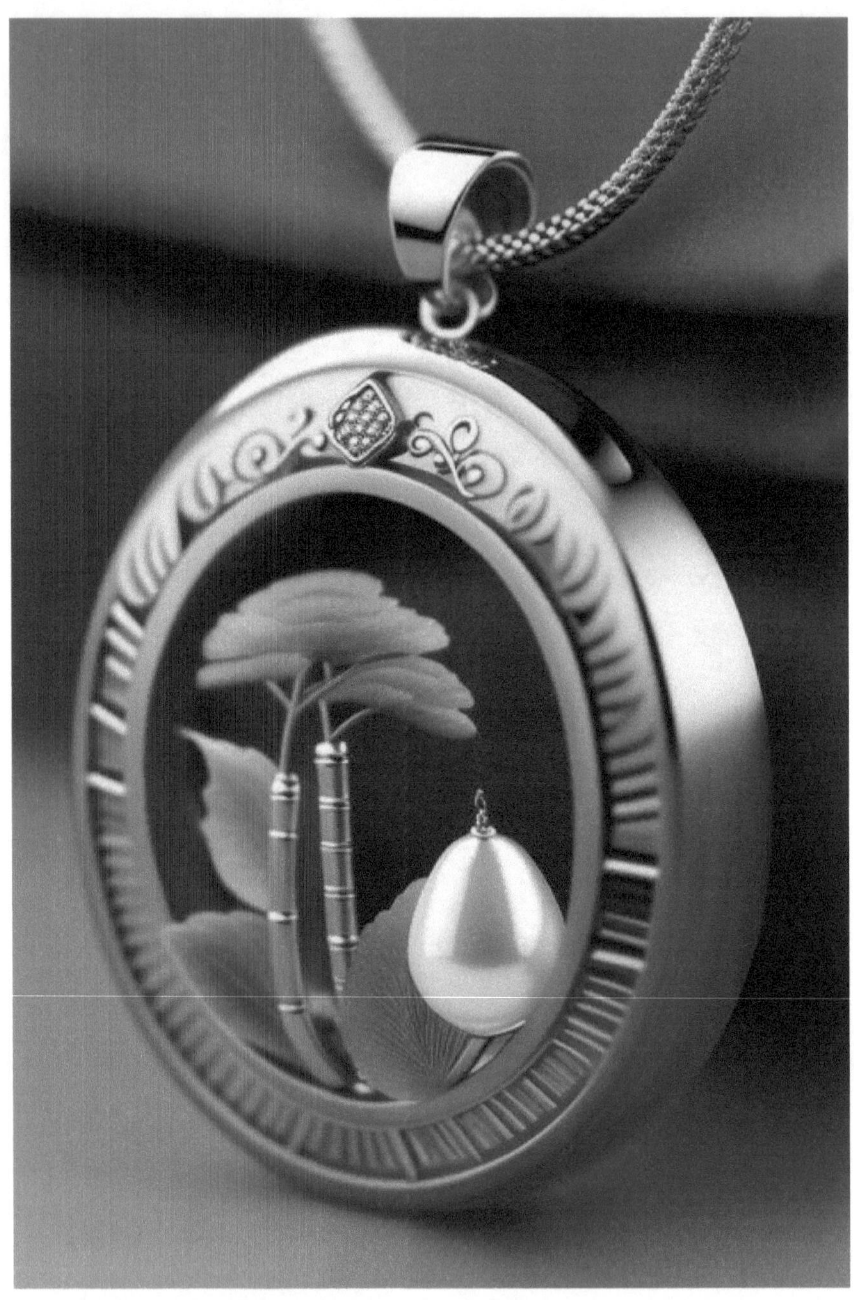

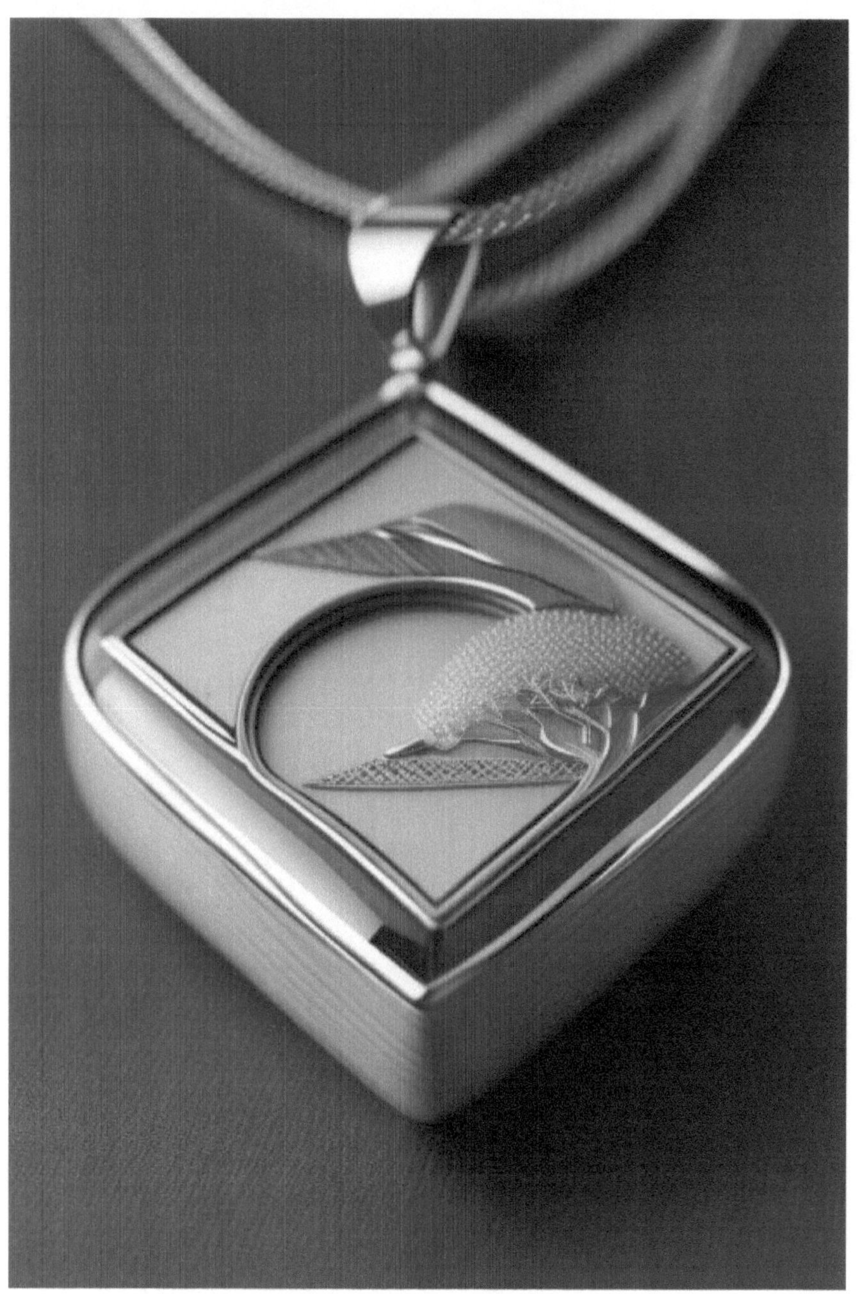

Classical Style:

The classical style is timeless, elegant, and refined. It draws inspiration from ancient Greece and Rome and features classical motifs such as laurel wreaths, scrolls, and cameos. Classical jewelry is typically made from gold and features pearls and gemstones such as amethysts, topaz, and garnets.

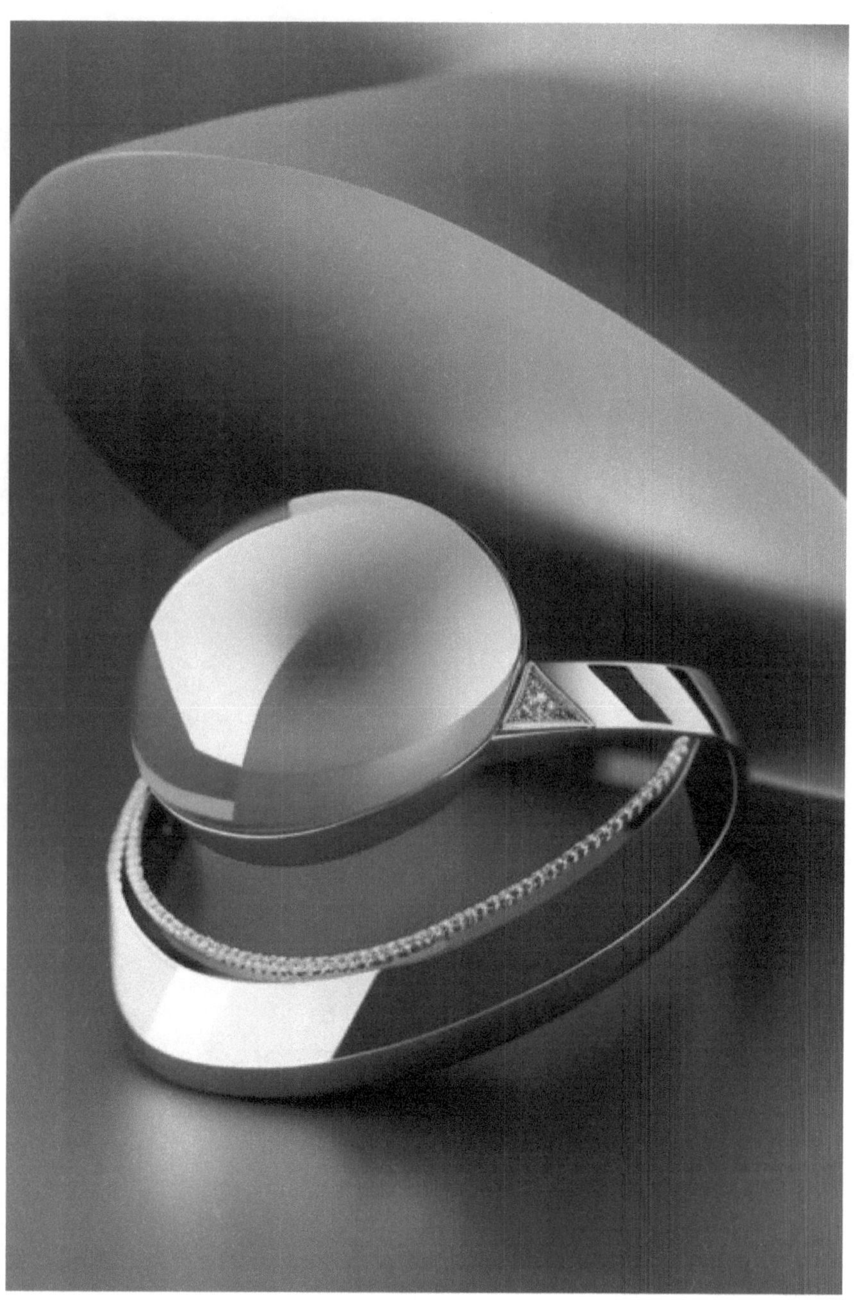

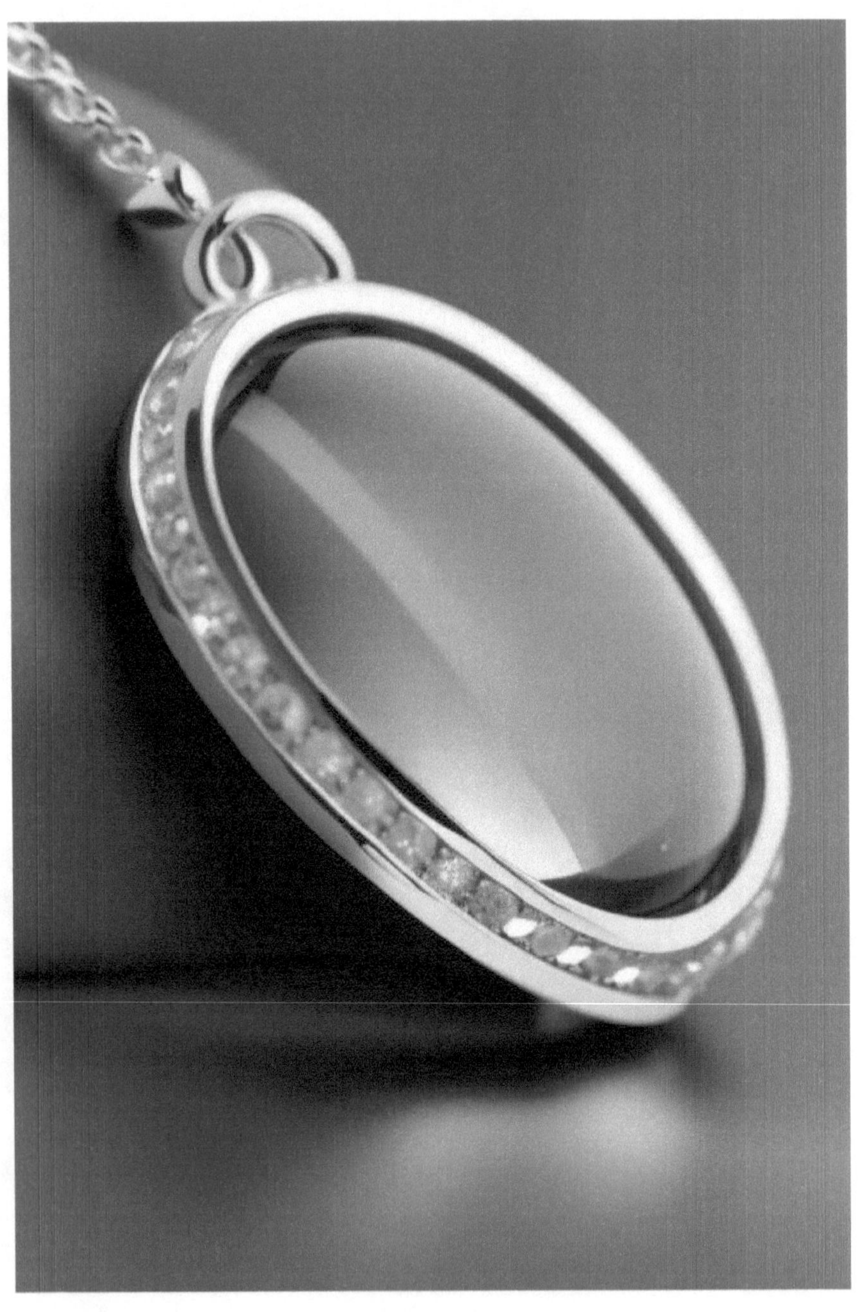

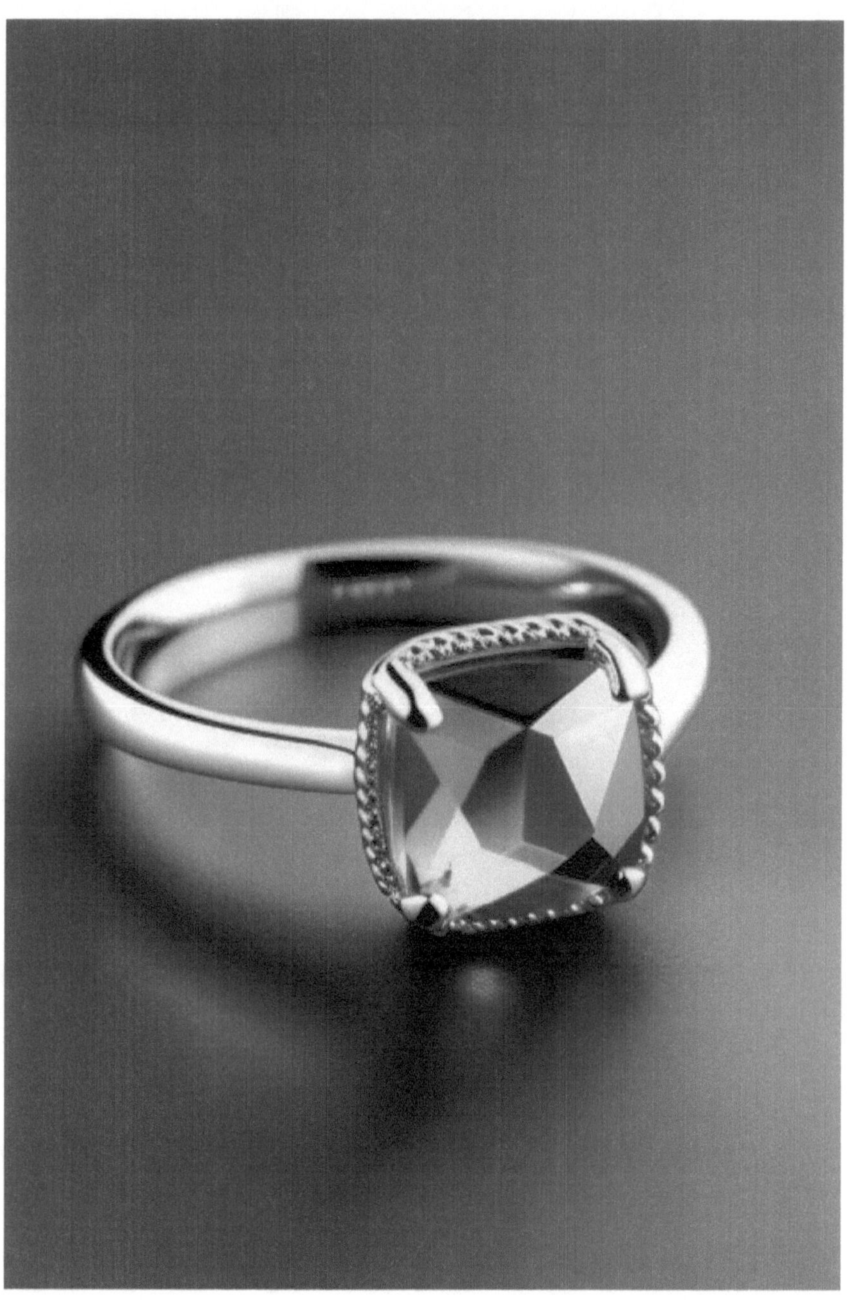

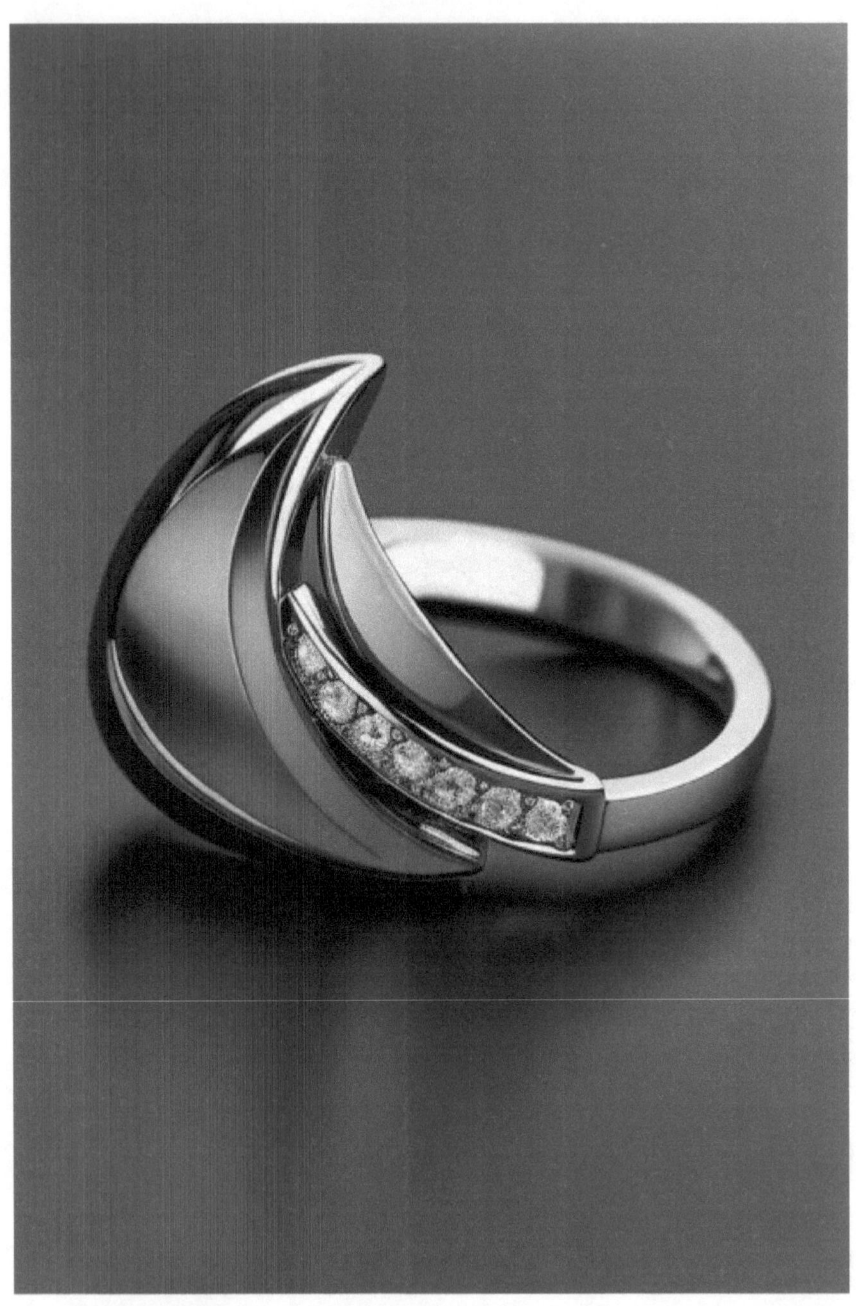

Modern Style:

Modern jewelry is edgy, bold, and innovative. It often features unusual materials such as acrylic, rubber, and leather and can incorporate non-traditional shapes and designs. Modern jewelry is perfect for those who want to make a statement and push the boundaries of traditional jewelry design.

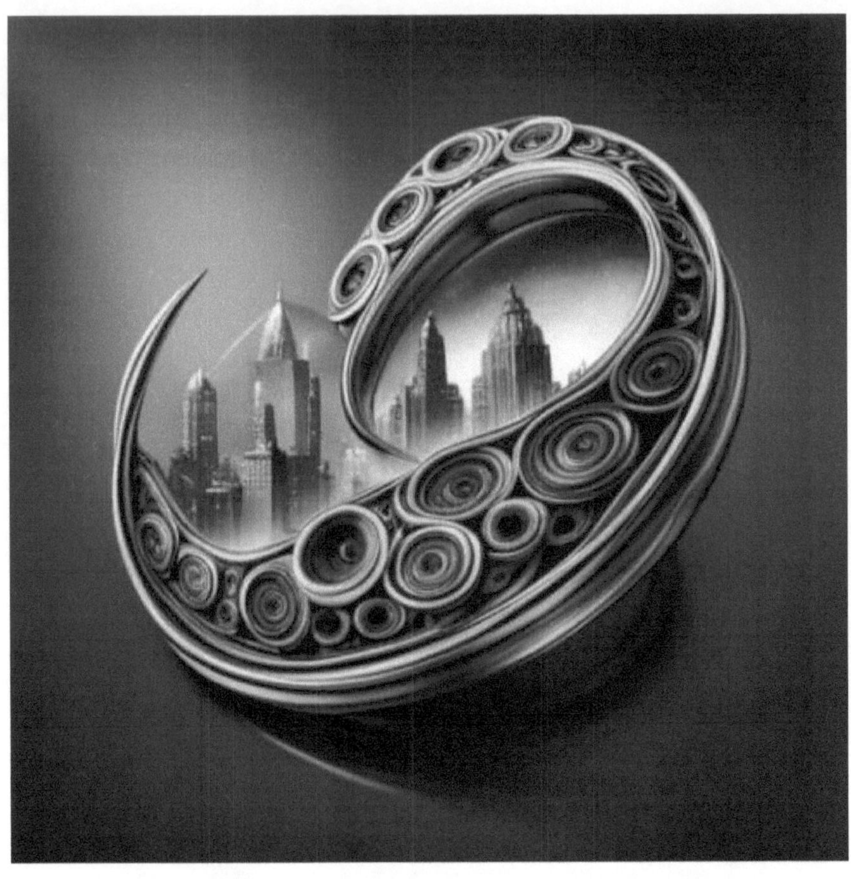

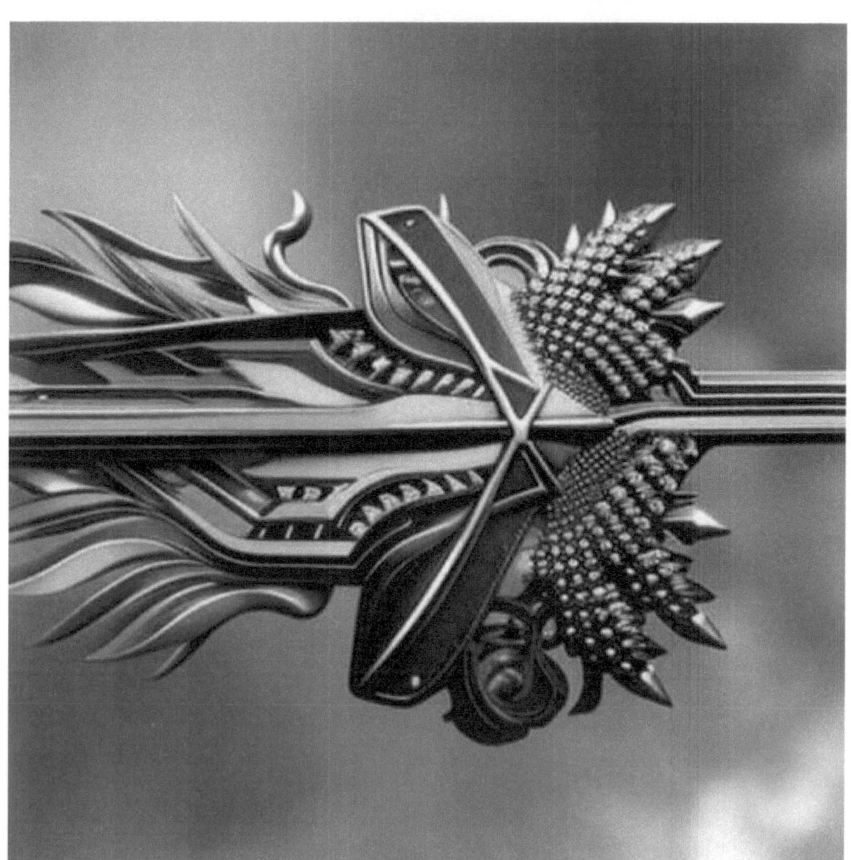

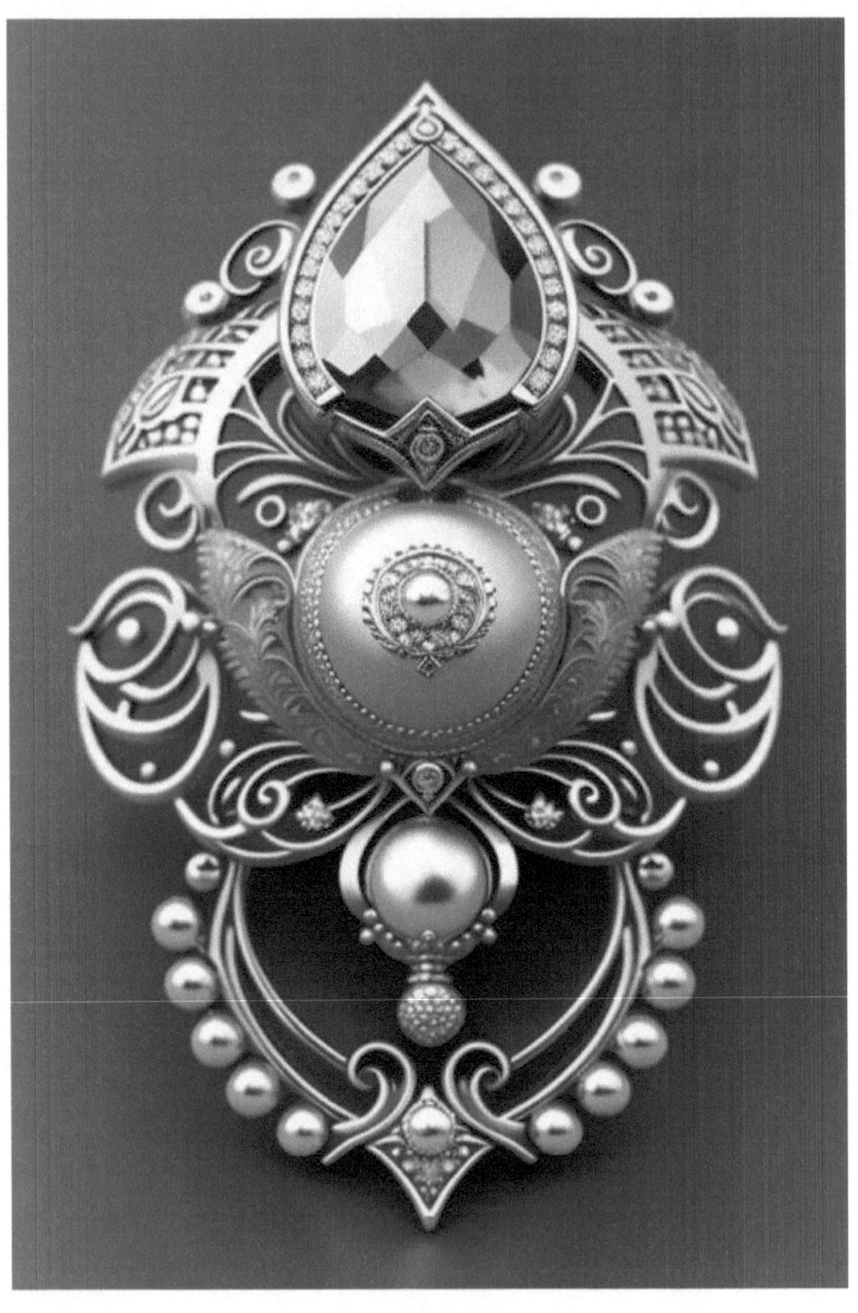

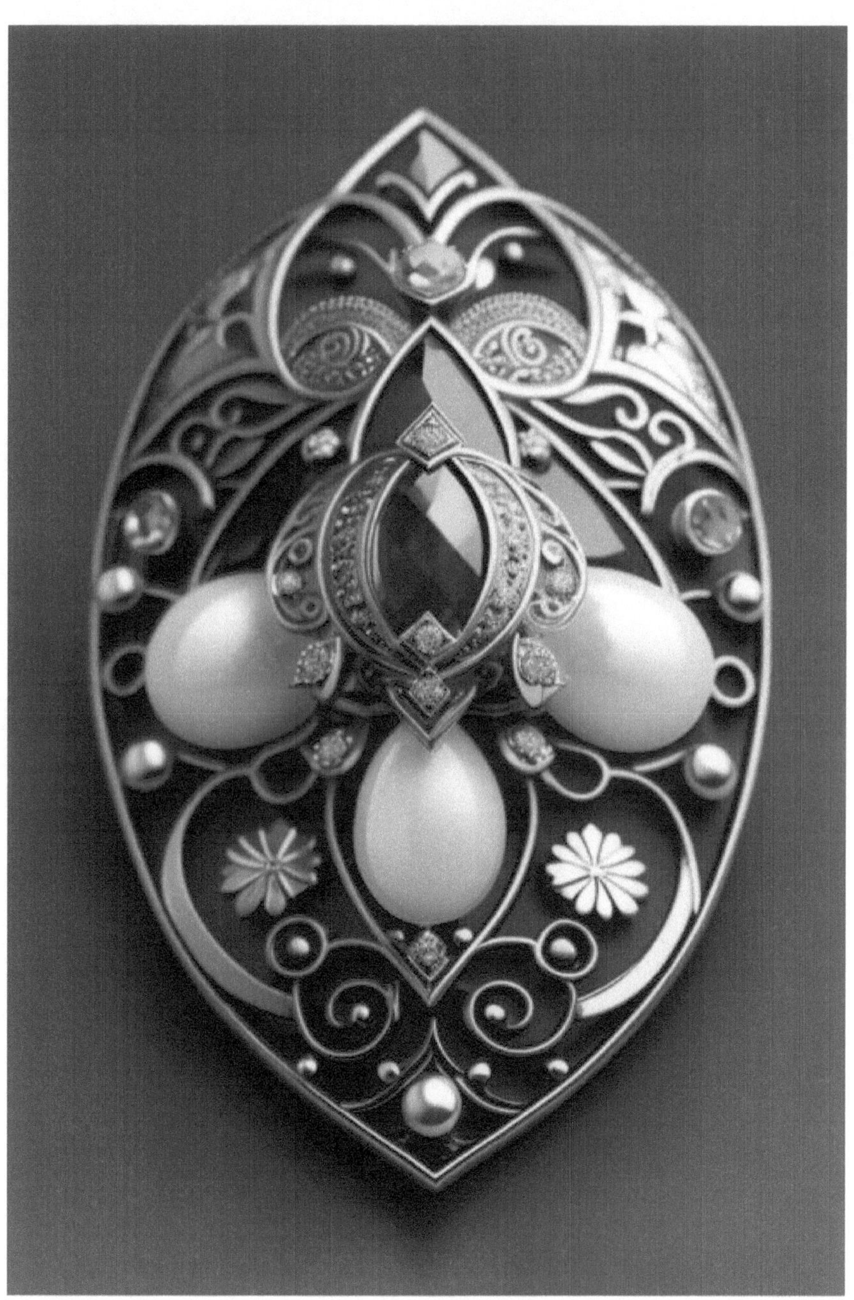

Abstract Style:

Abstract jewelry is unconventional, creative, and often incorporates unusual materials and shapes. It is less focused on traditional forms and more about creating unique and innovative designs. Abstract jewelry is perfect for those who want to express their individuality and stand out from the crowd.

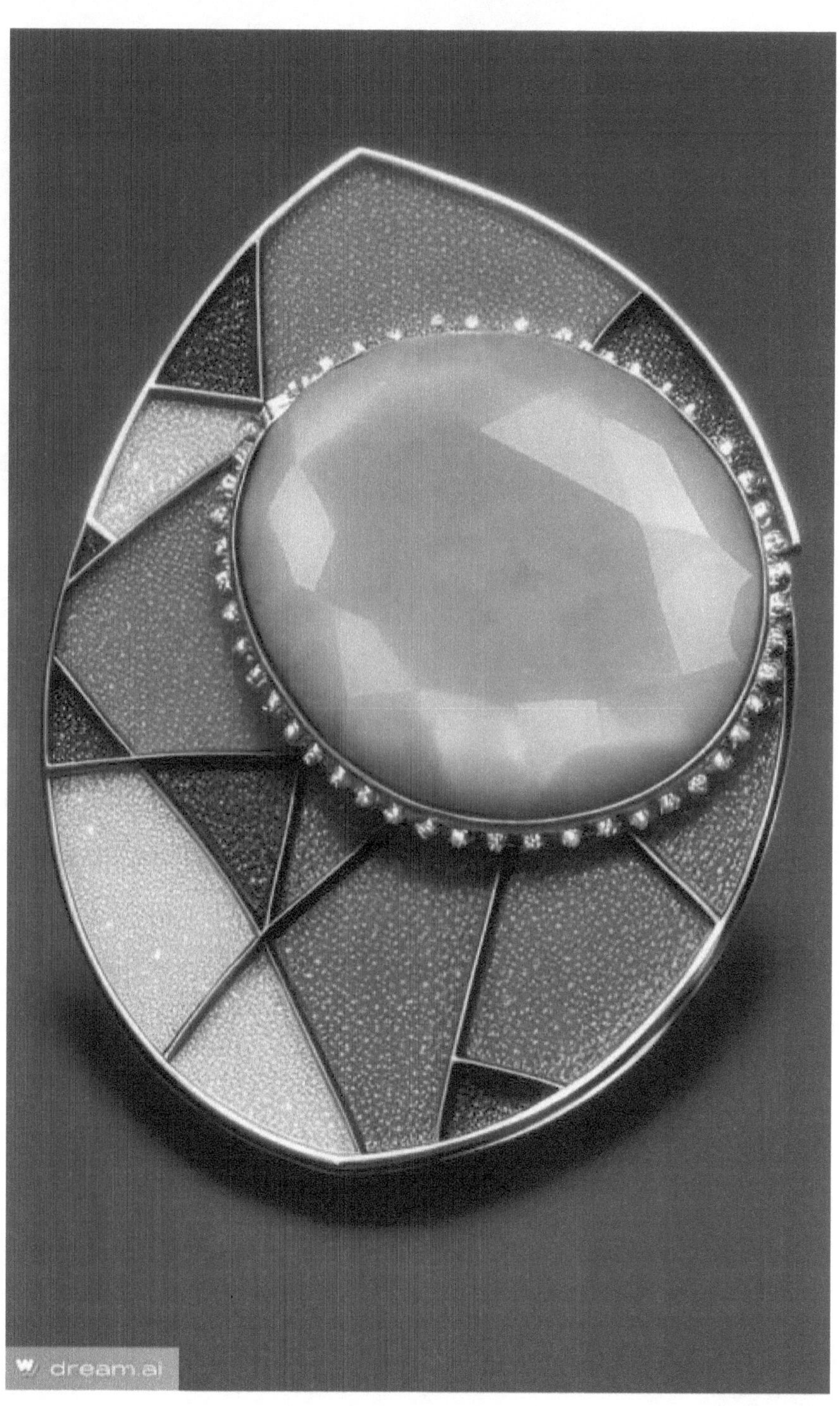

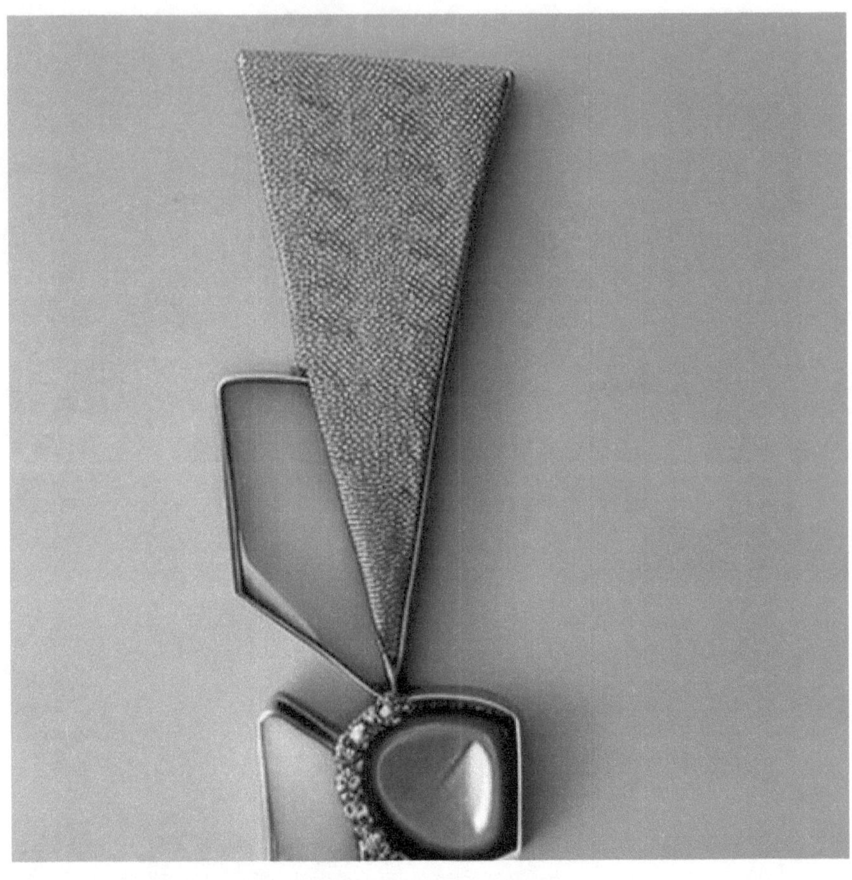

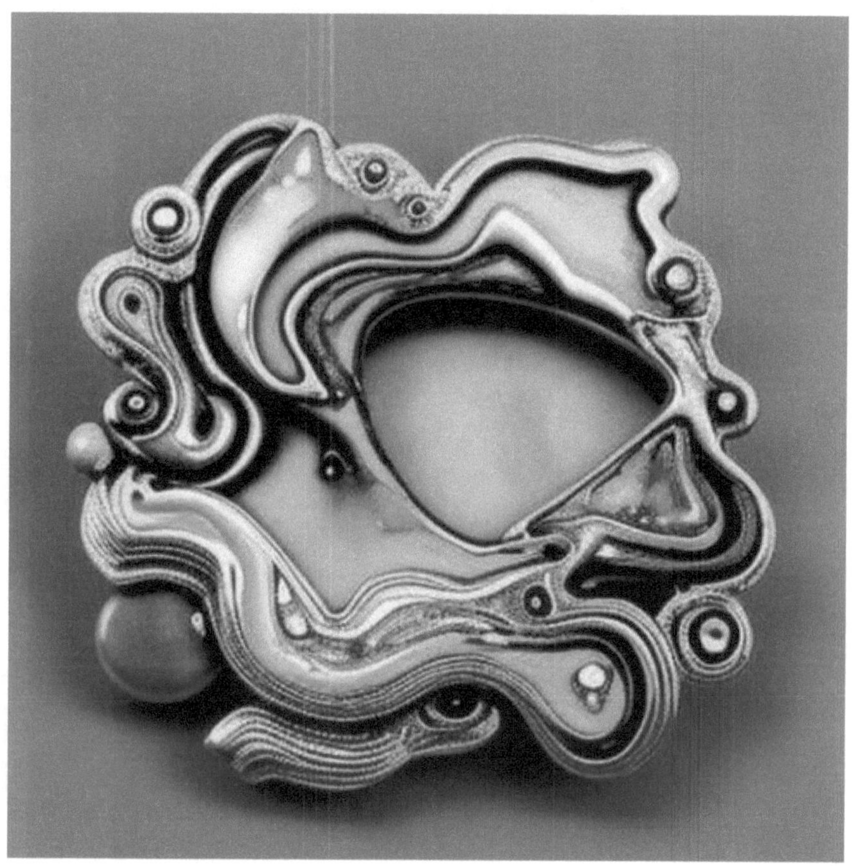

Impressionist Style:

The impressionist style is inspired by the art movement of the same name and features delicate, dreamy designs that evoke a sense of tranquility and beauty. Jewelry in this style often features pastel colors, floral motifs, and the use of enamel and other decorative techniques.

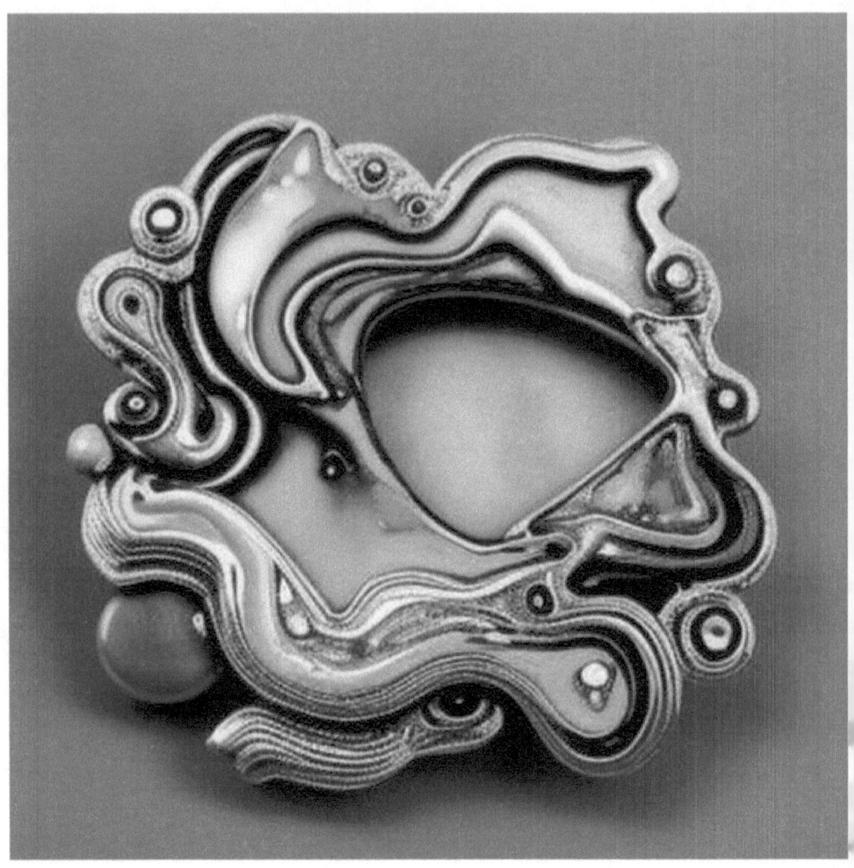

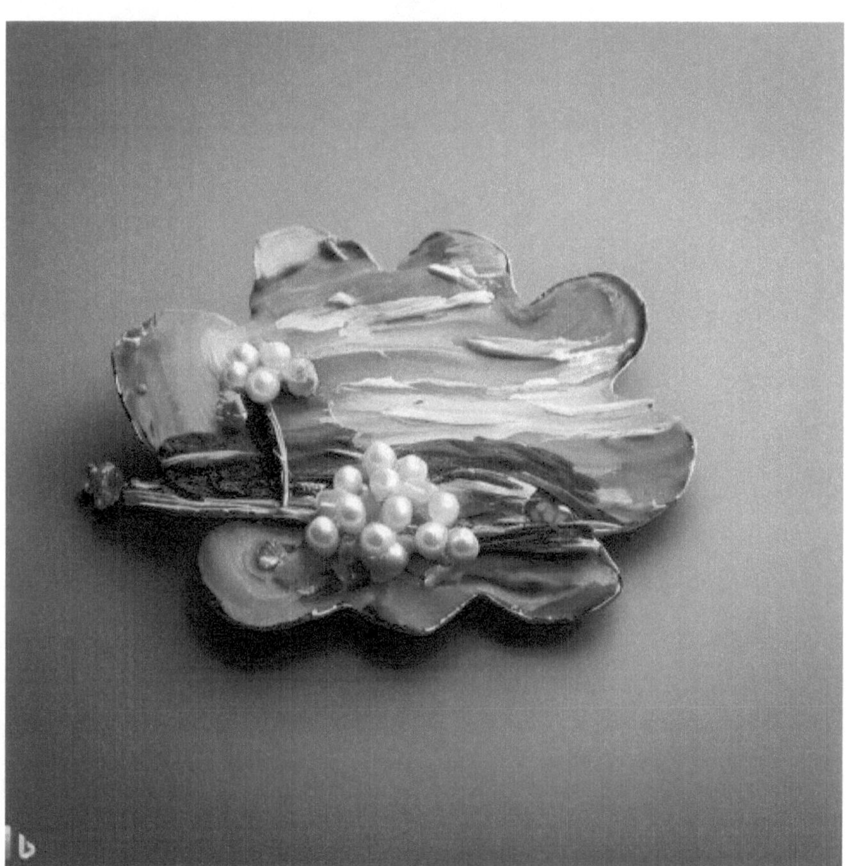

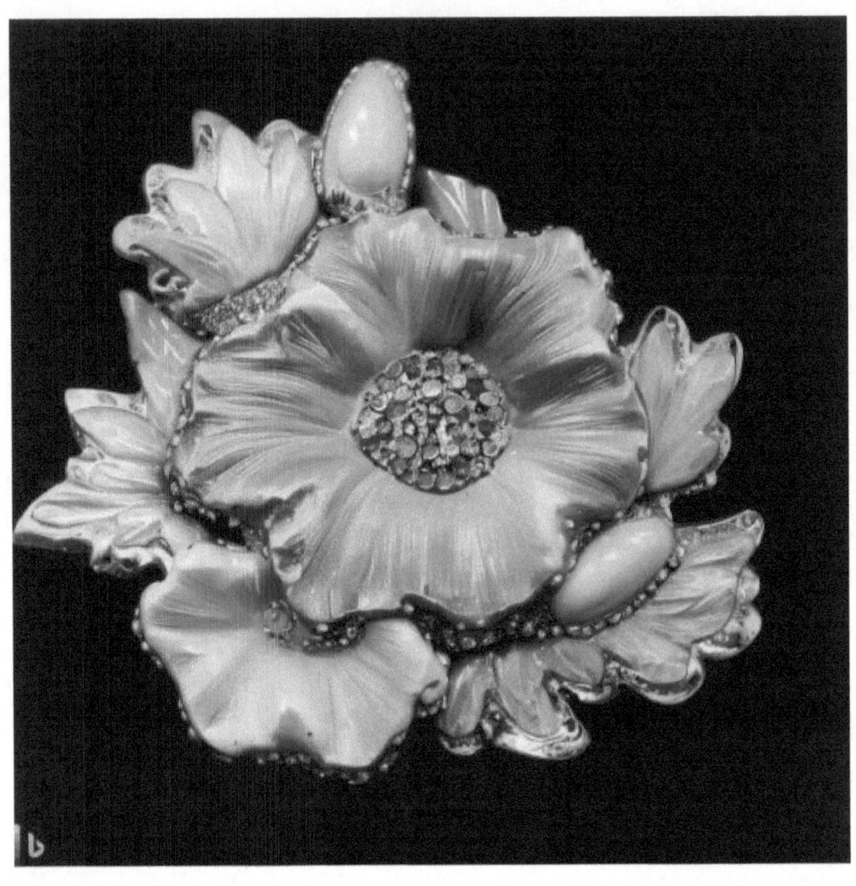

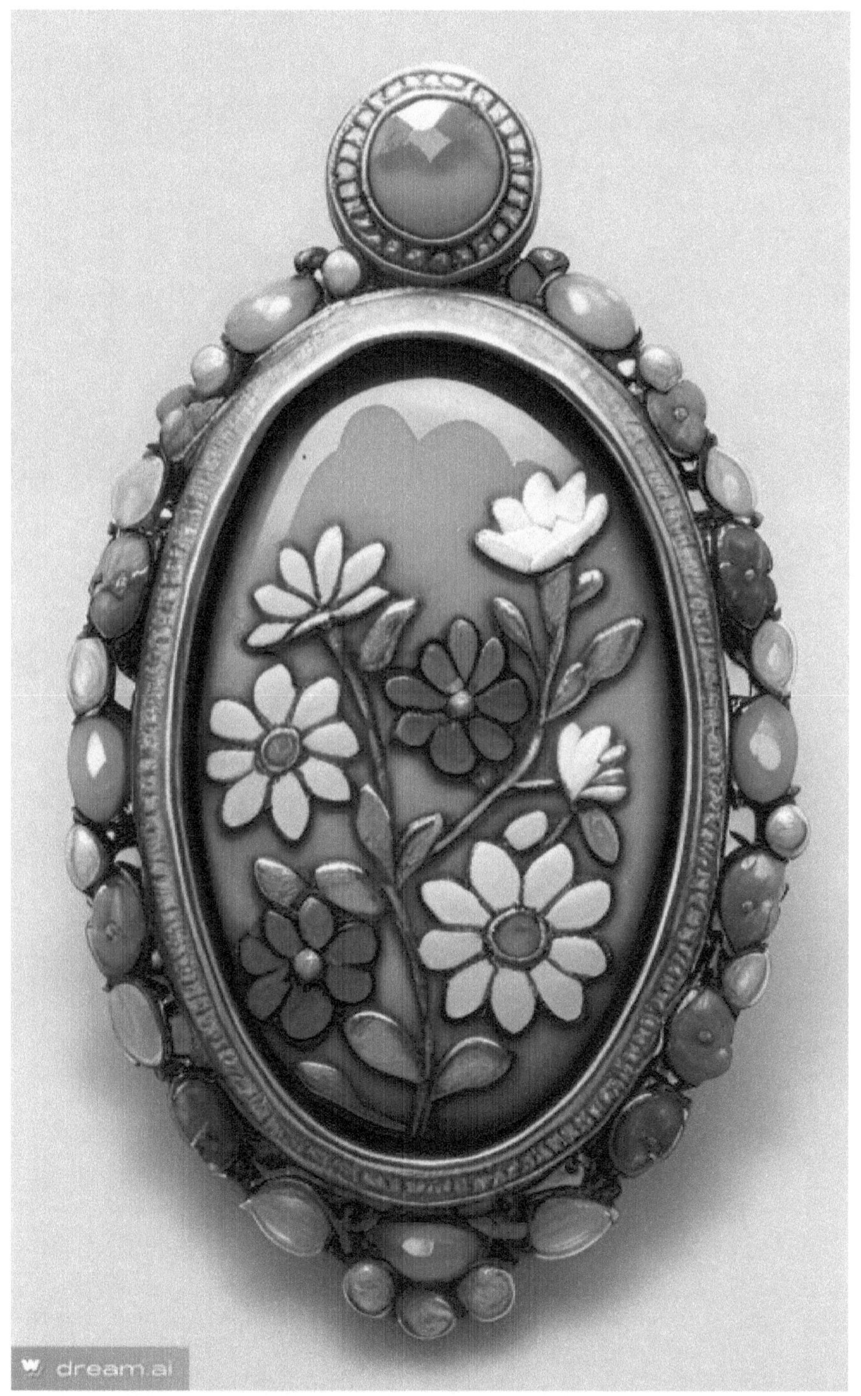

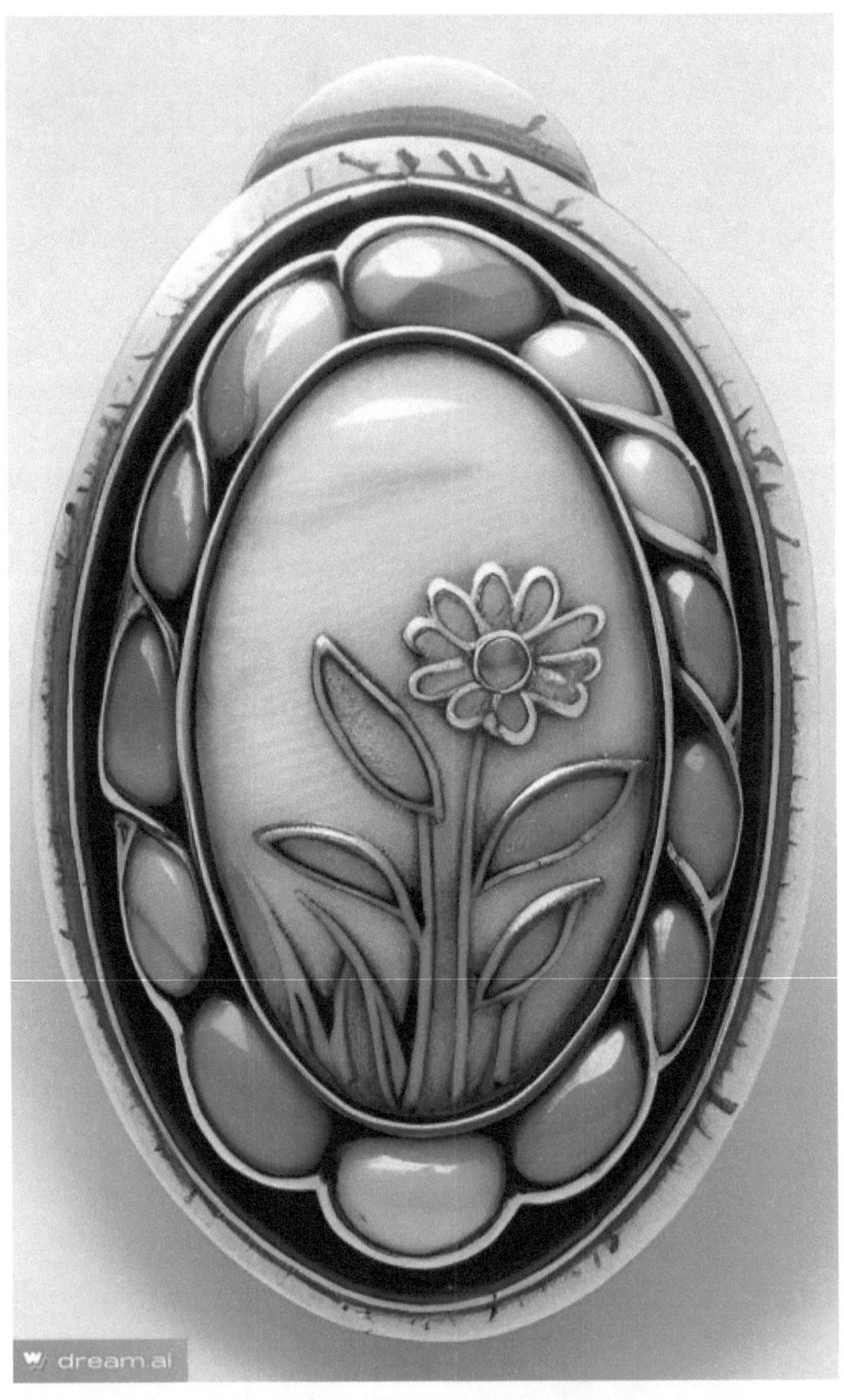

Viking Style:

Viking jewelry is bold, rugged, and inspired by the Viking culture of Scandinavia. It often features intricate patterns and symbols such as runes, knots, and Thor's hammer. Viking jewelry is typically made from silver or bronze and has a distinct and powerful look that is perfect for those who want to make a statement.

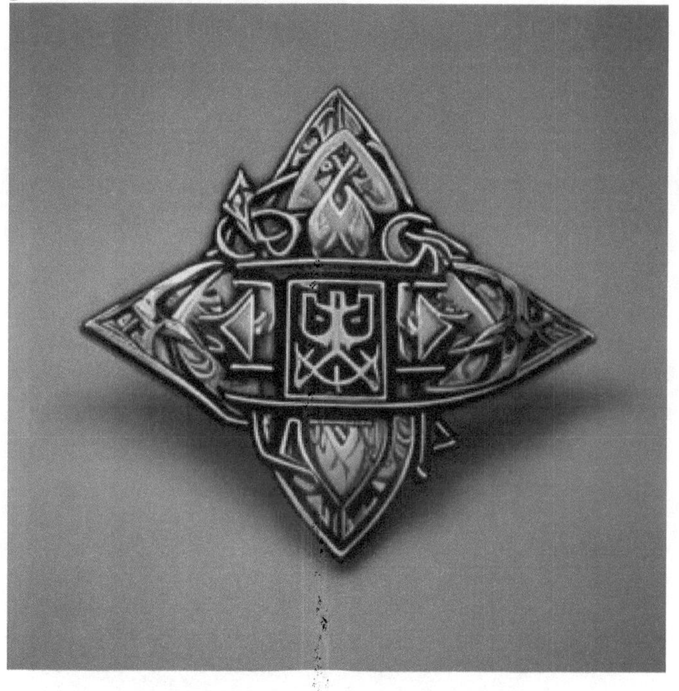

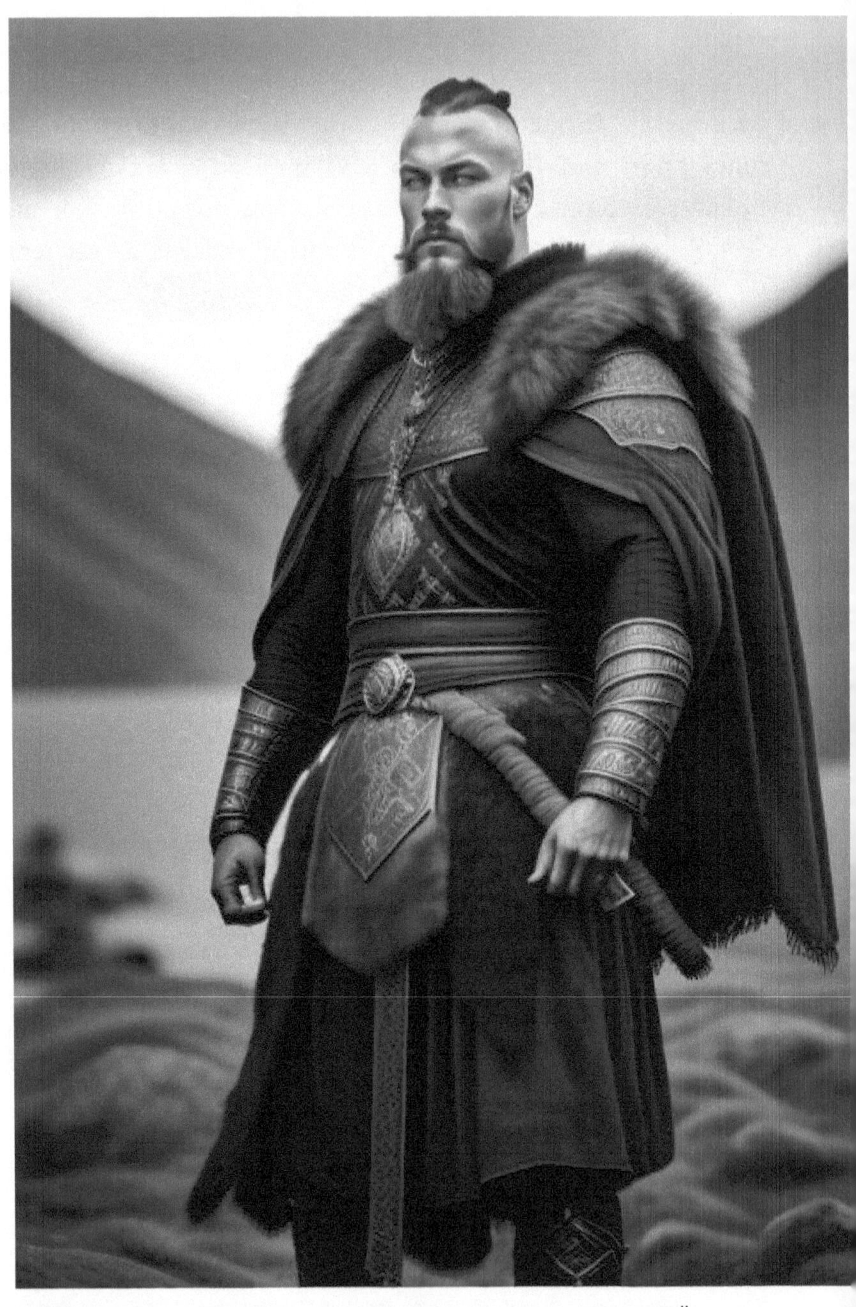

пользуем стили художников для создания ювелирных украшений.
ChatGPT

In conclusion, these styles are just a few of the many fascinating and diverse jewelry styles that have captured the imagination.

Harnessing the Styles of Artists in Jewelry Design

Art has always served as a wellspring of inspiration for designers across various creative industries. In the realm of jewelry design, artists' styles have been harnessed to create unique and captivating pieces. Drawing from the techniques, aesthetics, and iconic elements of renowned painters, sculptors, and visionaries, jewelry designers have embarked on a journey to translate art into wearable form. This article explores how the styles of famous artists have been utilized to create stunning and expressive jewelry pieces.

The Fusion of Art and Jewelry:

The intersection of art and jewelry design offers a realm of boundless possibilities. By incorporating the styles of famous artists, jewelry designers infuse their creations with a touch of artistic brilliance, transcending mere adornment to become wearable works of art. This convergence allows individuals to carry the spirit of their favorite artists with them, showcasing their appreciation for art while enhancing their personal style.

The Techniques and Aesthetics of Artists:

Each artist brings a unique set of techniques, aesthetics, and themes to their work. By harnessing these elements, jewelry designers can create pieces that pay homage to the artist's vision while adding their own interpretive flair. For example, the bold and vibrant brushstrokes of Van Gogh can be translated into enamel designs, capturing the essence of his masterpieces on a small canvas of precious metal. Similarly, the intricate and surreal motifs of Salvador Dali can find expression in sculptural and avant-garde jewelry pieces.

Iconic Elements and Symbolism:

Famous artists often have distinct motifs, symbols, or themes that define their body of work. These iconic elements can be woven into jewelry designs to create pieces that reflect the essence of the artist's style. For instance, the use of geometric patterns and vibrant colors in the style of Piet Mondrian can be translated into sleek, contemporary jewelry pieces that exude a sense of artistic abstraction.

Prompt: Necklace in style of Piet Mondrian

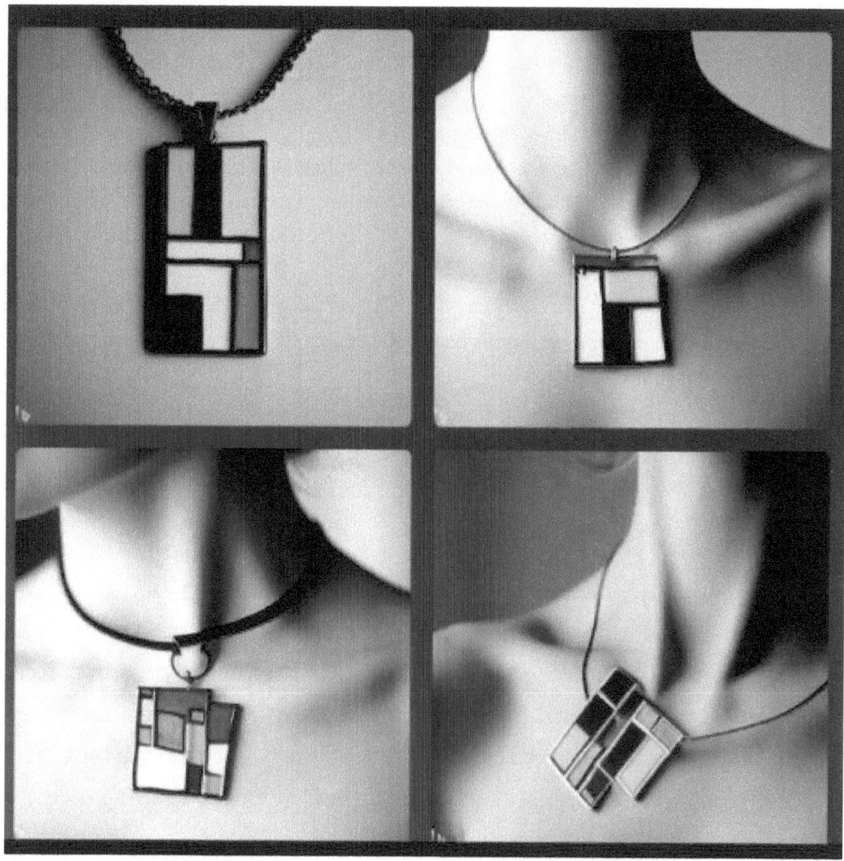

Likewise, the organic forms and fluid lines of Art Nouveau, as seen in the works of Alphonse Mucha, can inspire intricate and delicate jewelry designs.

Jewelry Houses and Collaborations:

In collaboration with museums, art foundations, or the estates of renowned artists, jewelry houses have embarked on exciting projects to bring art to life in the form of jewelry. These collaborations often involve licensing agreements, allowing designers to access the artist's archives and create collections inspired by their works. By fusing the artist's style with their expertise in jewelry craftsmanship, these houses offer individuals the opportunity to own wearable art pieces that embody the spirit of their favorite artists.

Personal Expression and Cultural Appreciation:

The utilization of artists' styles in jewelry design goes beyond mere imitation; it is a means of personal expression and cultural appreciation. By wearing jewelry inspired by famous artists, individuals can convey their artistic sensibilities, showcase their love for a particular art movement, or pay homage to an artist whose work resonates with them. It becomes a wearable statement that reflects their unique personality, interests, and artistic tastes.

The fusion of art and jewelry design creates a captivating synergy, allowing individuals to carry the essence of renowned artists wherever they go. By harnessing the techniques, aesthetics, and iconic elements of artists, jewelry designers create wearable art that speaks to the beauty and inspiration found in the world of art. Whether it's Van Gogh's expressive brushstrokes, Dali's surreal motifs, or the organic forms of Art Nouveau, these styles provide an avenue for individuals to celebrate their love for art while adorning themselves with one-of-a-kind jewelry pieces that embody the spirit of artistic brilliance.

The Influence of Gustav Klimt's Style on Jewelry Design

Introduction:

Gustav Klimt, renowned for his mesmerizing paintings, was a prominent figure in the Art Nouveau movement and a leading proponent of the Vienna Secession. His distinct style, characterized by opulent ornamentation, intricate patterns, and symbolic imagery, continues to captivate art enthusiasts and inspire various artistic disciplines. One such area is jewelry design, where Klimt's techniques and aesthetics have found a new medium of expression. In this article, we will explore how Klimt's style, rooted in Secession and Modernism, has influenced the creation of exquisite jewelry pieces. We will also delve into the example of the jewelry house Freywille, which has released a collection inspired by Gustav Klimt's masterpieces.

The Artistic Language of Gustav Klimt:

Gustav Klimt's artistic language was defined by several distinctive features, which have made a profound impact on the world of art and design. His works were characterized by the lavish use of gold leaf, intricate patterns, and a harmonious fusion of symbolism and sensuality. Klimt's emphasis on decorative elements, such as ornate borders and mosaic-like compositions, created a visual language that exuded opulence and refinement.

The Influence on Jewelry Design:

Klimt's artistic techniques and motifs have seamlessly translated into the realm of jewelry design. Jewelry artisans have drawn inspiration from his elaborate patterns, flowing lines, and intricate details to create stunning wearable art pieces. The use of gold, often in the form of gilding or gold-plated elements, pays homage to Klimt's fondness for this precious metal. The incorporation of delicate enamel work and gemstones further enriches the jewelry, echoing the richness and depth found in Klimt's paintings.

Prompt: Bracelet, metal painting in the style of Gustav Klimt

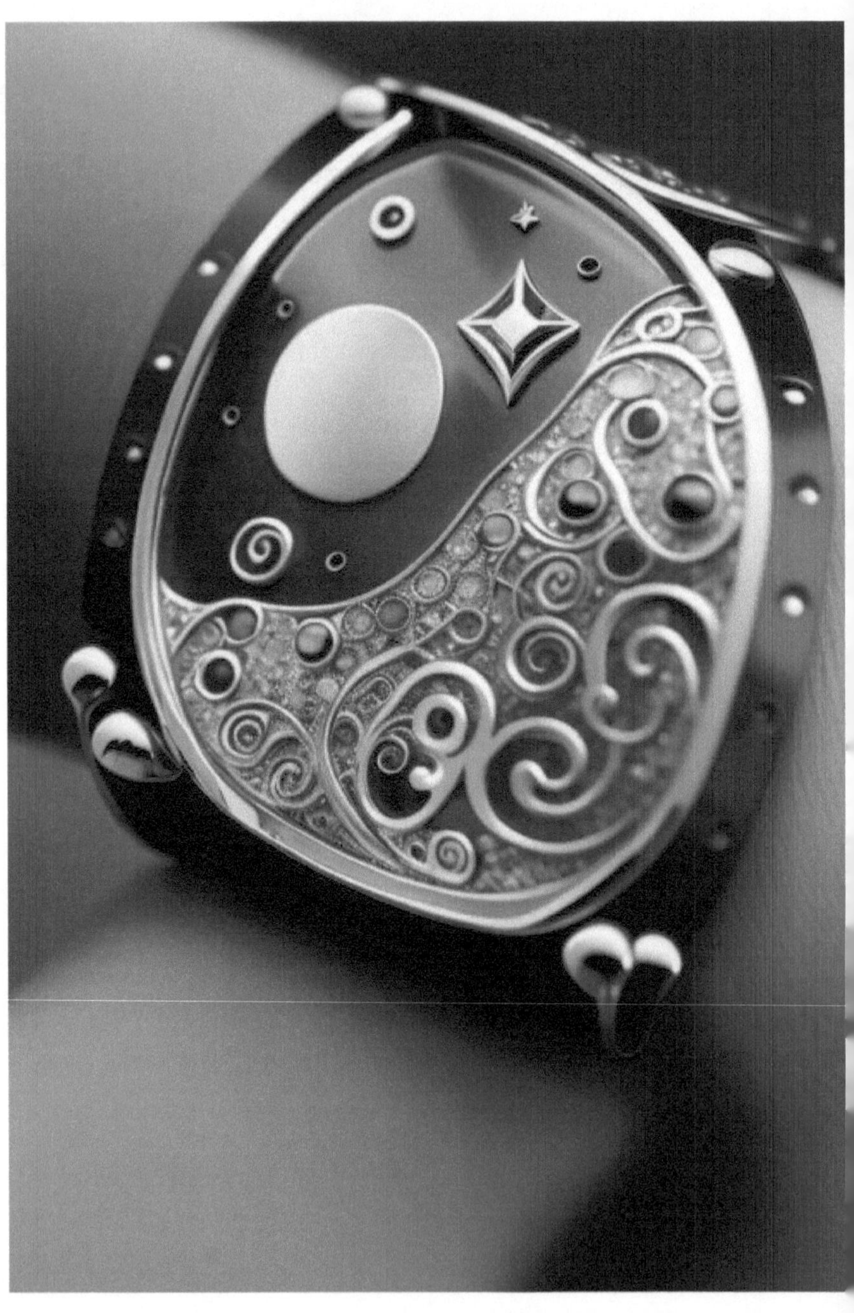

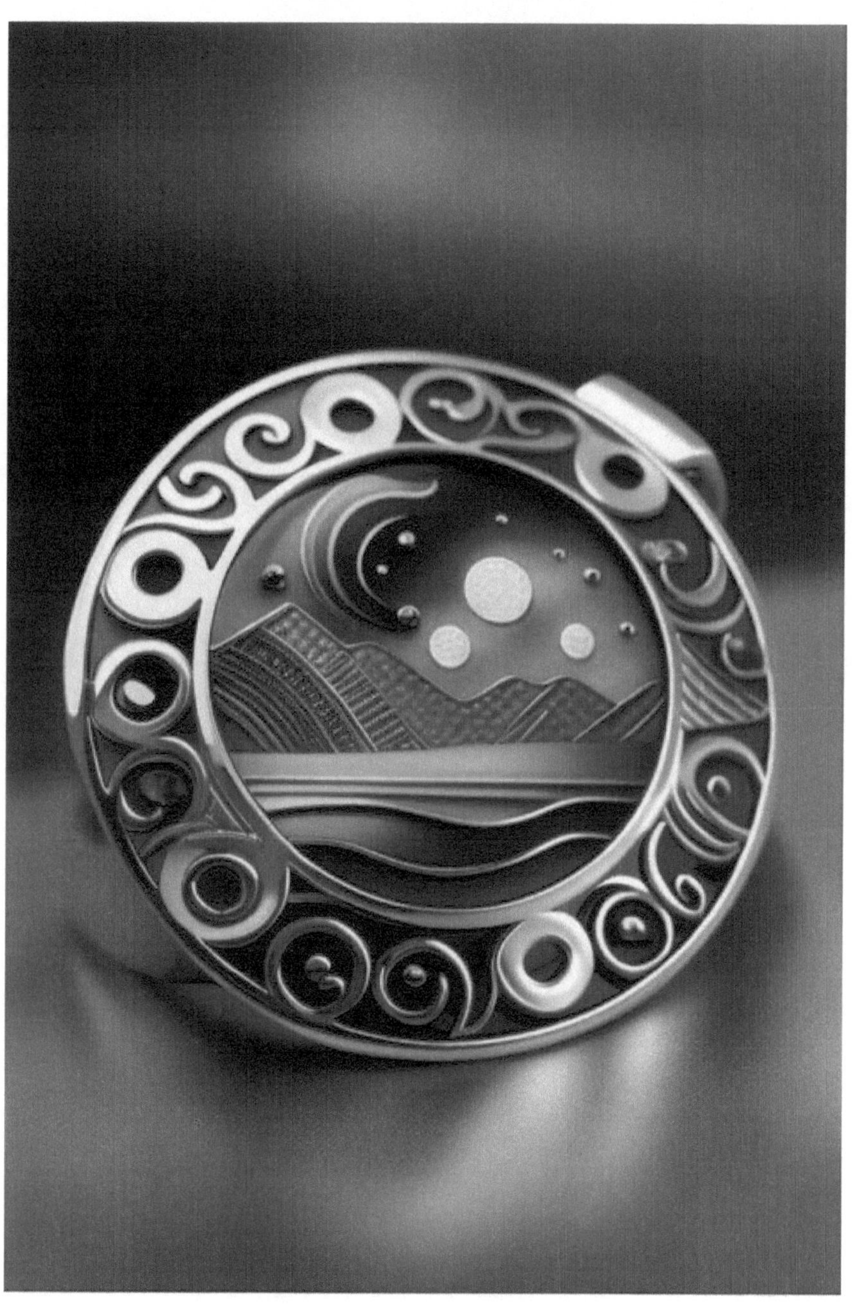

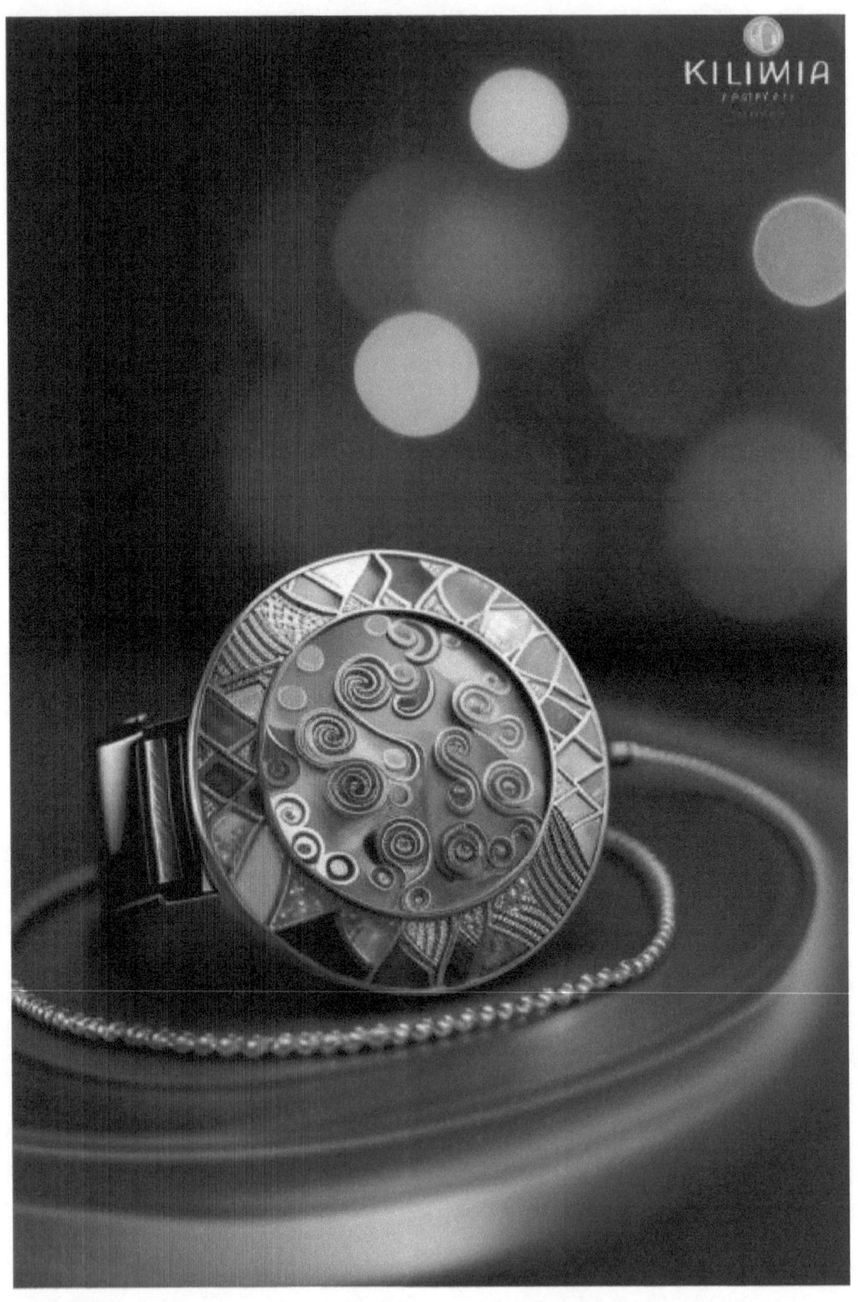
KILIMIA

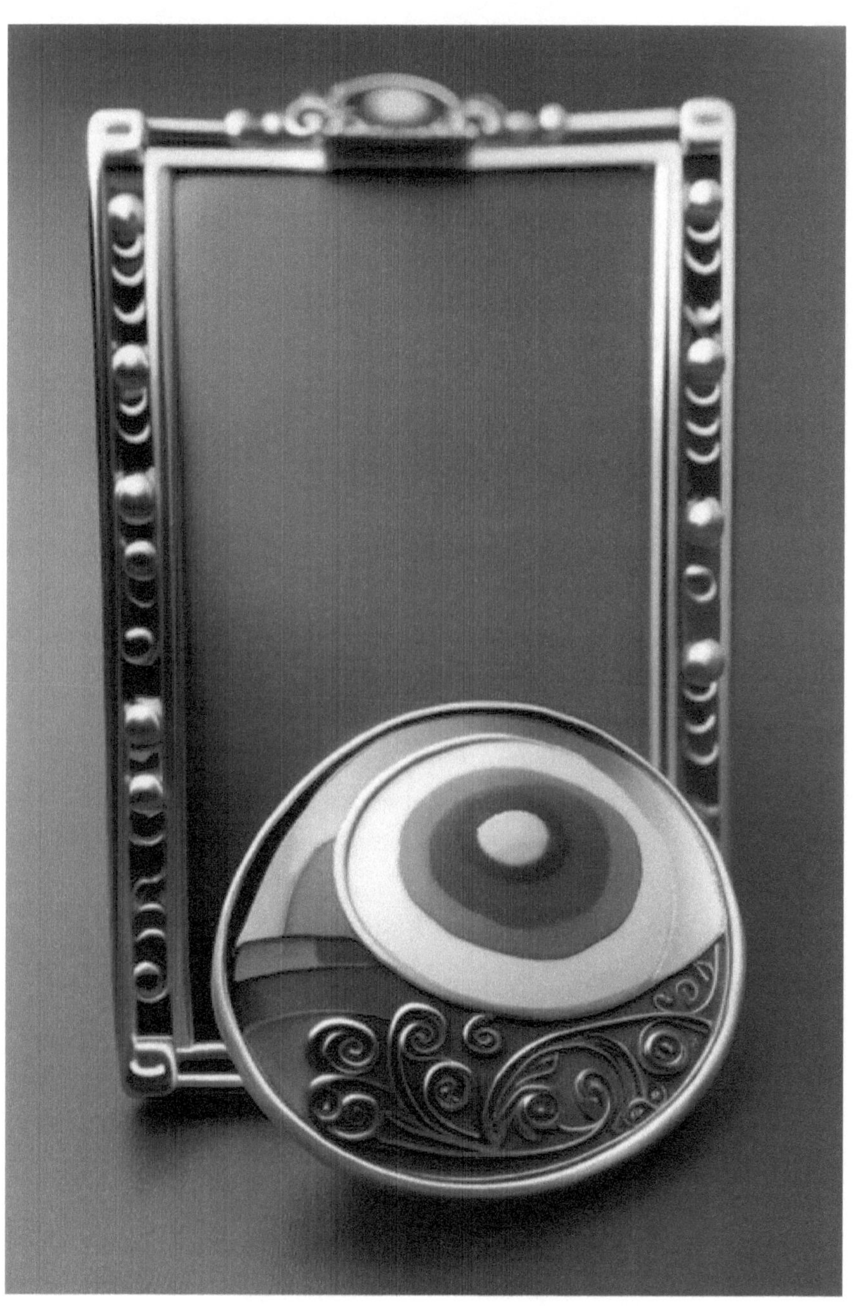

Symbolism and Mythology:

One of the notable aspects of Klimt's work is the symbolism and mythological references he incorporated. From the embracing lovers in "The Kiss" to the intertwining serpents in "Judith and the Head of Holofernes," these symbolic elements have found their way into jewelry design. Artists have adopted Klimt's use of motifs like flowers, birds, and geometric abstractions to imbue their creations with a deeper meaning and evoke a sense of mystery and allure.

Freywille: A Tribute to Gustav Klimt:

Freywille, a renowned jewelry house known for its artistic enamel techniques, has paid homage to Gustav Klimt in a remarkable collection. This collection, inspired by Klimt's iconic paintings, brings his mesmerizing art to life in the form of wearable masterpieces. Each jewelry piece showcases intricate enamel designs, reminiscent of Klimt's distinctive patterns and color palette. The motifs chosen reflect the ethereal beauty and sensuality found in Klimt's works, such as the intertwining bodies, graceful curves, and ornate borders.

By incorporating Klimt's visual vocabulary into their jewelry, Freywille has successfully transformed his artistic legacy into elegant and timeless accessories. The collection not only serves as a tribute to Klimt's genius but also allows art enthusiasts to carry a piece of his enchanting world wherever they go.

Prompt: brooch style Gustav Klimt

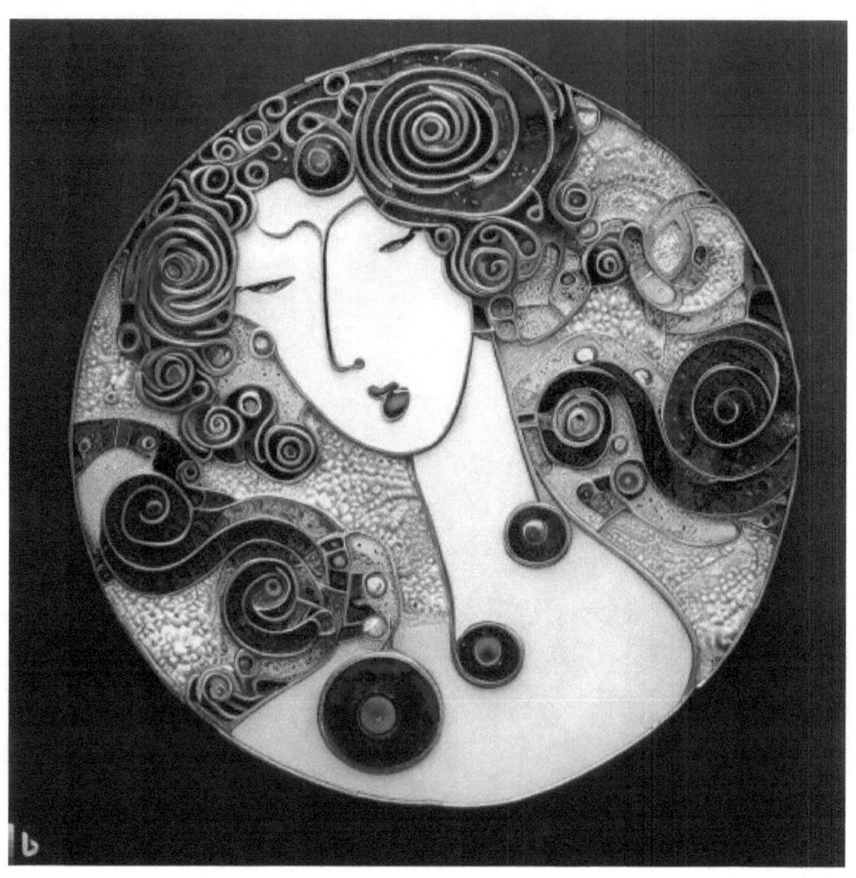

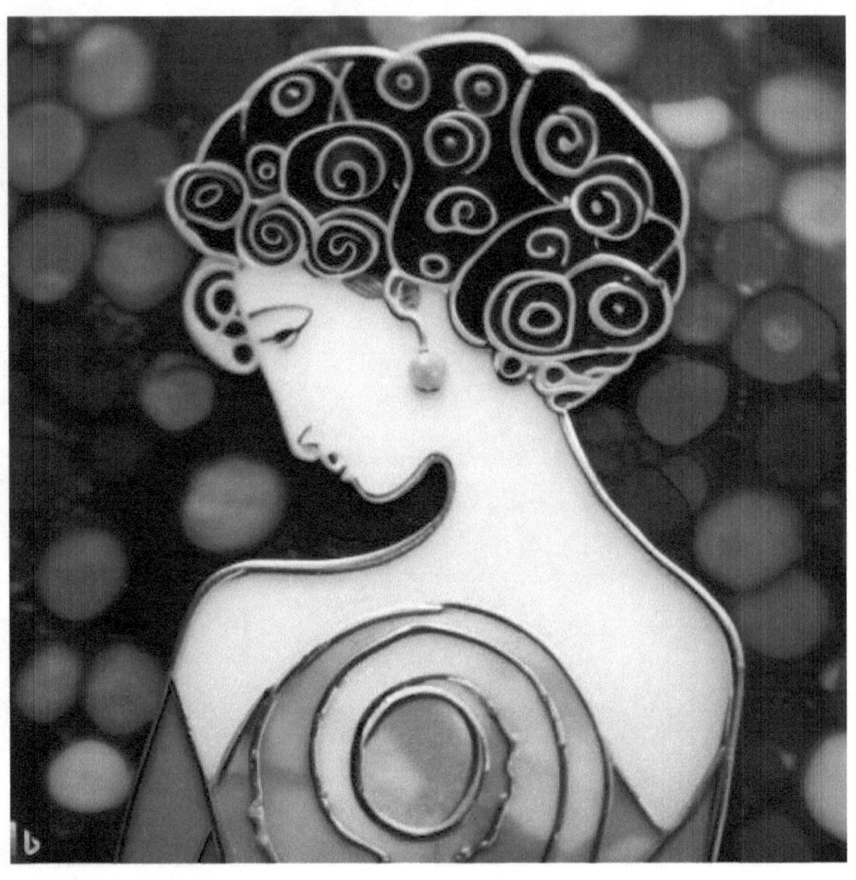

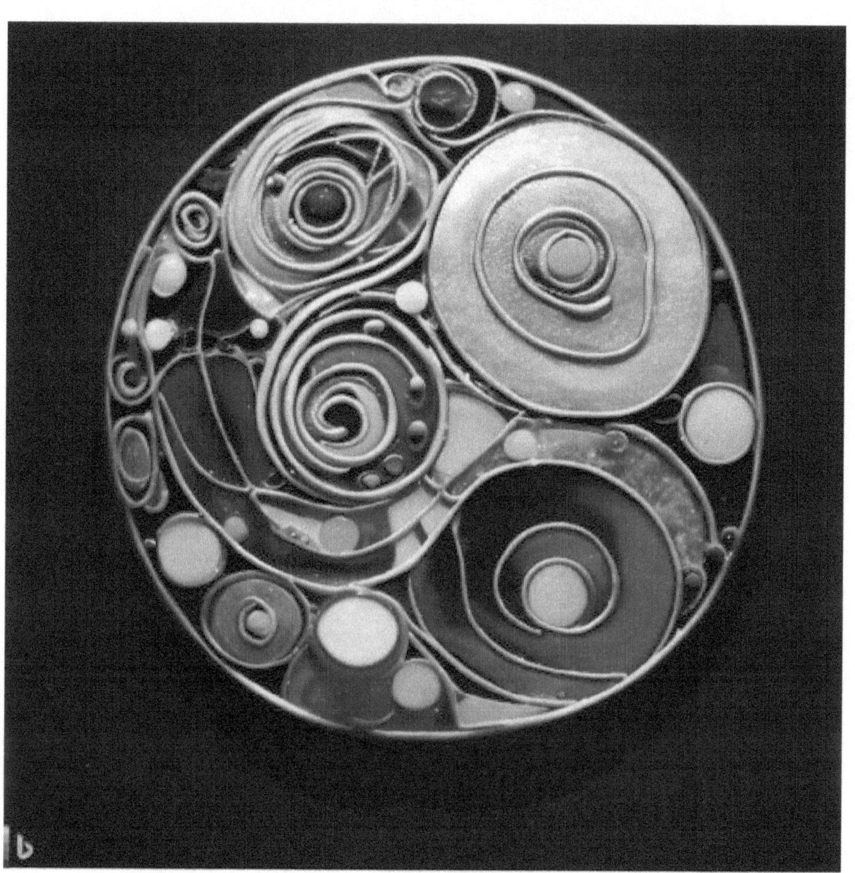

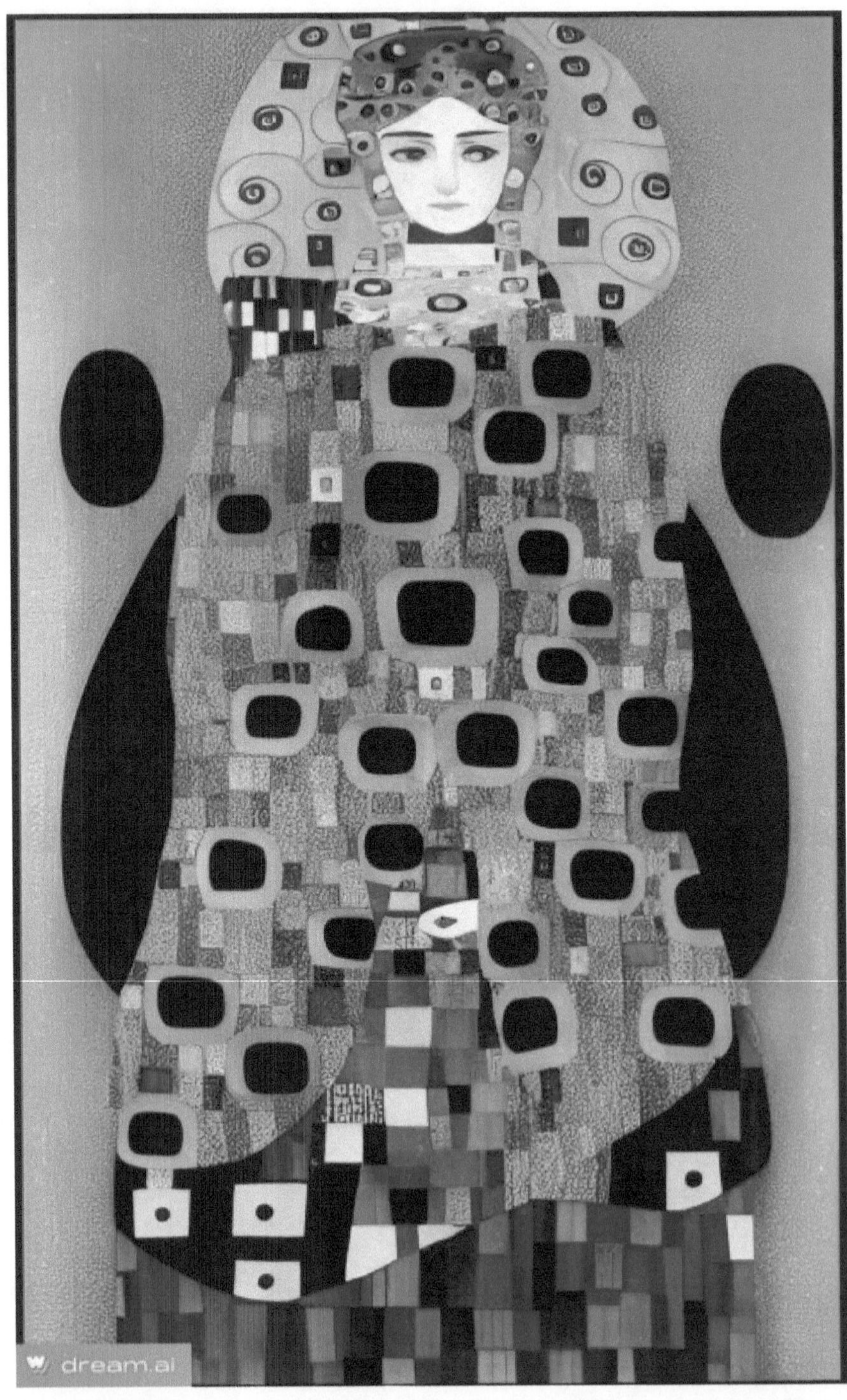

dream.ai

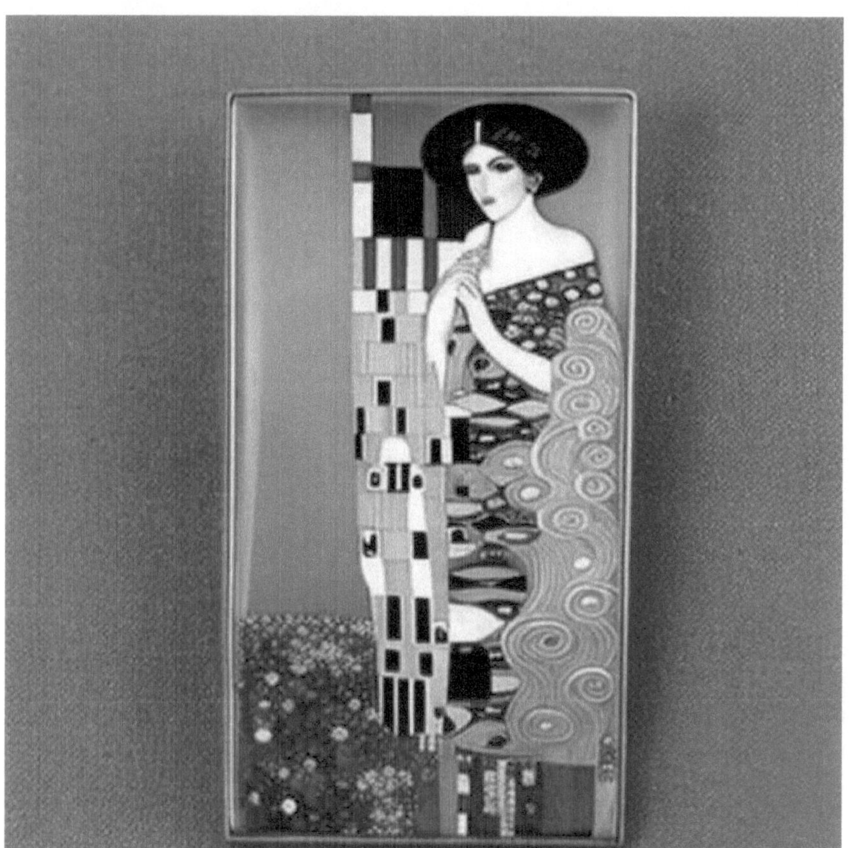

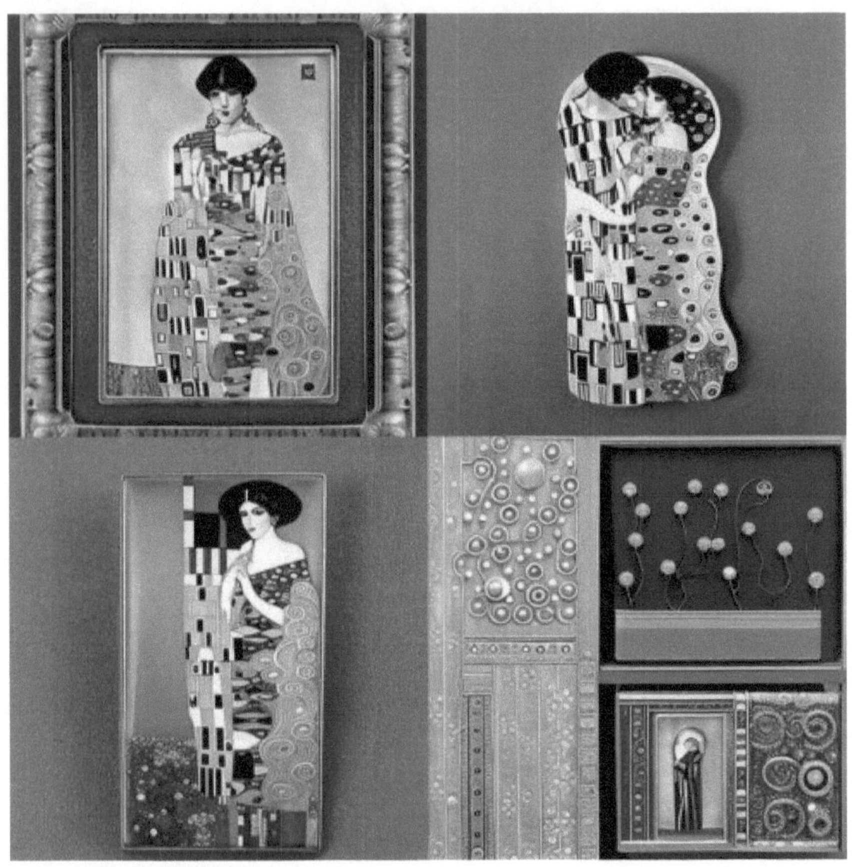

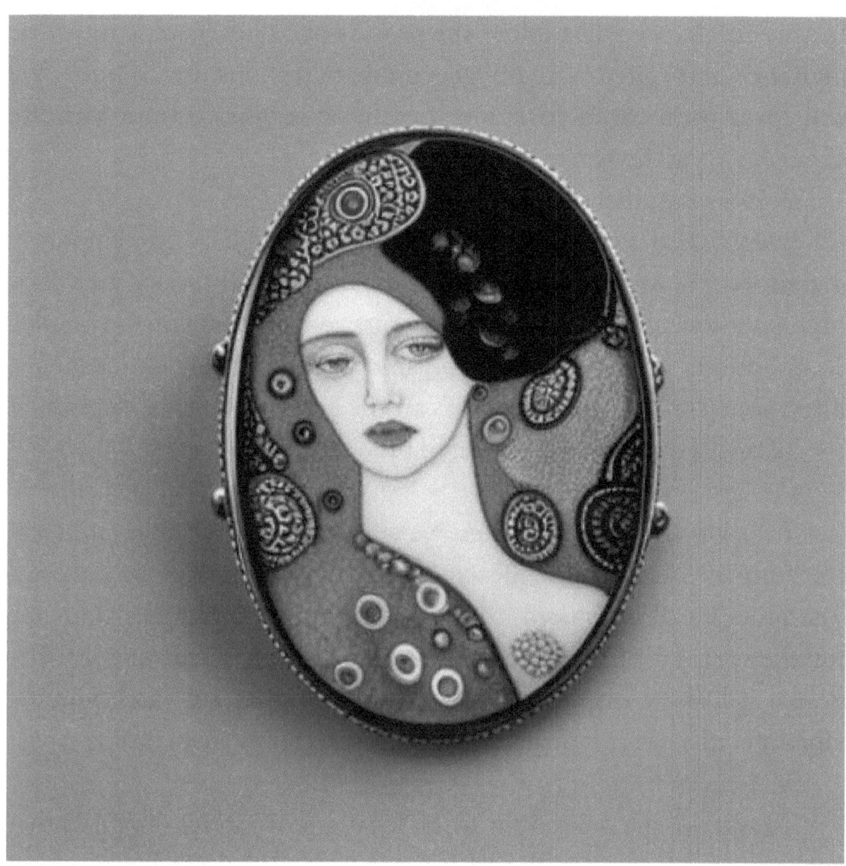

Conclusion:

Gustav Klimt's unique style, rooted in the Vienna Secession and the Art Nouveau movement, continues to inspire and influence artists across various disciplines. The world of jewelry design has embraced Klimt's techniques, aesthetics, and symbolism, resulting in the creation of exquisite pieces that reflect his opulent and symbolic vision. The example of Freywille's collection demonstrates how Klimt's art can be seamlessly translated into wearable art, allowing individuals to adorn themselves with the allure and beauty of his iconic

Creating a Modern, Tech-Inspired Brooch with Beeple's Futuristic Art

In this article, we will explore the process of using Beeple's futuristic digital art as inspiration to design a modern, tech-inspired brooch. We will focus on incorporating metal painting techniques and intricate details to bring this artistic vision to life.

Beeple's Futuristic Digital Art:

Beeple, also known as Mike Winkelmann, is a contemporary digital artist renowned for his groundbreaking and futuristic artworks. His captivating pieces often feature vibrant colors, complex compositions, and a blend of organic and technological elements. These characteristics make Beeple's art the perfect source of inspiration for creating a modern, tech-inspired brooch.

Design Concept:

To begin the design process, we envision a brooch that embraces the futuristic aesthetic while incorporating elements of technology. The brooch will be crafted using metal painting techniques, allowing for the creation of intricate details and a striking visual impact. The design will draw inspiration from Beeple's digital art, incorporating vibrant colors, geometric patterns, and a sense of movement.

Material Selection:

To achieve the desired futuristic look, we will select materials that evoke a sense of modernity and technology. Stainless steel or titanium can be excellent choices due to their sleek and contemporary appearance. These metals provide a solid foundation for the intricate detailing that will be applied through metal painting techniques.

Metal Painting Techniques:

Metal painting involves applying pigments and enamels directly onto the surface of the metal to create intricate designs and patterns. In our Beeple-inspired brooch, this technique will be utilized to bring the vibrant colors and geometric shapes to life. The careful layering of translucent and opaque enamels will add depth and dimension to the design, mimicking the digital effects often seen in Beeple's art.

Prompt: Use Beeple's futuristic digital art as inspiration for a modern, tech-inspired brooch, Metal painting, intricate details

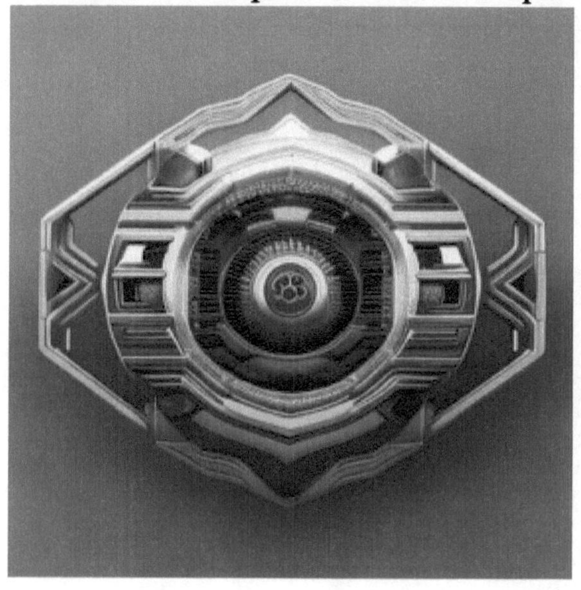

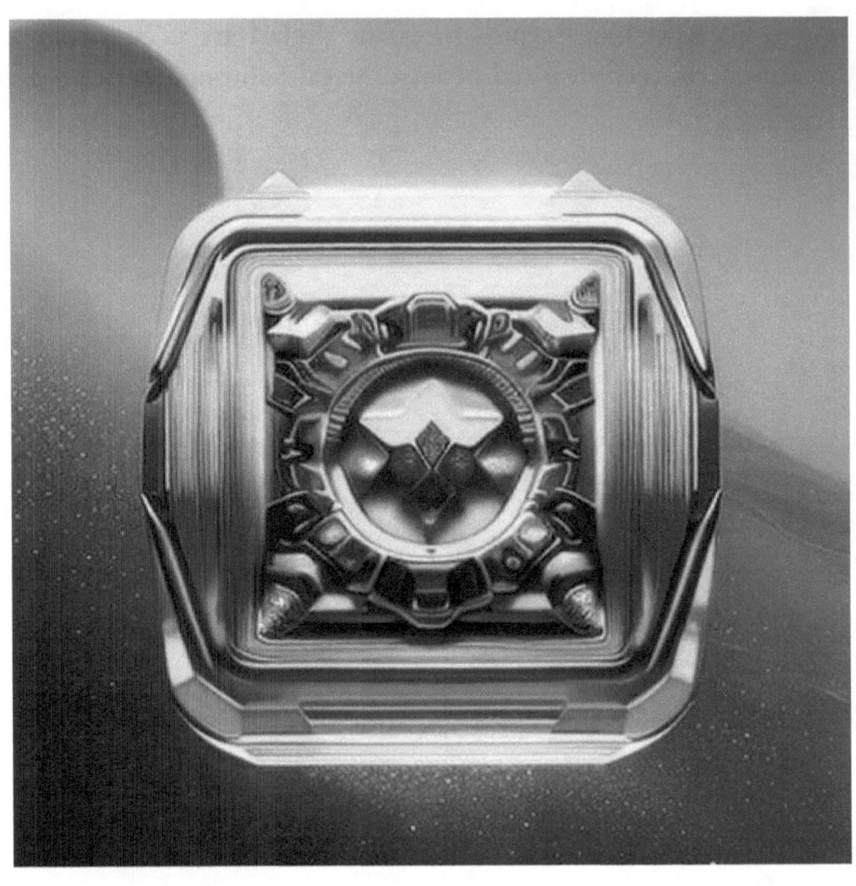

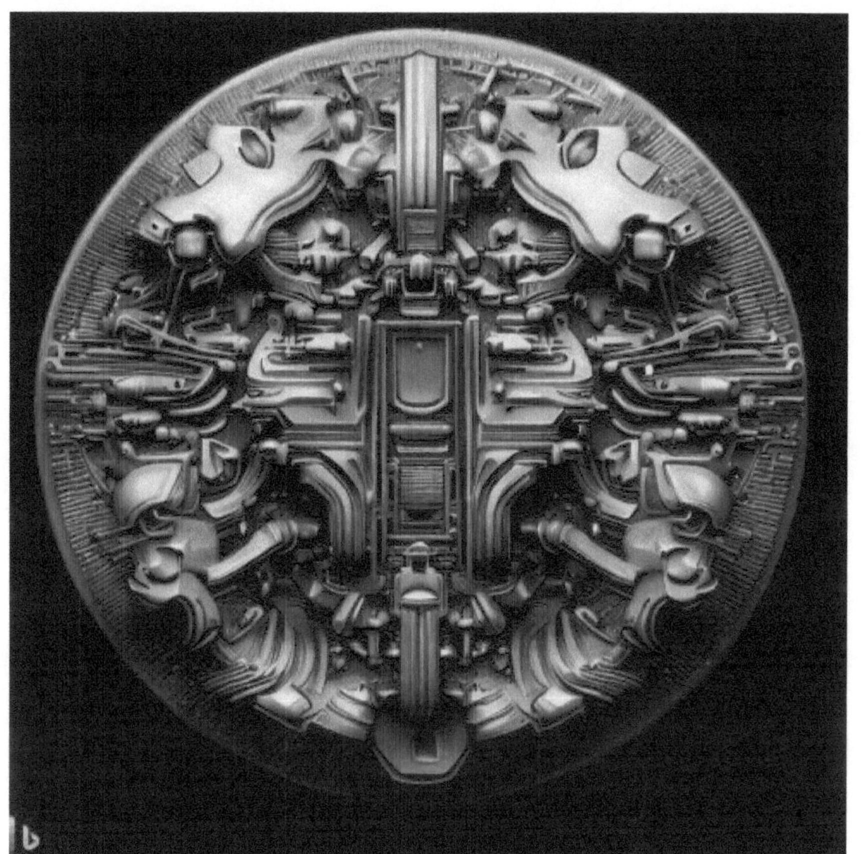

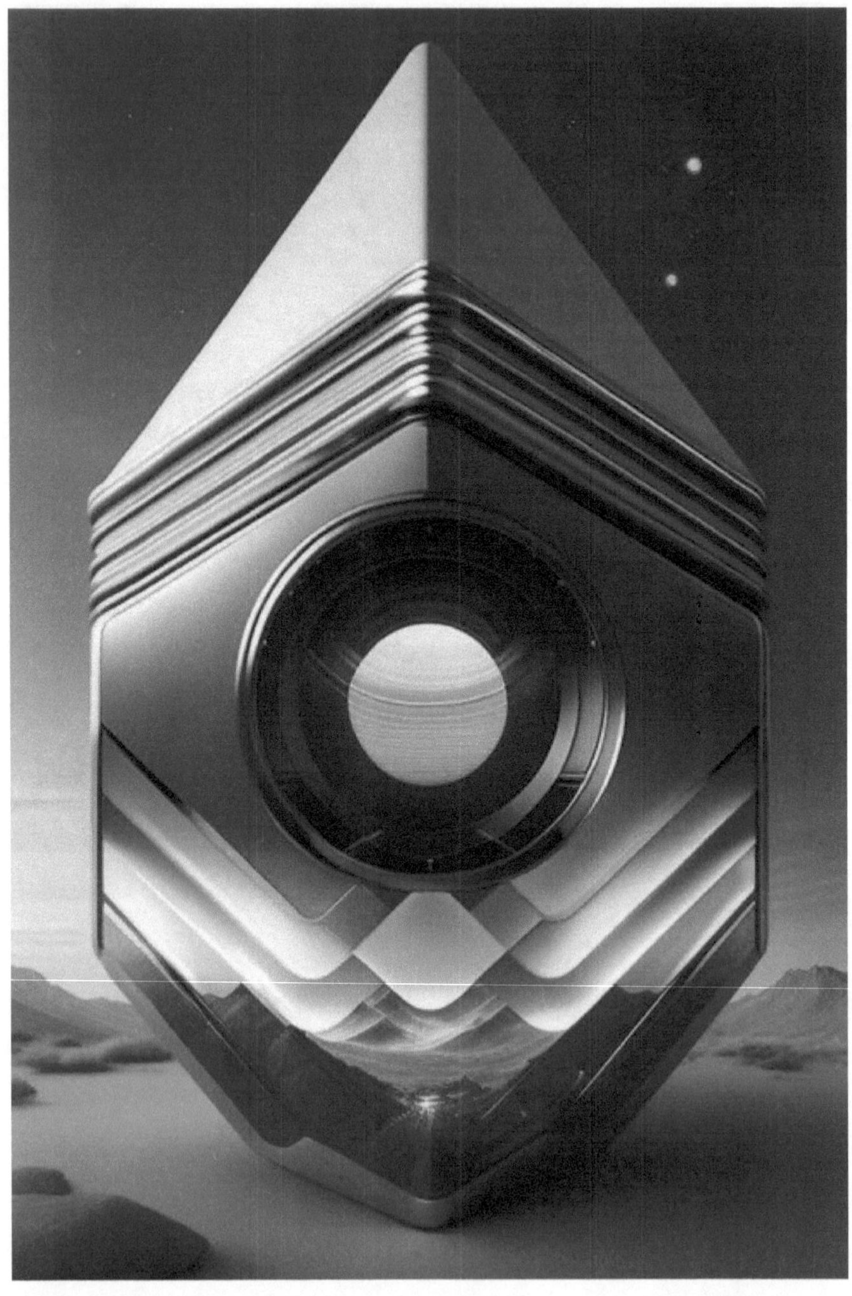

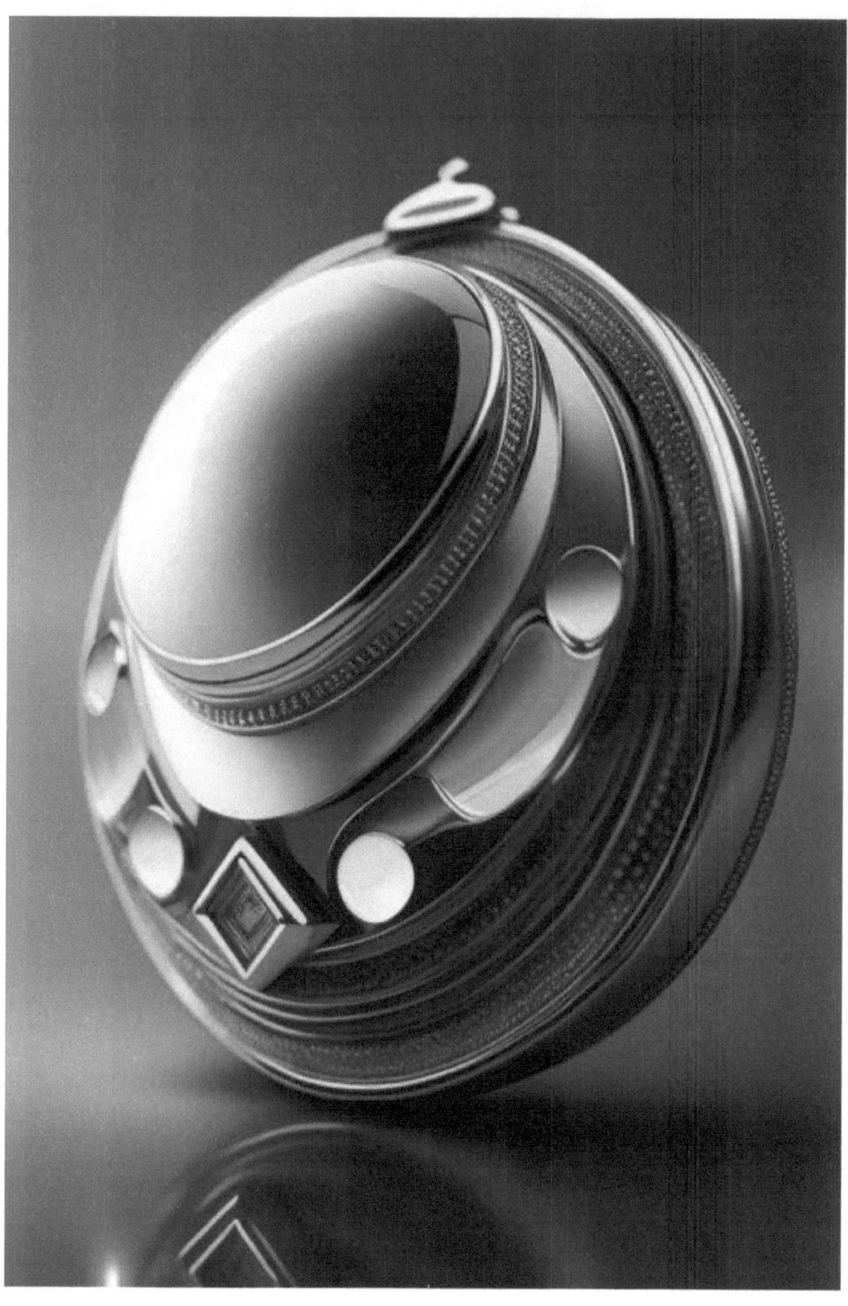

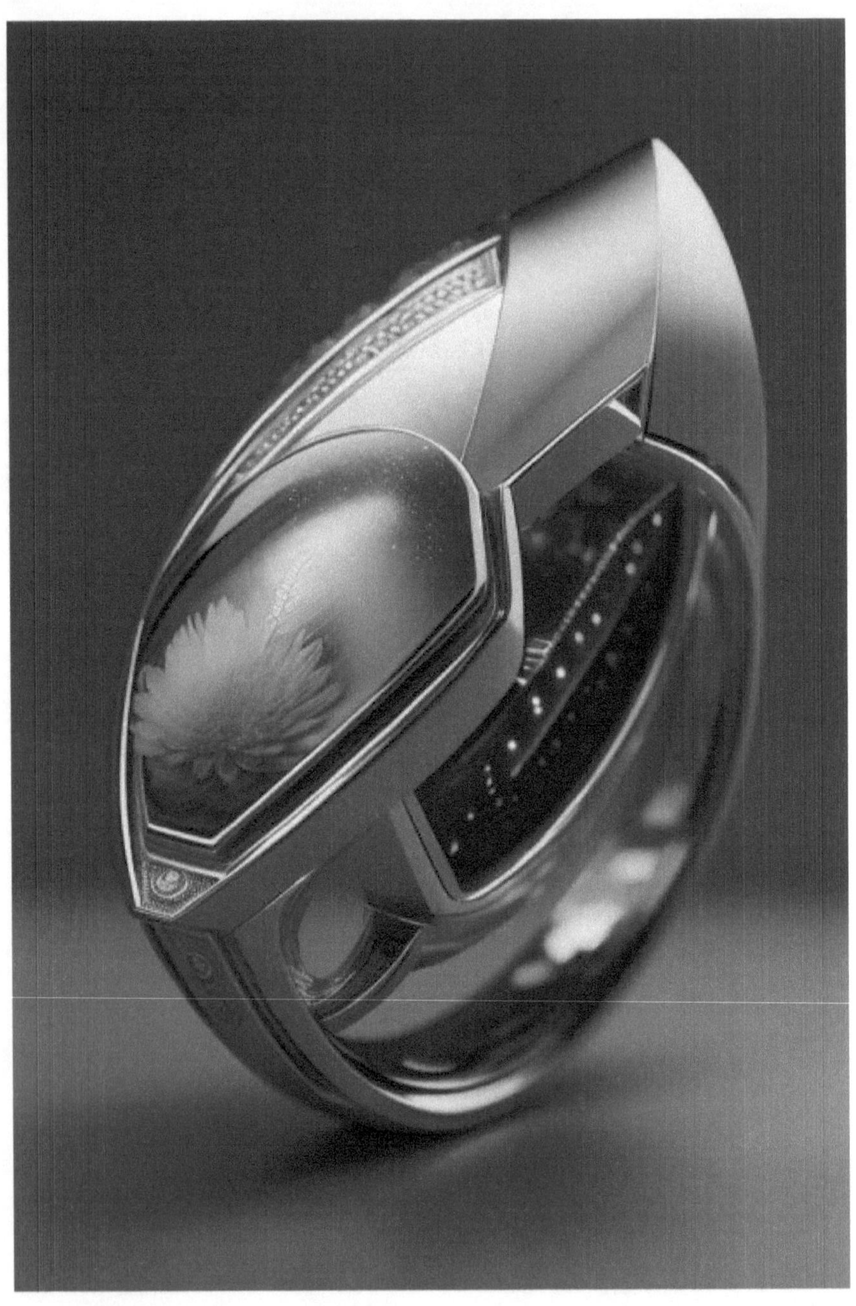

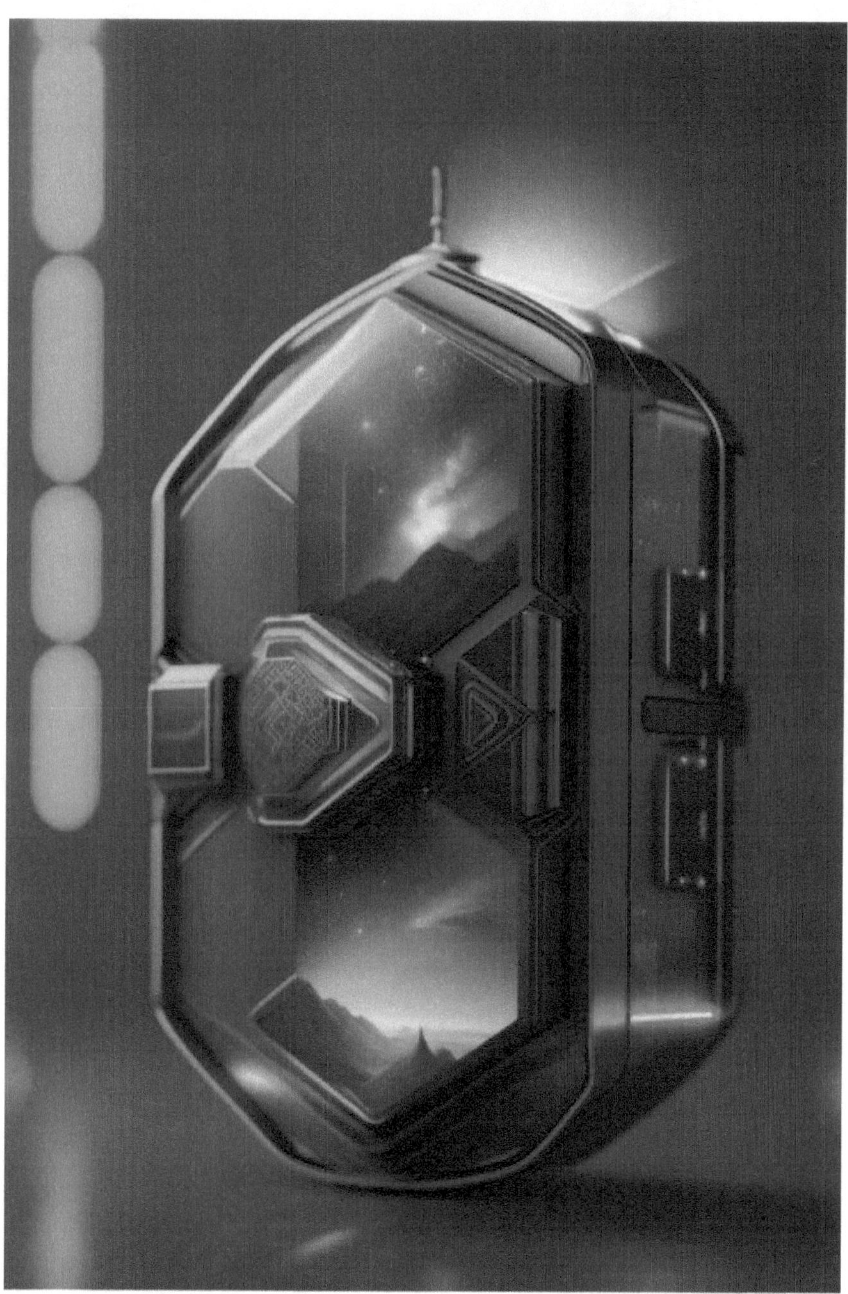

Intricate Details:

Incorporating intricate details is crucial to capturing the essence of Beeple's futuristic art. The brooch can feature delicate engravings or laser-cut designs, inspired by the intricate patterns found in Beeple's digital creations. These details will enhance the visual interest of the brooch, creating a captivating interplay between the metal base and the painted elements.

Pablo Picasso: A Multi-Talented Artist and Jewelry Designer

Pablo Picasso is widely celebrated as one of the greatest artists of the 20th century. His groundbreaking contributions to various art movements have left an indelible mark on the art world. However, Picasso's artistic prowess extended beyond painting and sculpture. He also ventured into the realm of jewelry design, creating exquisite pieces for his family and close friends. In this article, we will explore Picasso's foray into jewelry design and how his distinctive style, characterized by geometric forms and vibrant colors, continues to inspire contemporary jewelry makers and artisans.

Picasso's Jewelry Design:

Picasso's exploration of jewelry design was an extension of his artistic vision. He approached jewelry with the same innovative spirit and boldness that defined his paintings. While his jewelry creations were not as prolific as his paintings, each piece showcased his unique artistic flair and attention to detail.

Geometric Forms and Vibrant Colors:

Picasso's distinctive style, characterized by the use of geometric forms and vibrant colors, permeated his jewelry designs. Inspired by Cubism, an art movement he co-founded, Picasso incorporated angular shapes, abstract motifs, and bold color palettes into his jewelry pieces. His use of unconventional materials, such as found objects and non-precious materials, added an element of artistic experimentation to his designs.

Incorporating Picasso's Techniques:
Contemporary jewelry designers and artisans draw inspiration from Picasso's techniques to create unique and expressive pieces. Some of the key techniques utilized include:

1. Asymmetry: Picasso often embraced asymmetry in his jewelry designs, challenging traditional notions of balance and symmetry. Contemporary jewelry makers incorporate this technique to create visually dynamic and unconventional pieces that break away from conventional design norms.

2. Mixed Materials: Picasso's penchant for using unconventional materials in his artwork translates into jewelry design as well. Contemporary designers experiment with a mix of materials, combining precious metals with unexpected elements such as wood, ceramics, or even recycled materials. This approach adds a touch of eclecticism and artistic individuality to the final pieces.

3. Expressive Forms: Picasso's jewelry designs often featured bold, sculptural forms that evoke a sense of movement and energy. These expressive forms continue to inspire contemporary jewelry makers who seek to create statement pieces that captivate the viewer's attention and convey a strong artistic message.

Prompt: bracelet, Picasso's style, use Picasso's paintings, Metal painting, intricate details,

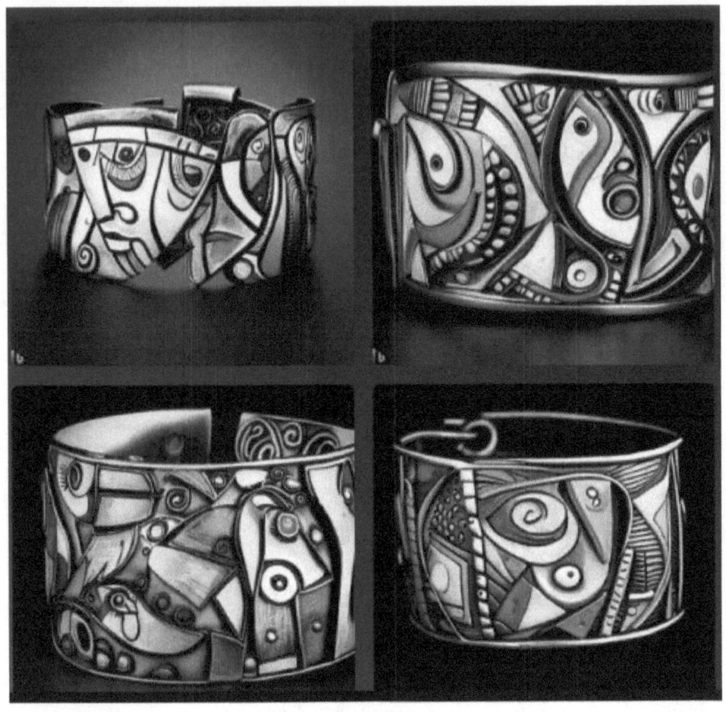

Handmade Artistry:

In recent years, there has been a resurgence of interest in handmade jewelry and artisanal craftsmanship. Picasso's jewelry designs serve as a source of inspiration for these contemporary artisans. They study his pieces, seeking to understand his design principles and reinterpret his artistic language in their own creations. By referencing Picasso's work, these craftsmen infuse their jewelry pieces with a sense of artistic heritage and pay homage to one of the greatest artists in history.

Prompt: brooch, Picasso's style, use of geometric forms and vibrant colors, Metal painting, intricate details,

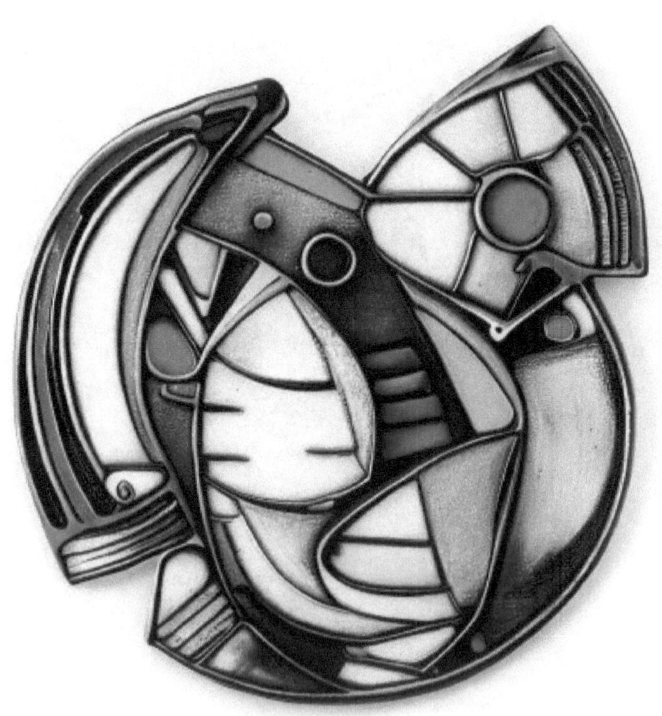

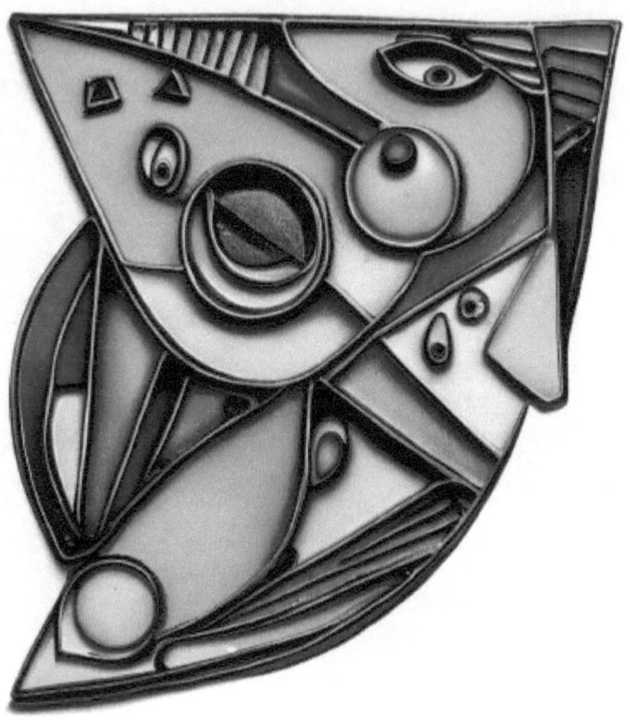

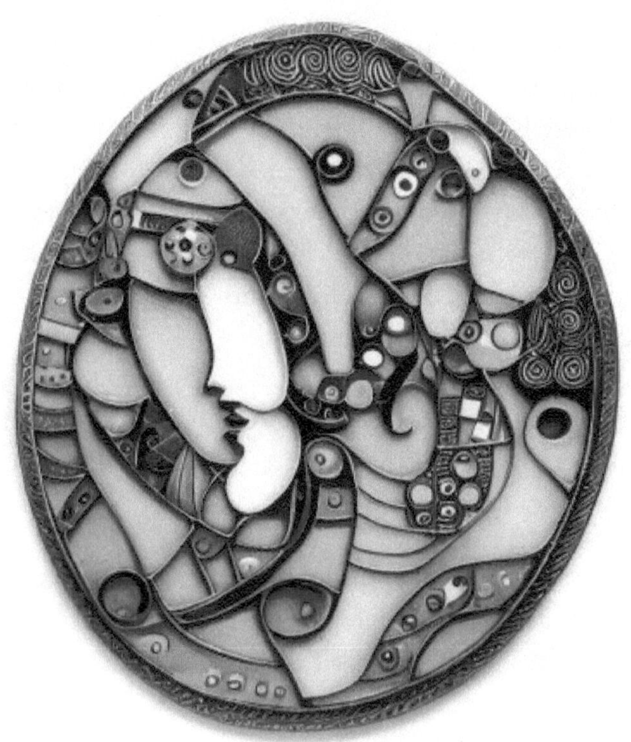

Pablo Picasso's legacy as a multifaceted artist extends beyond his paintings and sculptures. His foray into jewelry design exemplifies his creative versatility and innovative approach. Through his exploration of geometric forms, vibrant colors, and unconventional materials, Picasso left an enduring impact on the world of jewelry design. Today, contemporary jewelry makers continue to draw inspiration from his techniques, incorporating his artistic language into their own creations. Picasso's influence in the realm of jewelry design serves as a testament to his enduring artistic genius and the timeless appeal of his visionary approach to art.

Salvador Dalí: The Artistic Alchemy of Jewelry Design

Salvador Dalí, known for his surrealist masterpieces, ventured beyond the realms of painting and sculpture to explore the world of jewelry design. With his signature blend of imagination, symbolism, and unconventional creativity, Dalí created dozens of remarkable jewelry pieces. In this article, we will delve into Dalí's journey as a jewelry designer, explore his unique techniques, and admire the distinctive collection of jewelry that bears his unmistakable touch.

Dalí's Jewelry Design Techniques:

Dalí approached jewelry design with the same avant-garde spirit that defined his artistic career. His jewelry pieces showcased an array of techniques and concepts that reflected his surrealistic vision. Some of the key techniques employed by Dalí include:

1. Symbolism and Narrative: Like his paintings, Dalí's jewelry designs were imbued with symbolism and narrative. His pieces often featured intricate details and hidden meanings, inviting viewers to unravel the enigmatic stories behind each creation. Symbolic motifs, such as melting clocks, ants, and distorted faces, were meticulously crafted to evoke a sense of mystery and intrigue.

2. Transformation and Metamorphosis: Dalí's fascination with transformation and metamorphosis manifested in his jewelry designs. He explored the idea of objects evolving into unexpected forms, blurring the boundaries between reality and the subconscious. His pieces often featured intricate mechanisms that allowed them to transform, revealing hidden elements or shifting shapes.

3. Unconventional Materials: Dalí's jewelry designs were characterized by his innovative use of materials. He embraced a wide range of materials, from precious metals

and gemstones to unconventional elements such as feathers, glass, and even natural objects like seashells. This eclectic combination of materials added an element of surprise and intrigue to his jewelry pieces.

The Dalí Jewelry Collection:
Salvador Dalí's jewelry collection is a testament to his boundless creativity and artistic vision. The collection encompasses a unique ensemble of treasures, each possessing an extraordinary blend of themes, materials, colors, and forms. From the famous lobster telephone pendant to the iconic lips brooch, each piece captures the essence of Dalí's surrealistic world.

Legacy and Contemporary Influence:
Dalí's jewelry designs continue to captivate and inspire contemporary jewelry designers and artisans. His audacious exploration of techniques, his commitment to storytelling through jewelry, and his unorthodox use of materials serve as a source of inspiration for those seeking to push the boundaries of traditional jewelry design. By channeling Dalí's innovative spirit, contemporary jewelers create pieces that challenge conventions, provoke thought, and ignite the imagination of the wearer and viewer alike.

Prompt: pendant in the style of Salvador Dali, surrealism,

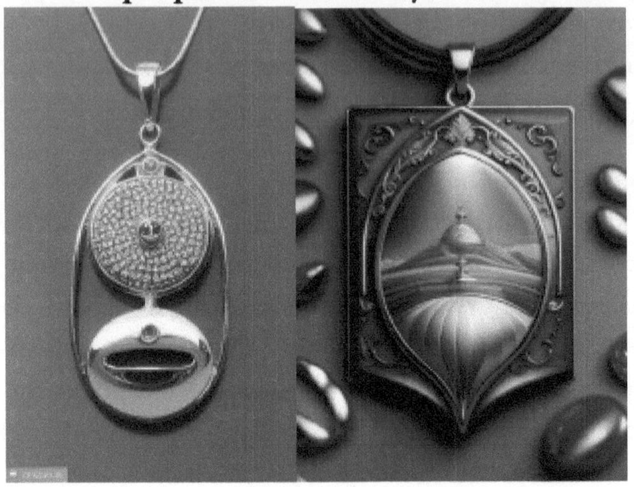

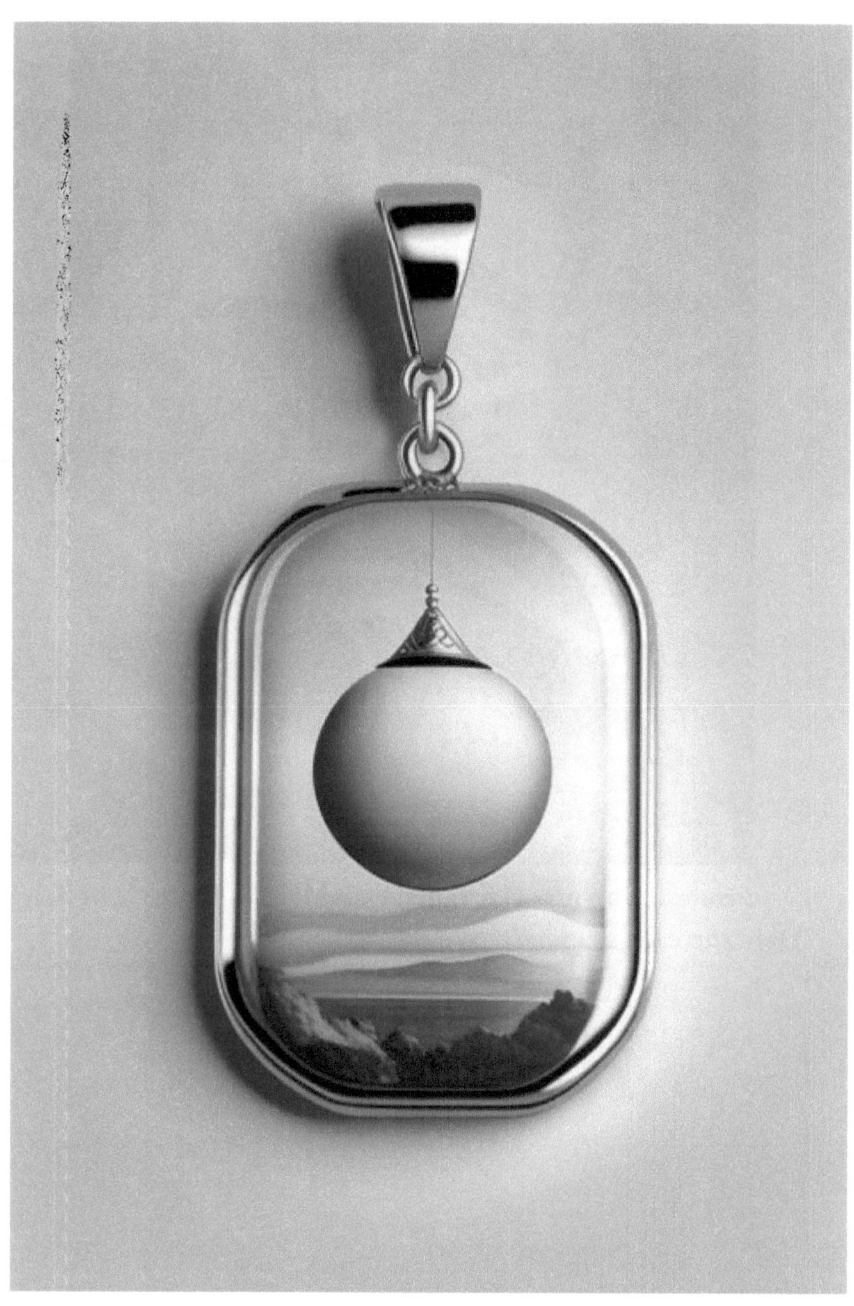

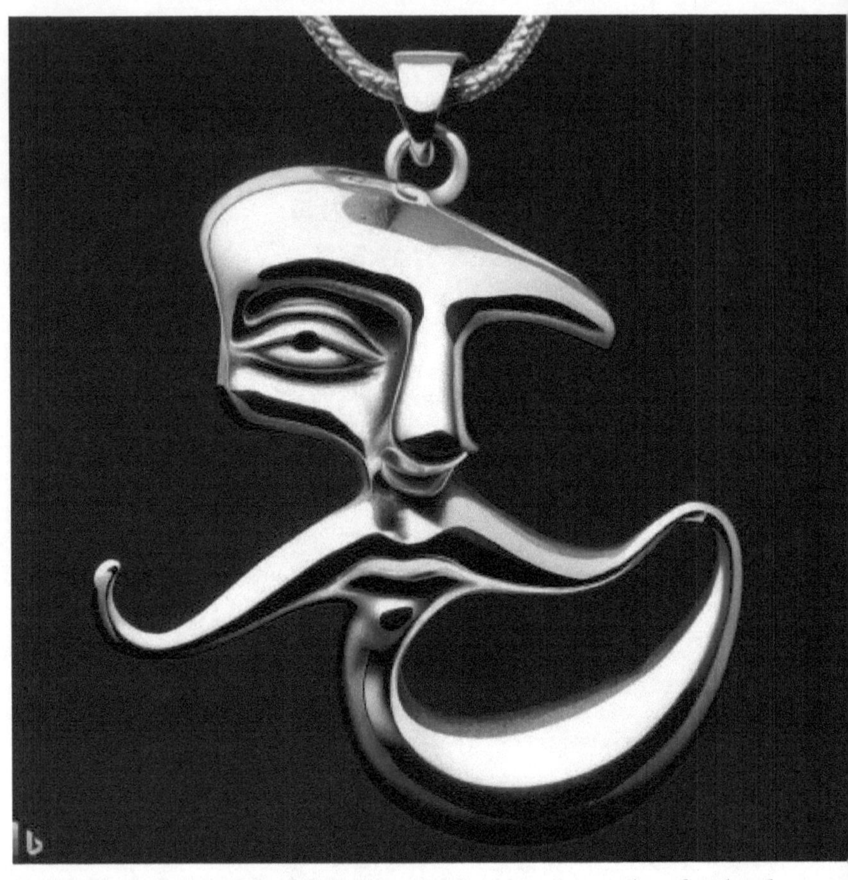

Prompt: Polymer clay fantasy necklace in the style of Salvador Dali, surrealism, metal,

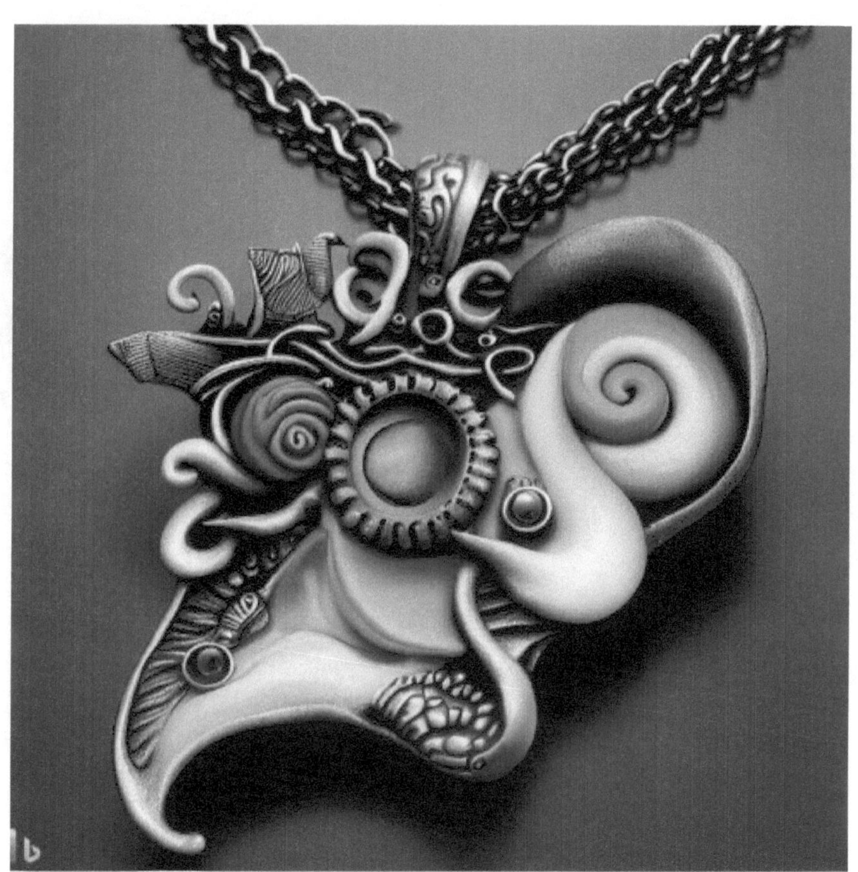

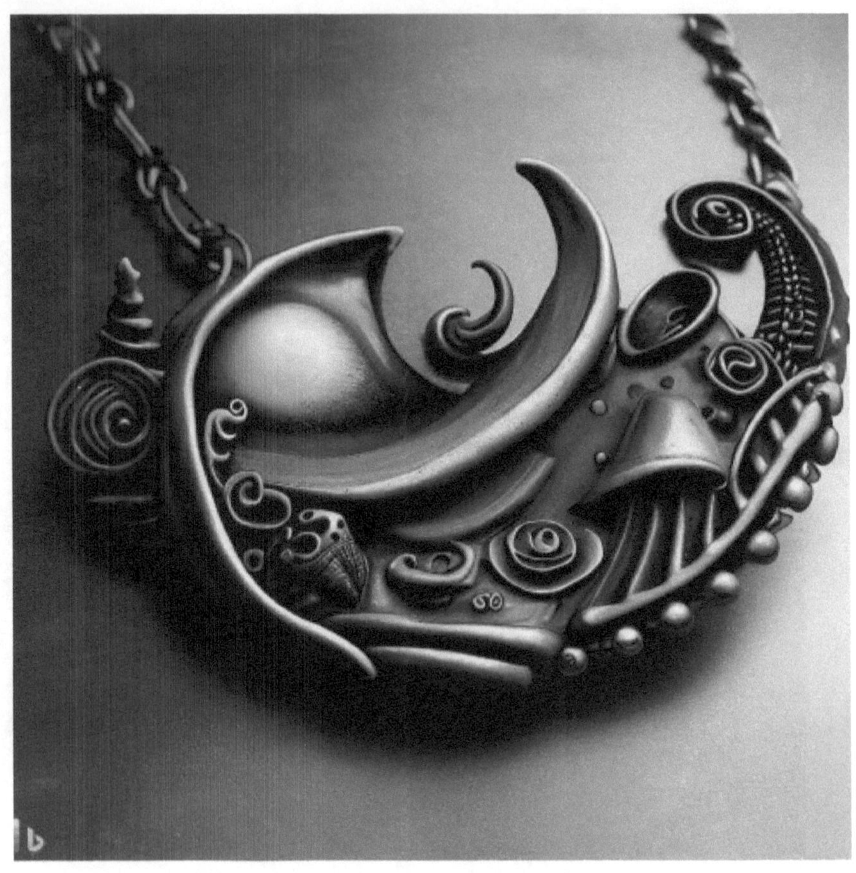

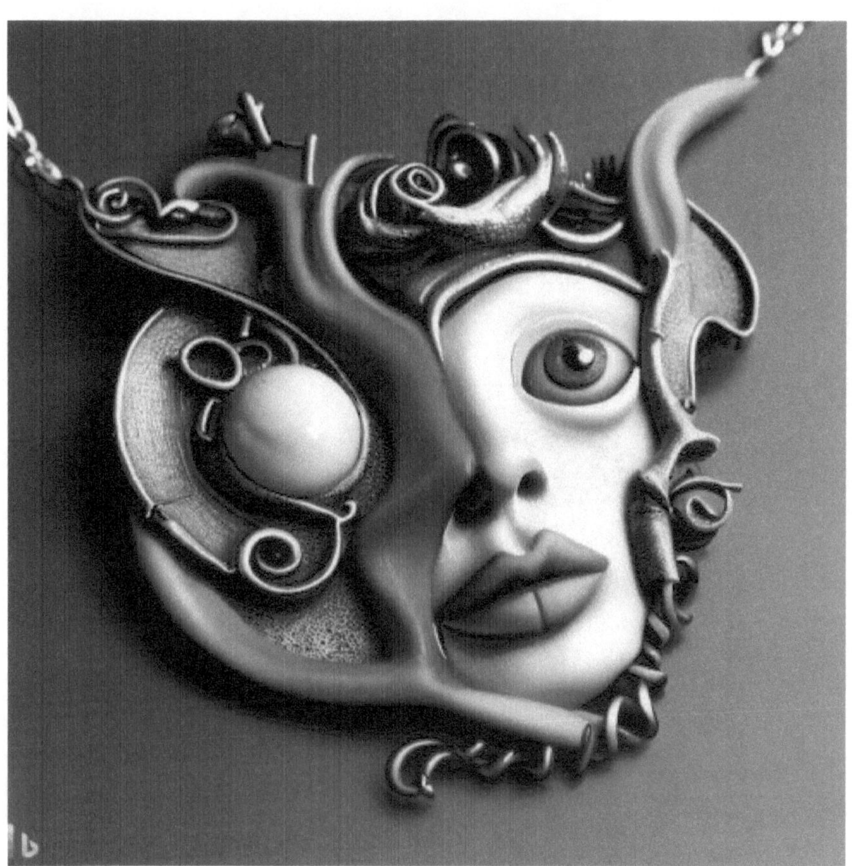

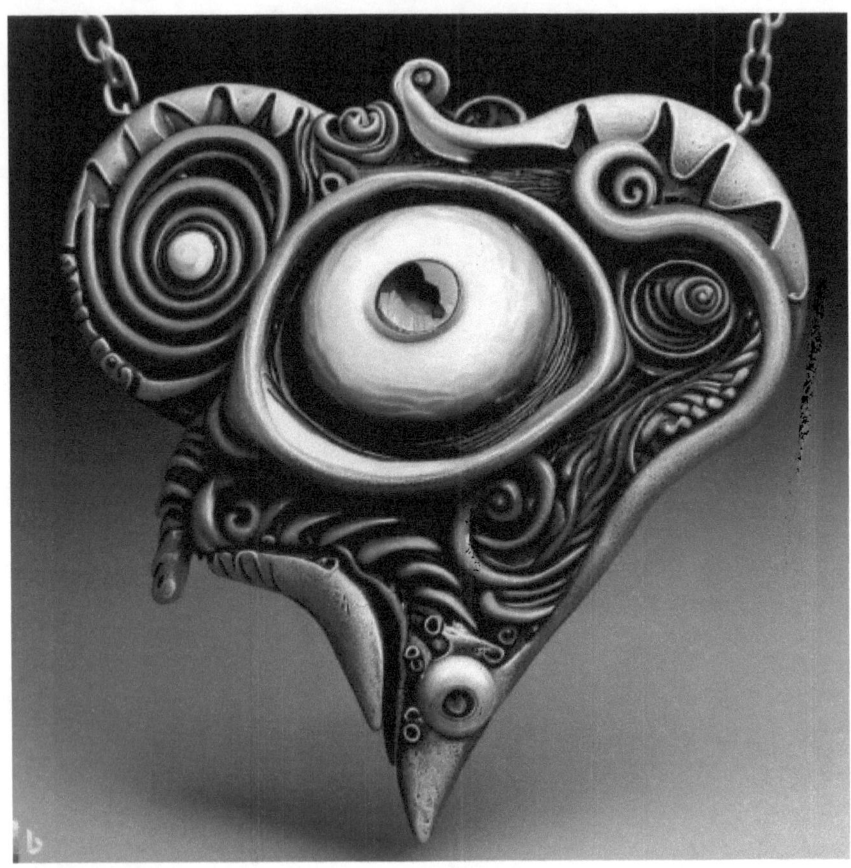

Salvador Dalí's venture into jewelry design adds another layer to his artistic legacy. His imaginative and unconventional approach brought forth a collection of jewelry that echoes the essence of surrealism. With his unique techniques, symbolic narratives, and innovative use of materials, Dalí's jewelry designs continue to mesmerize and inspire generations of artists and jewelry enthusiasts. The Dalí jewelry collection stands as a testament to his genius and his ability to transform the ordinary into the extraordinary, making a lasting impression in the world of jewelry design.

The Enigmatic Artistry of Alex Grey: Inspiring Jewelry Design

Enter the realm of renowned artist Alex Grey, whose distinctive style has captivated audiences with its ethereal beauty and spiritual depth. Not only has Grey left an indelible mark on the art world, but his unique techniques and visionary approach have also found their way into the realm of jewelry design. In this article, we will explore the enigmatic world of Alex Grey, his characteristic style, and how his artistic techniques are translated into mesmerizing jewelry creations that embody his unmistakable essence.

Prompt: painting in the style of Alex Grey

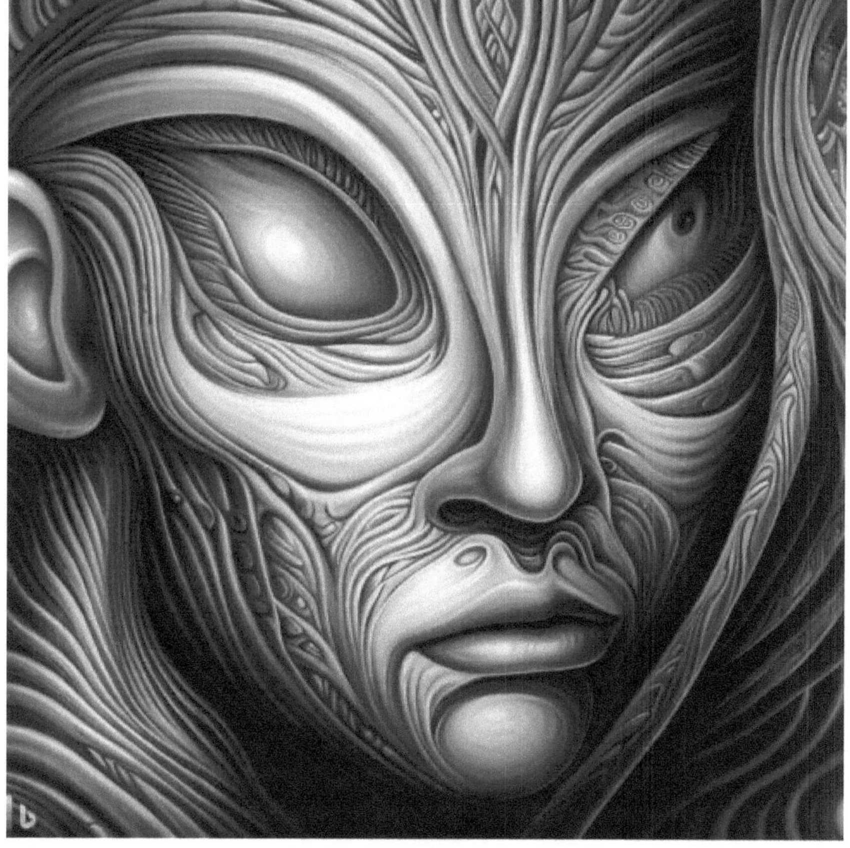

The Style of Alex Grey:

Alex Grey's style is a marriage of the mystical and the anatomical, a transcendental exploration of the human experience and the interconnectedness of all beings. His visionary artworks often depict intricate and detailed renditions of the human body, infused with vibrant colors, cosmic imagery, and spiritual symbolism. Grey's style is characterized by the following key elements:

1. Sacred Geometry: Grey's works frequently incorporate sacred geometric patterns, such as the Flower of Life or fractal formations. These geometric elements add a sense of harmony, balance, and cosmic order to his compositions, reflecting his belief in the underlying unity of the universe.

2. Translucent Bodies: Grey's portrayal of the human form often features transparent or translucent layers, revealing the intricate network of energy and consciousness within. This technique symbolizes the interconnectedness of individuals and the spiritual essence that transcends physicality.

3. Spiritual Symbolism: Drawing inspiration from various spiritual traditions, Grey infuses his artworks with symbolic elements like eyes, hands, and sacred symbols. These symbols serve as gateways to the inner realms of the psyche and evoke a sense of higher consciousness and spiritual awakening.

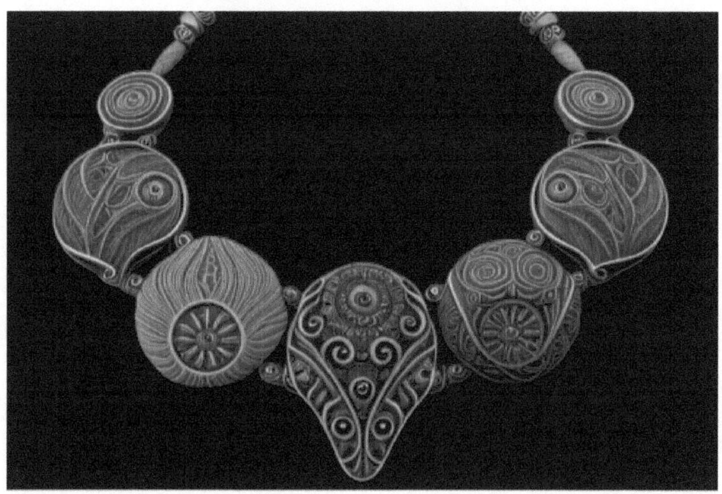

Influence on Jewelry Design:

The distinctive style of Alex Grey has made a significant impact on the world of jewelry design. Jewelry artisans and designers have been inspired by Grey's visionary art, adapting his techniques to create captivating and evocative jewelry pieces. Some of the ways Grey's artistic techniques are incorporated into jewelry design include:

1. Intricate Filigree: Grey's attention to detail and intricate line work have found their way into the realm of jewelry through delicate filigree designs. Filigree artisans use fine metal wires to create lacy patterns that resemble the ethereal quality of Grey's artwork.

2. Gemstone Symbolism: Just as Grey incorporates symbolic elements in his art, jewelry designers take inspiration from his use of symbolism and infuse their creations with meaningful gemstones. Each gemstone is chosen for its unique properties and symbolic significance, adding depth and intention to the jewelry piece.

3. Vibrant Color Schemes: The vibrant color palettes employed by Grey serve as inspiration for jewelry designers who incorporate gemstones, enamels, and vibrant materials into their creations. The resulting jewelry pieces become vibrant, wearable works of art, reminiscent of Grey's mesmerizing compositions.

Prompt: Intricate Filigree Jewelry Brooch in Alex Grey Style

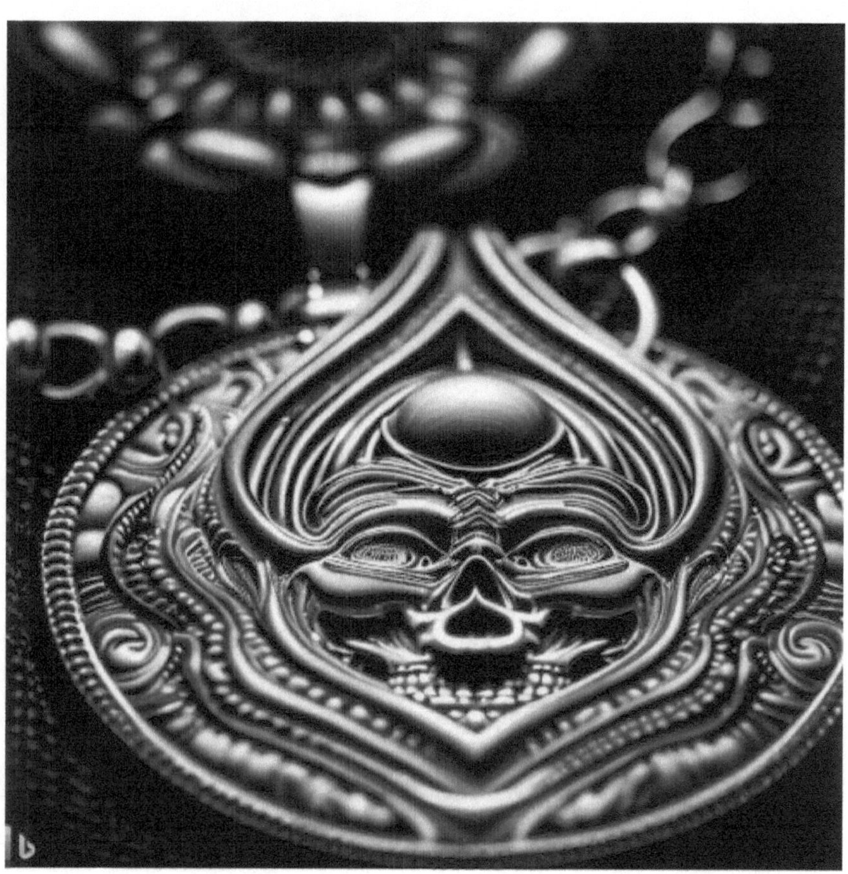

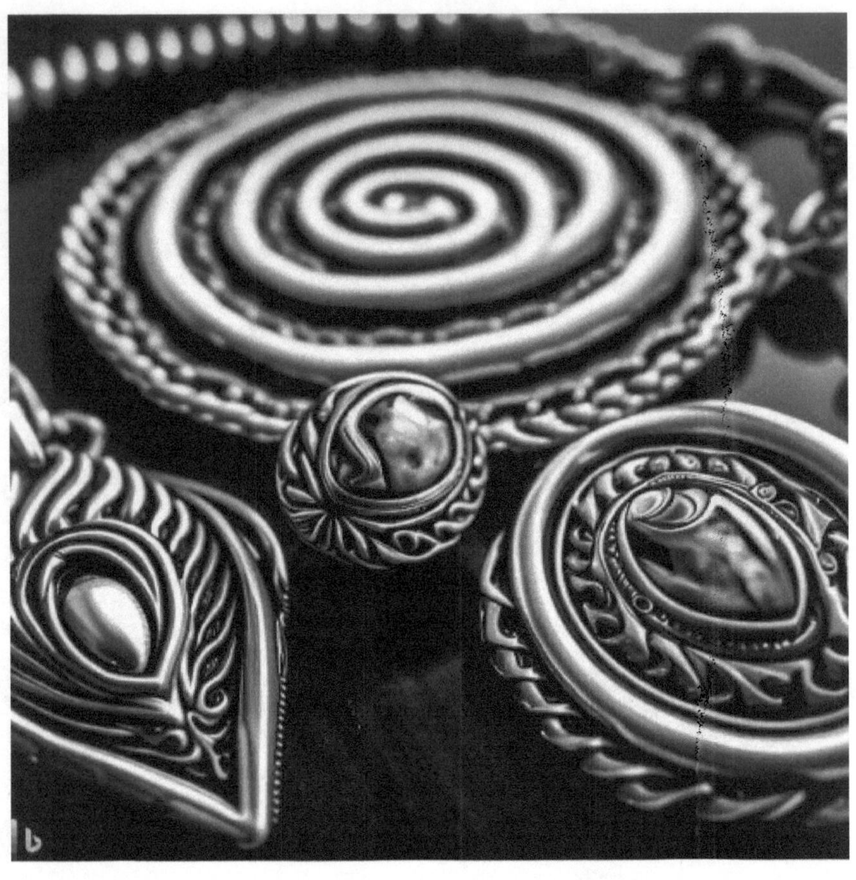

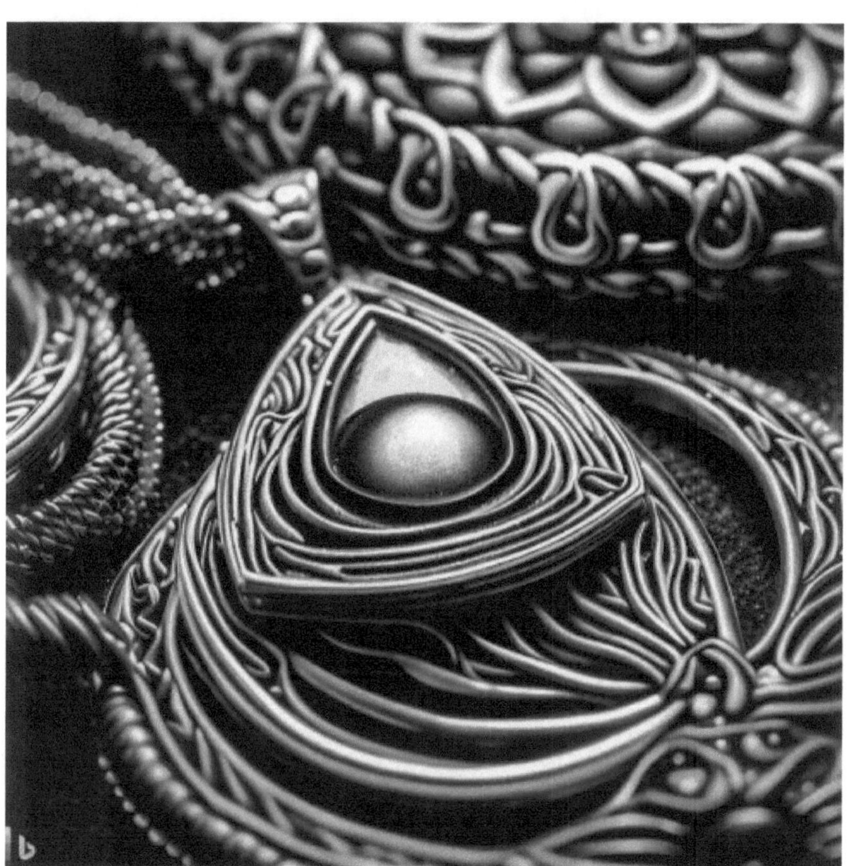

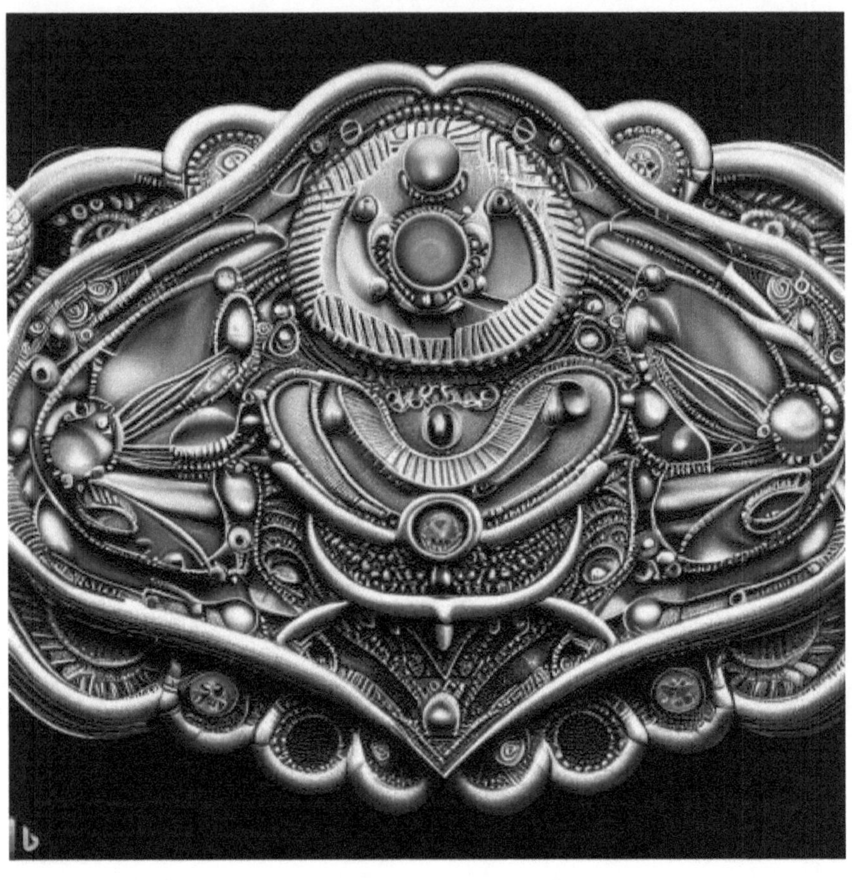

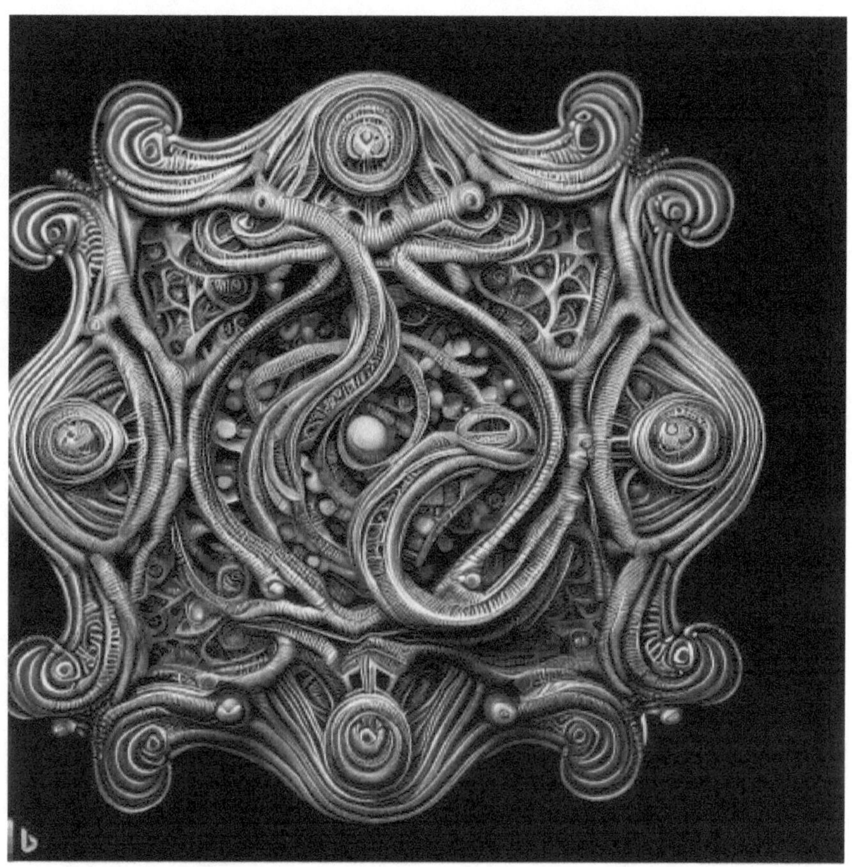

Alex Grey-inspired Jewelry:

The allure of Alex Grey's artistry has given rise to a distinct genre of jewelry that bears his influence. Alex Grey-inspired jewelry pieces embody the transcendent beauty, spiritual symbolism, and intricate details that define Grey's style. These pieces serve as tangible expressions of the wearer's connection to the spiritual realm and act as personal talismans, carrying the transformative energy of Grey's visionary art.

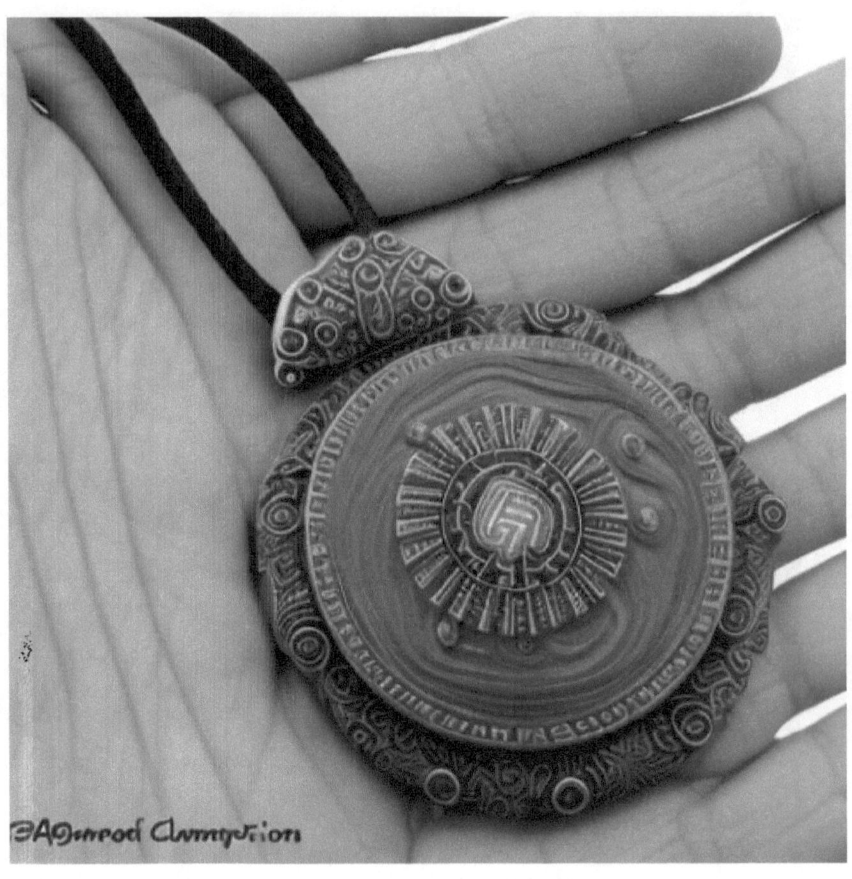

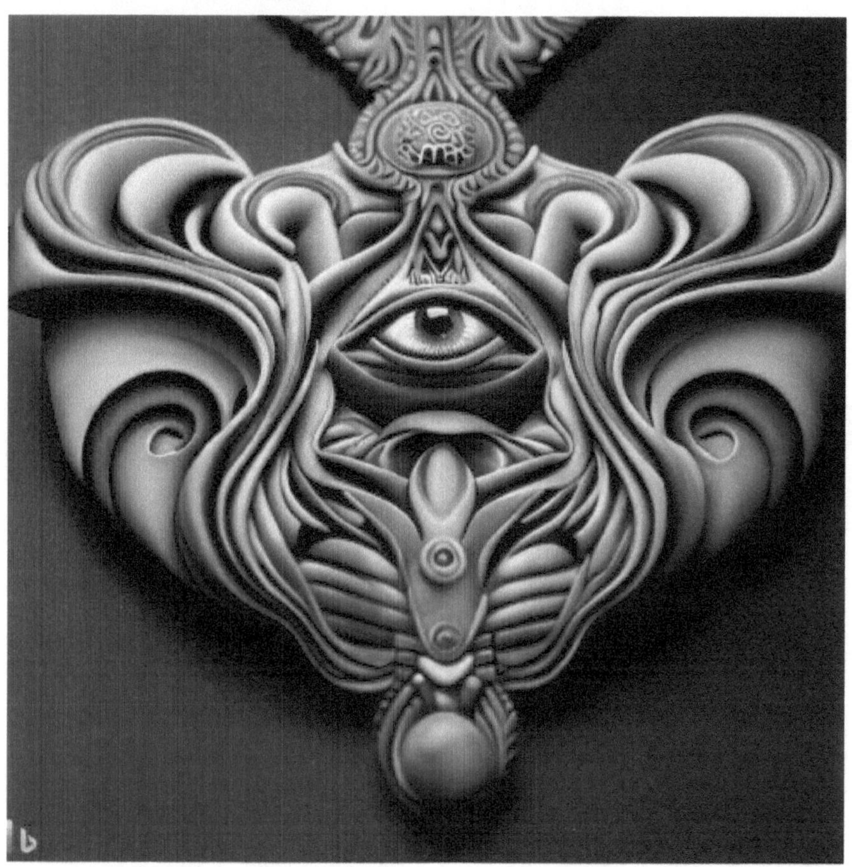

Alex Grey's profound artistic vision continues to resonate with audiences worldwide. His unique style, characterized by sacred geometry, translucent bodies, and spiritual symbolism, has found its way into the realm of jewelry design. Jewelry artisans and designers draw inspiration from Grey's techniques, infusing their creations with a sense of transcendence and spiritual depth. The world of jewelry design has been enriched by the enigmatic artistry of Alex Grey.

René Lalique: A Master of Art Nouveau Jewelry and Glass Design

René Lalique (1860-1945) was a renowned French designer, jeweler, and glassmaker who left an indelible mark on the world of art. He was one of the most significant figures in the Art Nouveau movement, which emerged in the late 19th century and flourished into the early 20th century. Lalique's creations, including jewelry and decorative objects, became iconic symbols of the era and continue to inspire jewelry designers today. In this article, we will explore the life and work of René Lalique, delve into the distinctive features of his style, and discover how his artistic legacy continues to shape the world of jewelry design.

The Artistic Style of René Lalique:

René Lalique's style was characterized by several key elements that set him apart as a visionary artist and designer:

1. Nature-Inspired Motifs: Lalique drew inspiration from the natural world, incorporating motifs of flora and fauna into his designs. He skillfully captured the delicate beauty of flowers, leaves, insects, and animals, infusing them with a sense of organic fluidity and grace. His jewelry pieces often featured intricate depictions of flowers, such as lilies, irises, and orchids, which exuded a sense of timeless elegance.

2. Innovative Use of Materials: Lalique was known for his pioneering use of materials in jewelry and glass design. He combined traditional precious metals and gemstones with unconventional materials such as enamel, horn, ivory, and glass. His innovative techniques, such as the use of molded glass and the incorporation of plique-à-jour enamel, brought a new dimension of artistic expression to his creations.

3. Symbolism and Whimsical Imagery: Lalique's designs often incorporated symbolic elements and whimsical imagery. He captured the essence of mythological creatures, such as dragons and nymphs, intertwining them with natural motifs. Lalique's pieces possessed a sense of mystique and enchantment, invoking a world of fantasy and imagination.

4. Fluidity and Movement: Lalique's designs exuded a sense of fluidity and movement, achieved through the use of curvilinear lines and dynamic compositions. His jewelry pieces seemed to effortlessly flow and interact with the wearer's body, creating an intimate and harmonious connection.

Prompt: a brooch in the style of René Lalique made with a glue gun, similar to his perfume bottles,

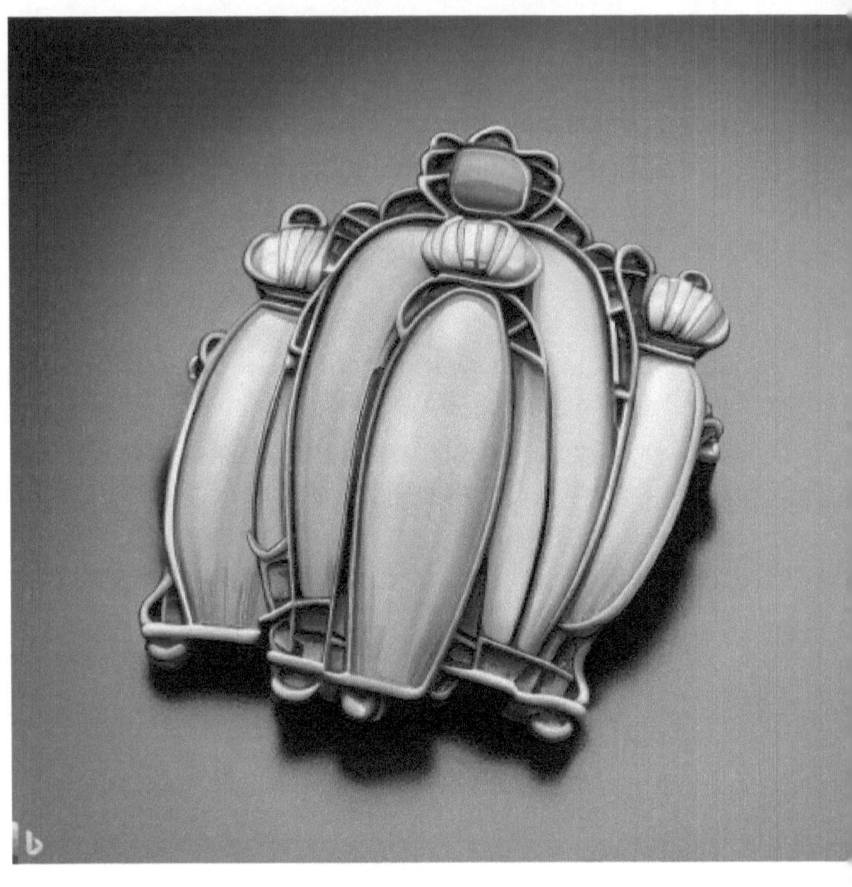

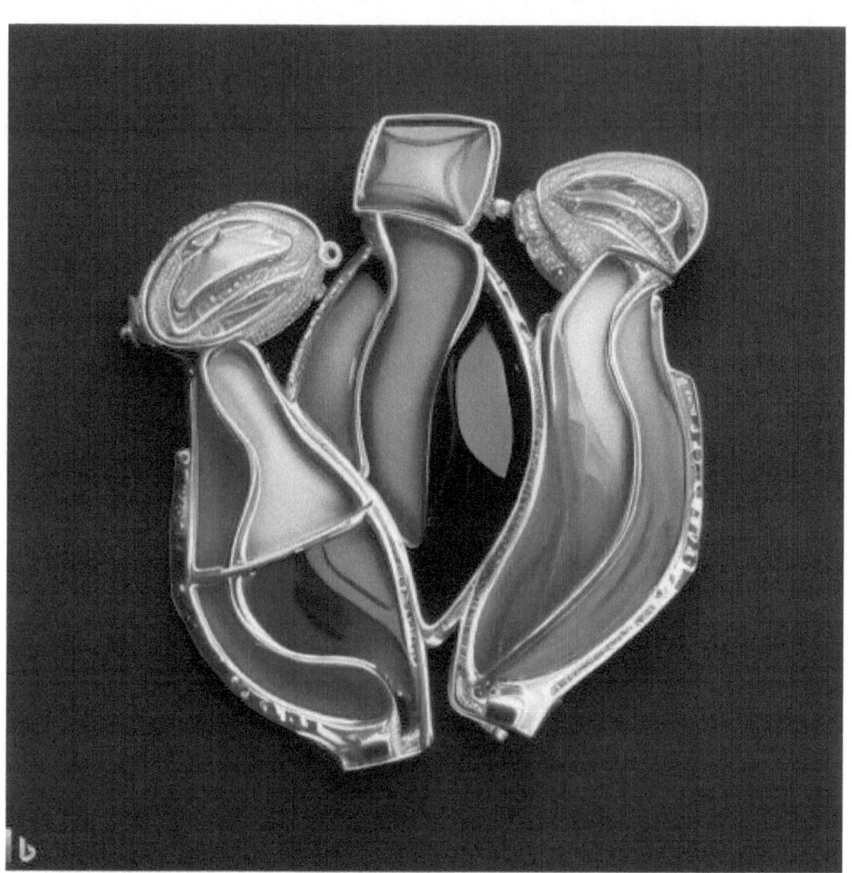

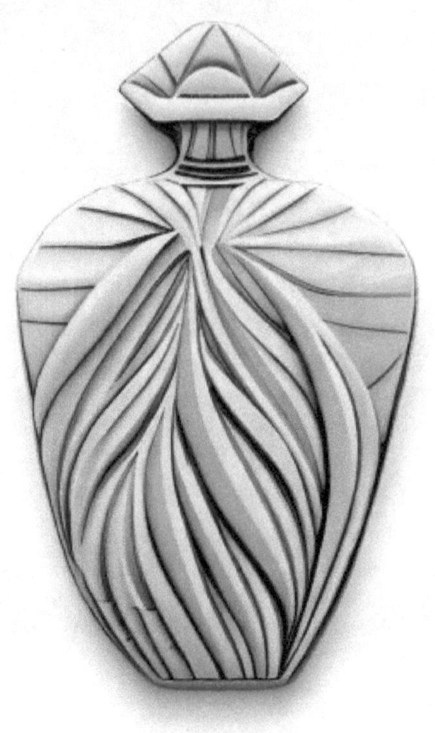

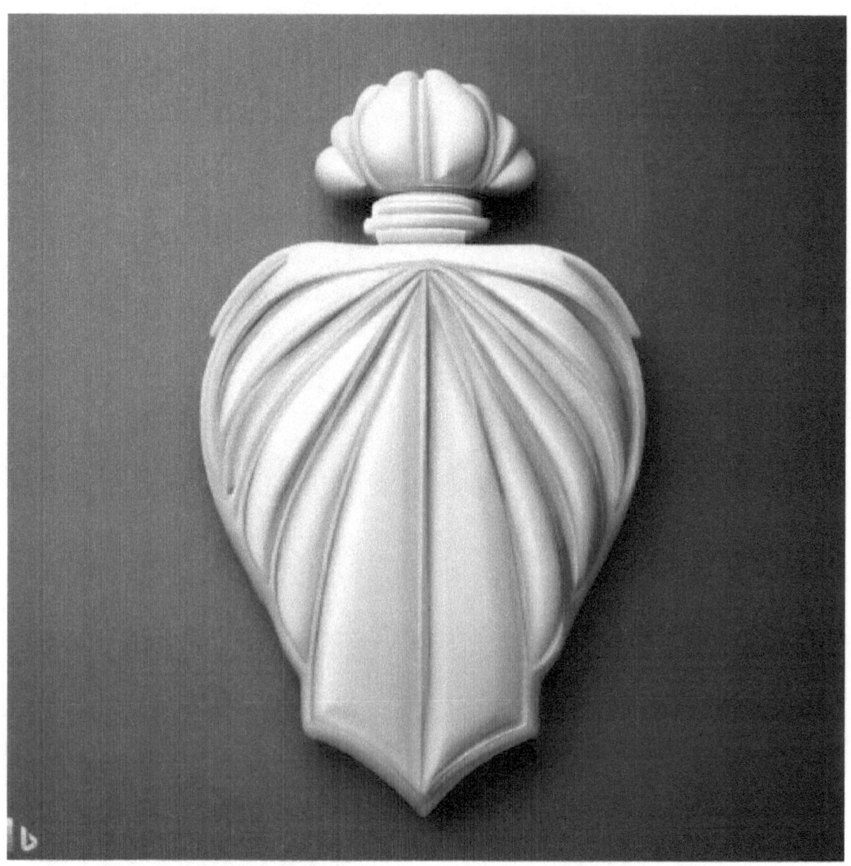

Lalique's Enduring Influence on Jewelry Design:

René Lalique's artistic legacy continues to inspire and influence contemporary jewelry designers. The distinct features of his style, which include nature-inspired motifs, innovative material usage, symbolism, and fluidity, serve as a rich source of inspiration for jewelry artisans around the world. Lalique's designs are celebrated for their timeless beauty, craftsmanship, and artistic vision. Many contemporary jewelers pay homage to Lalique by incorporating his techniques and motifs into their own creations, resulting in stunning pieces that embody the spirit of Lalique's art.

Prompt: brooch in the style of René Lalique, similar to his perfume bottles, glue gun

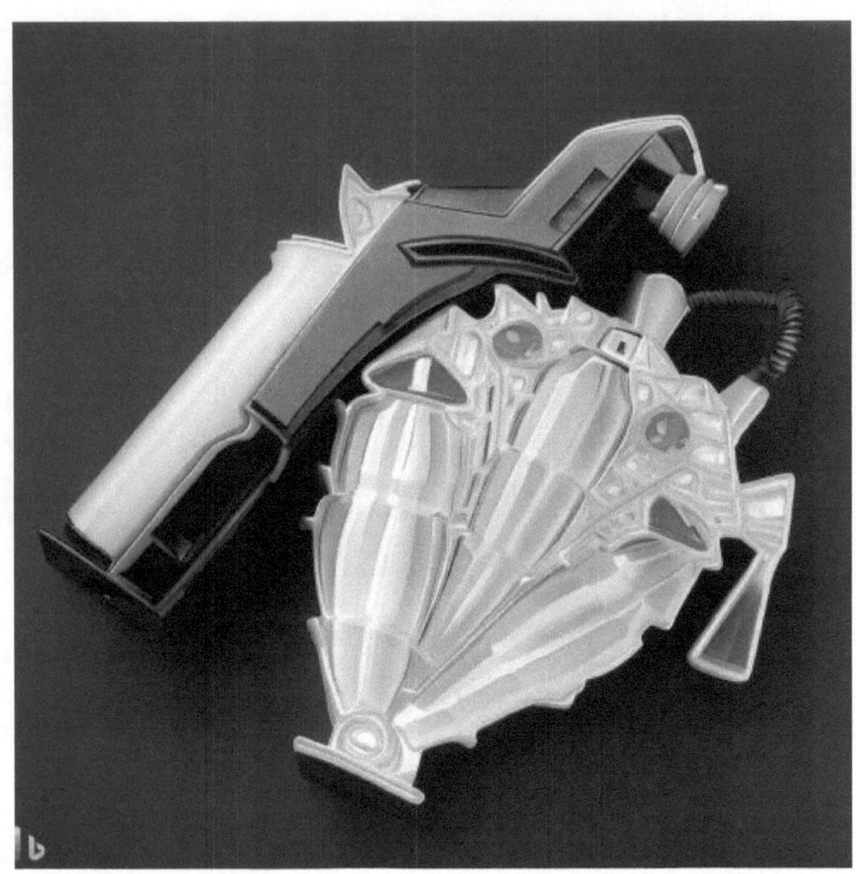

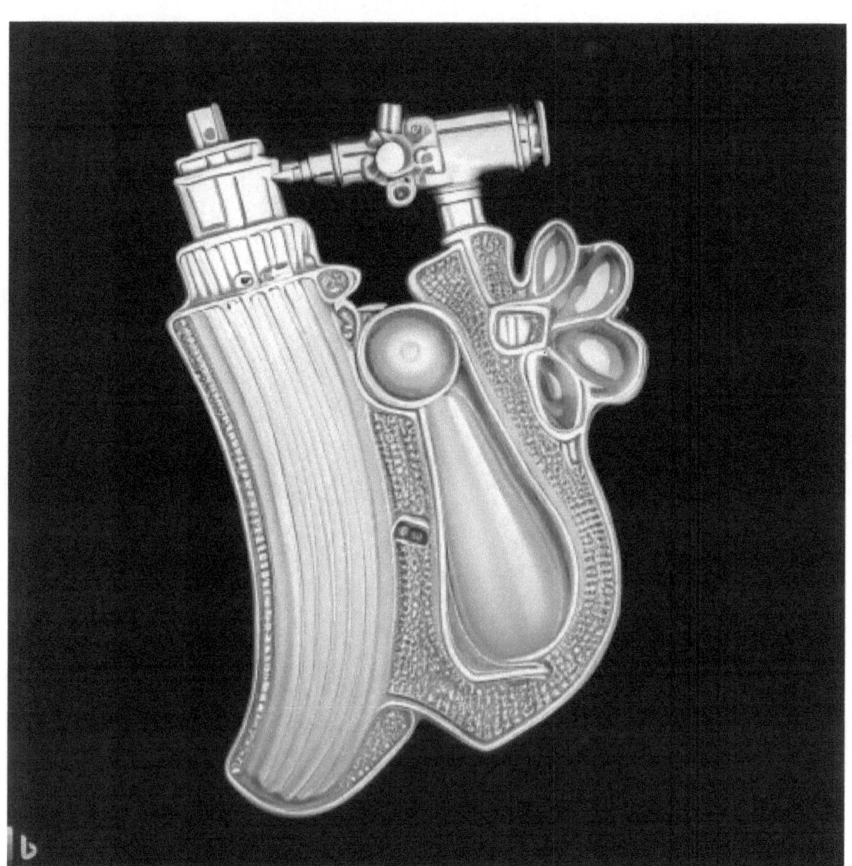

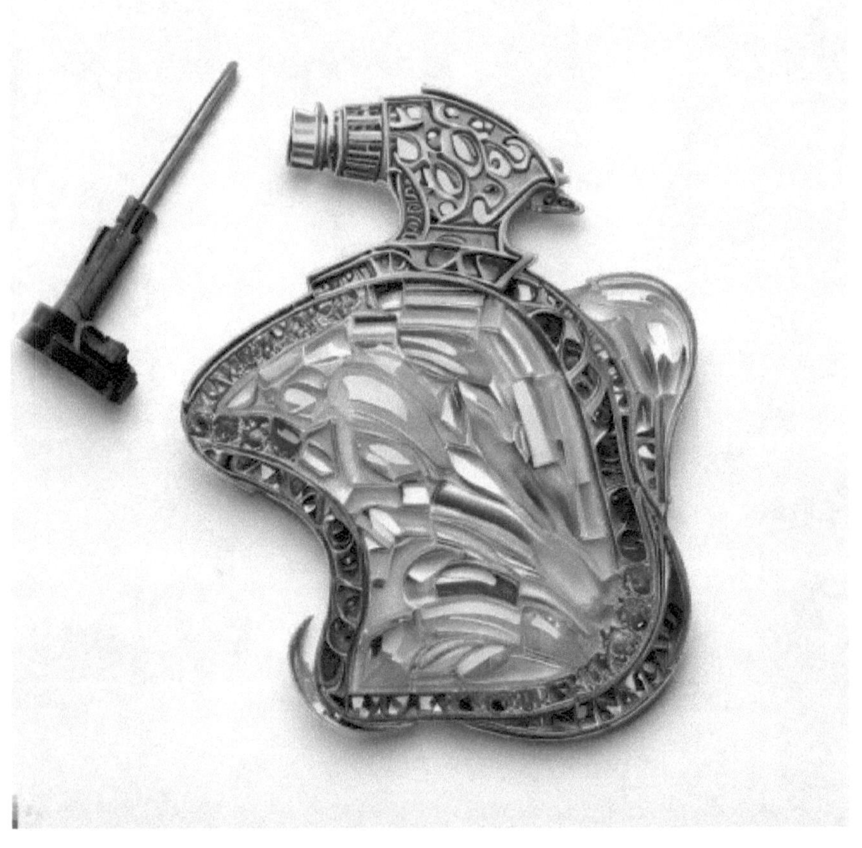

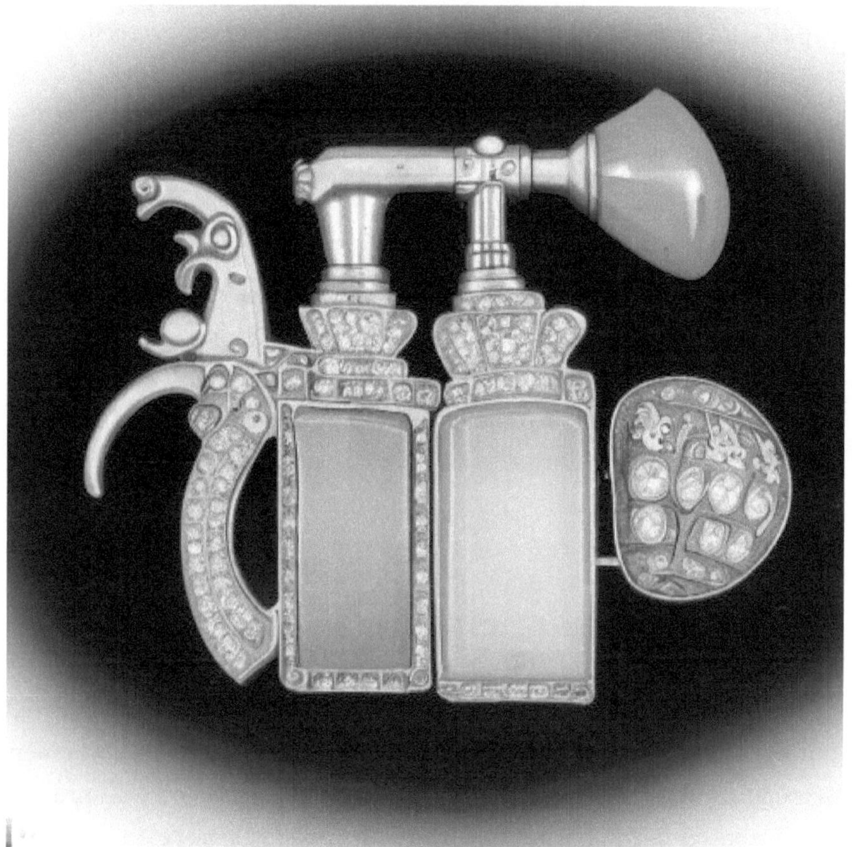

The Iconic Status of Lalique's Creations:

René Lalique's jewelry and decorative objects have achieved iconic status, symbolizing the artistry and innovation of the Art Nouveau movement. His creations, whether in the form of a brooch, pendant, vase, or chandelier, are highly sought after by collectors and enthusiasts. Lalique's unique ability to seamlessly blend art and craftsmanship into wearable and functional pieces of art established him as a master of his craft.

René Lalique's contributions to the world of jewelry and art cannot be overstated. His distinctive style, characterized by nature-inspired motifs, innovative use of materials, symbolism, and fluidity, set him apart as a visionary artist and designer. Lalique's legacy continues to inspire contemporary jewelry designers, who draw from his techniques and motifs to create breathtaking

Hundertwasser: The Visionary Artist and Architect

Friedensreich Hundertwasser, widely known as Hundertwasser, was a multifaceted artist and architect who left an indelible mark on the world of art and design. With his distinctive style and philosophy, he challenged conventional norms, embraced organic forms, and advocated for a harmonious coexistence between humanity and nature. In this article, we will explore the life and creative contributions of Hundertwasser, delve into the characteristics of his artistic style, and discover how his visionary concepts continue to inspire contemporary jewelry designers.

Hundertwasser's Artistic and Architectural Philosophy:

Hundertwasser rejected the rigidity of straight lines and sought to infuse his art and architecture with organic, flowing forms. His philosophy embraced the idea of "architecture in harmony with nature," emphasizing the importance of integrating natural elements and green spaces into urban environments. Hundertwasser believed that human beings should live in harmony with their surroundings, celebrating the uniqueness and diversity of nature.

Distinctive Features of Hundertwasser's Style:

1. Spirals and Whimsical Forms: Hundertwasser incorporated spirals, wavy lines, and playful, whimsical shapes into his artworks and architectural designs. These organic forms represented the interconnectedness and ever-changing nature of life, inviting viewers to embrace the beauty of imperfection.

2. Bold Colors and Patterns: Vibrant colors played a crucial role in Hundertwasser's artistic expression. His works

featured a vivid palette, often combined with intricate patterns and geometric motifs. Through the skillful use of color, he sought to evoke emotions and create a sense of joy and vitality.

3. Celebration of Nature: Nature served as a recurring theme in Hundertwasser's creations. He depicted forests, flowers, and landscapes, emphasizing the importance of environmental preservation and the need to reconnect with the natural world. Hundertwasser's artworks celebrated the beauty and diversity of nature, urging viewers to appreciate and protect it.

4. Rejection of Uniformity: Hundertwasser rebelled against uniformity and mass production, advocating for individuality and artistic freedom. He believed in the concept of the "third skin," which represented the idea that individuals should express their personalities through their surroundings, including their clothing and jewelry.

Prompt: bracelet, metal painting he those styles of hündertwasser

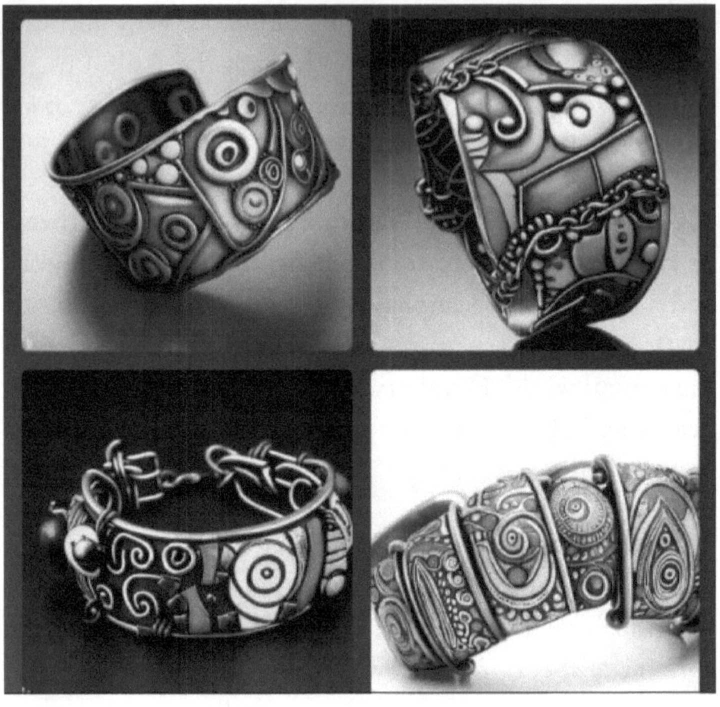

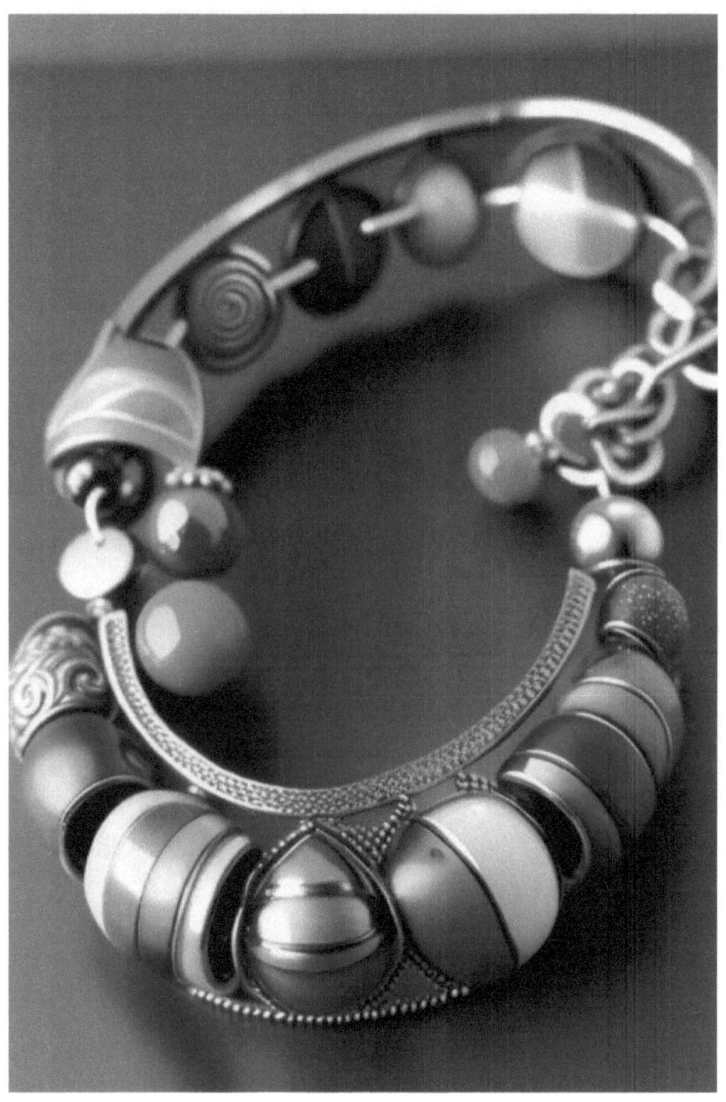

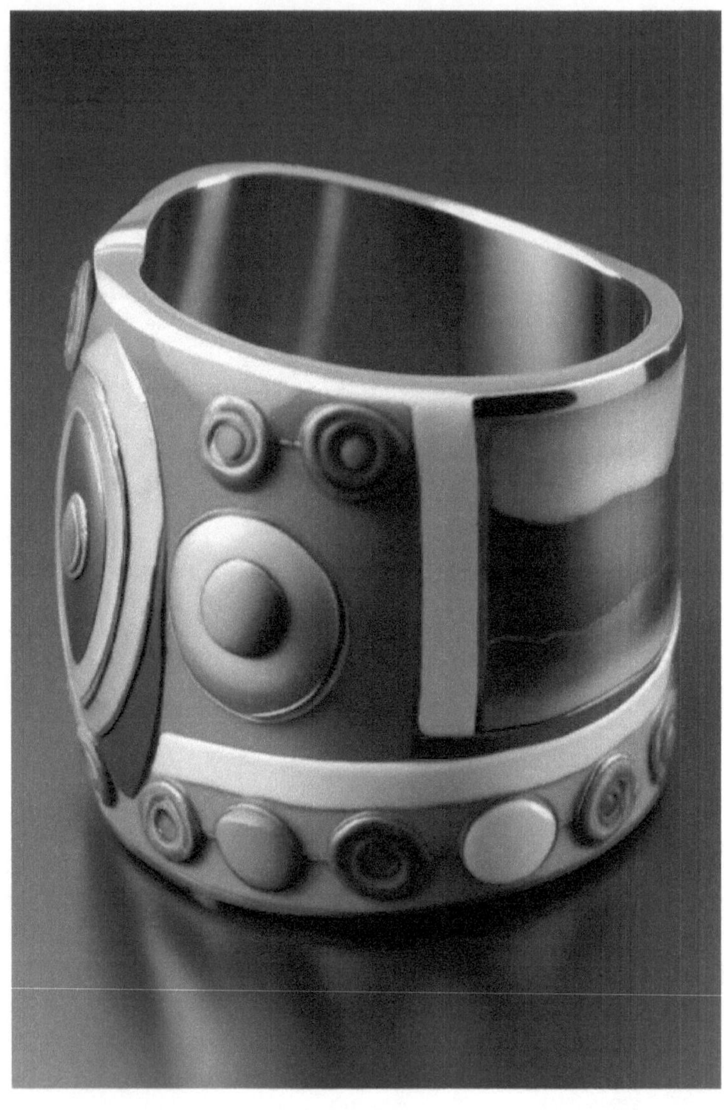

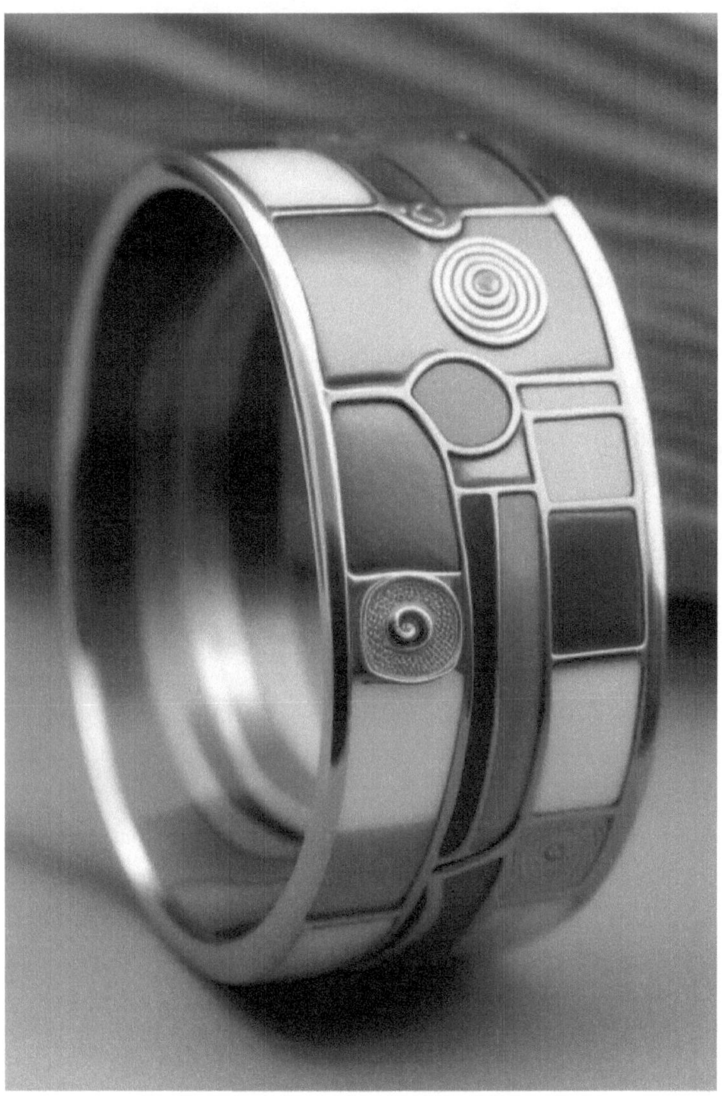

Hundertwasser's Influence on Jewelry Design:
Hundertwasser's artistic concepts have inspired contemporary jewelry designers to create unique and expressive pieces. Jewelry artisans draw inspiration from his distinctive style and philosophy to develop jewelry designs that embody the spirit of his work. Some of the

ways Hundertwasser's artistic principles are incorporated into jewelry design include:

1. Organic Forms and Fluid Lines: Jewelry designers integrate organic shapes, such as spirals and flowing lines, into their creations, echoing Hundertwasser's rejection of straight lines and his embrace of natural forms.

2. Bold Colors and Patterns: Jewelry pieces inspired by Hundertwasser often feature vibrant colors and intricate patterns, mirroring his use of bold and expressive color palettes.

3. Environmental Consciousness: Hundertwasser's focus on environmental sustainability and the connection between humanity and nature inspires jewelry designers to use recycled materials, responsibly sourced gemstones, and elements that reflect the beauty and fragility of the natural world.

4. Individuality and Self-Expression: Hundertwasser's concept of the "third skin" resonates with jewelry designers who aim to create pieces that reflect the wearer's unique personality and celebrate individuality.

Prompt: brooch, metal painting on those styles of hündertwasser

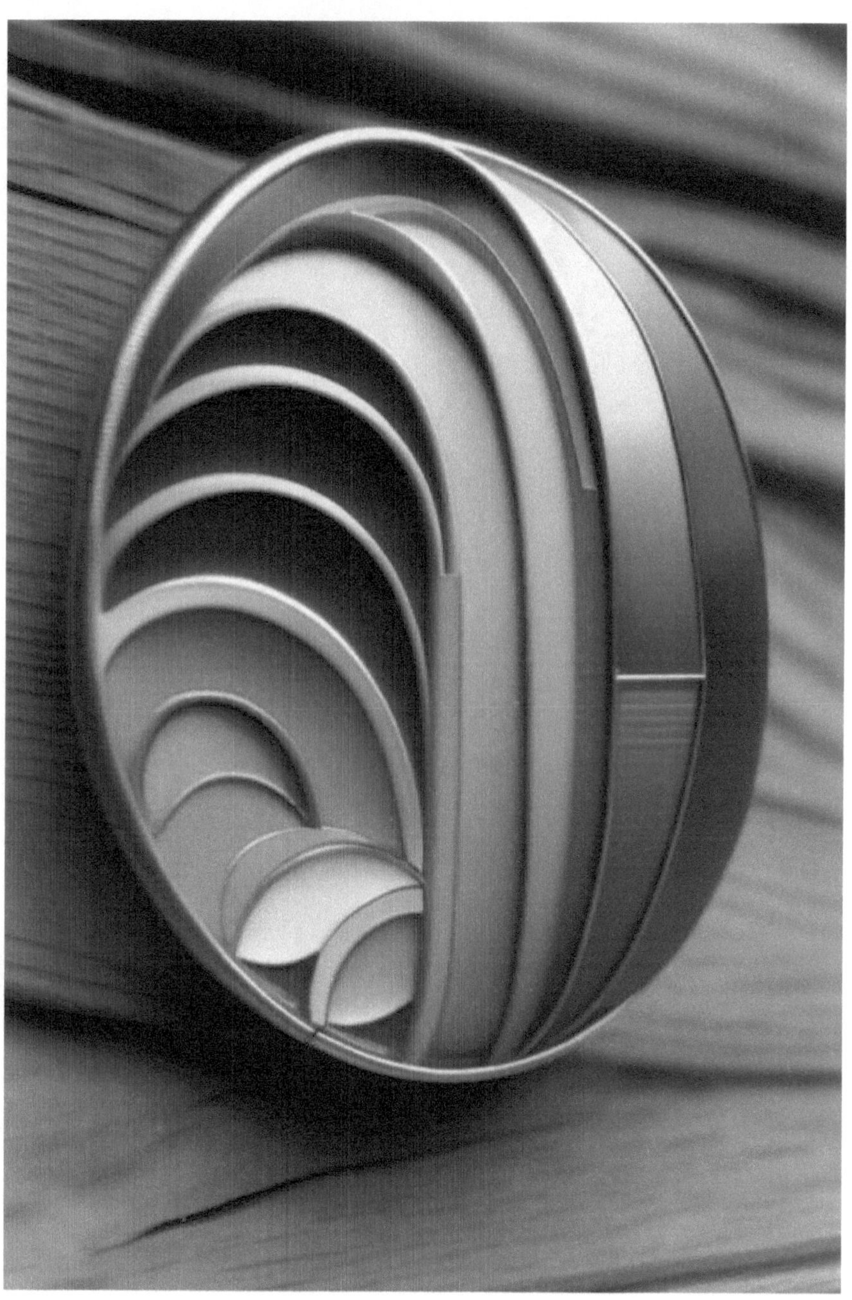

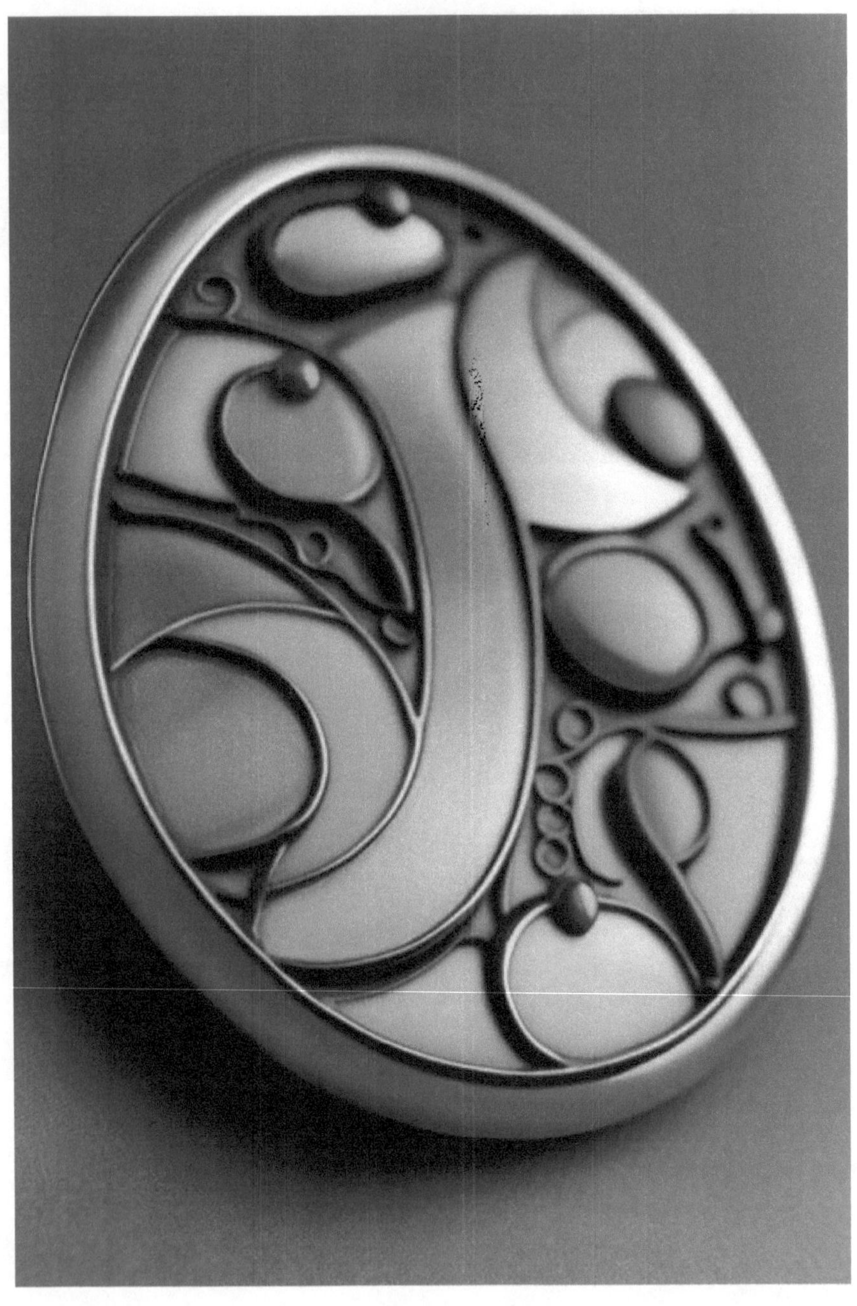

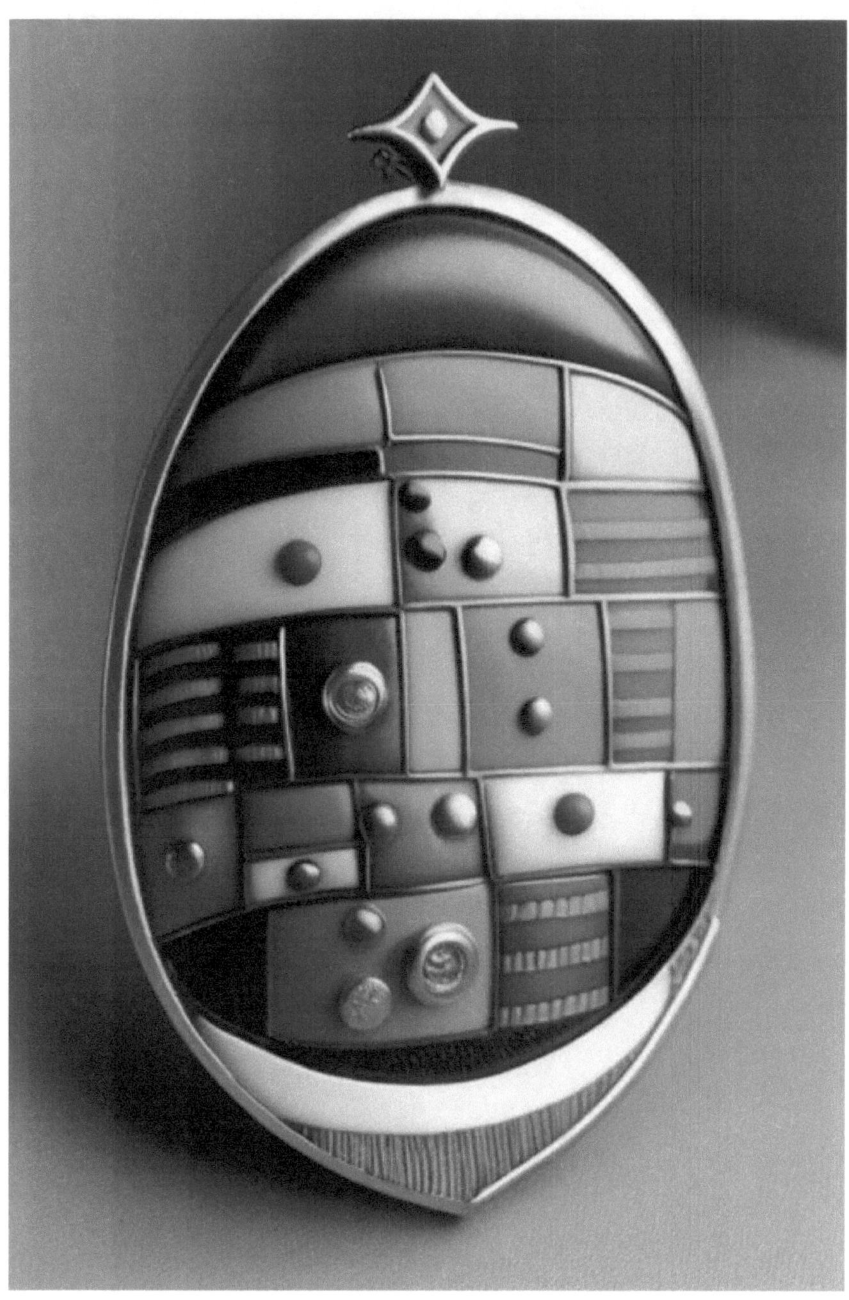

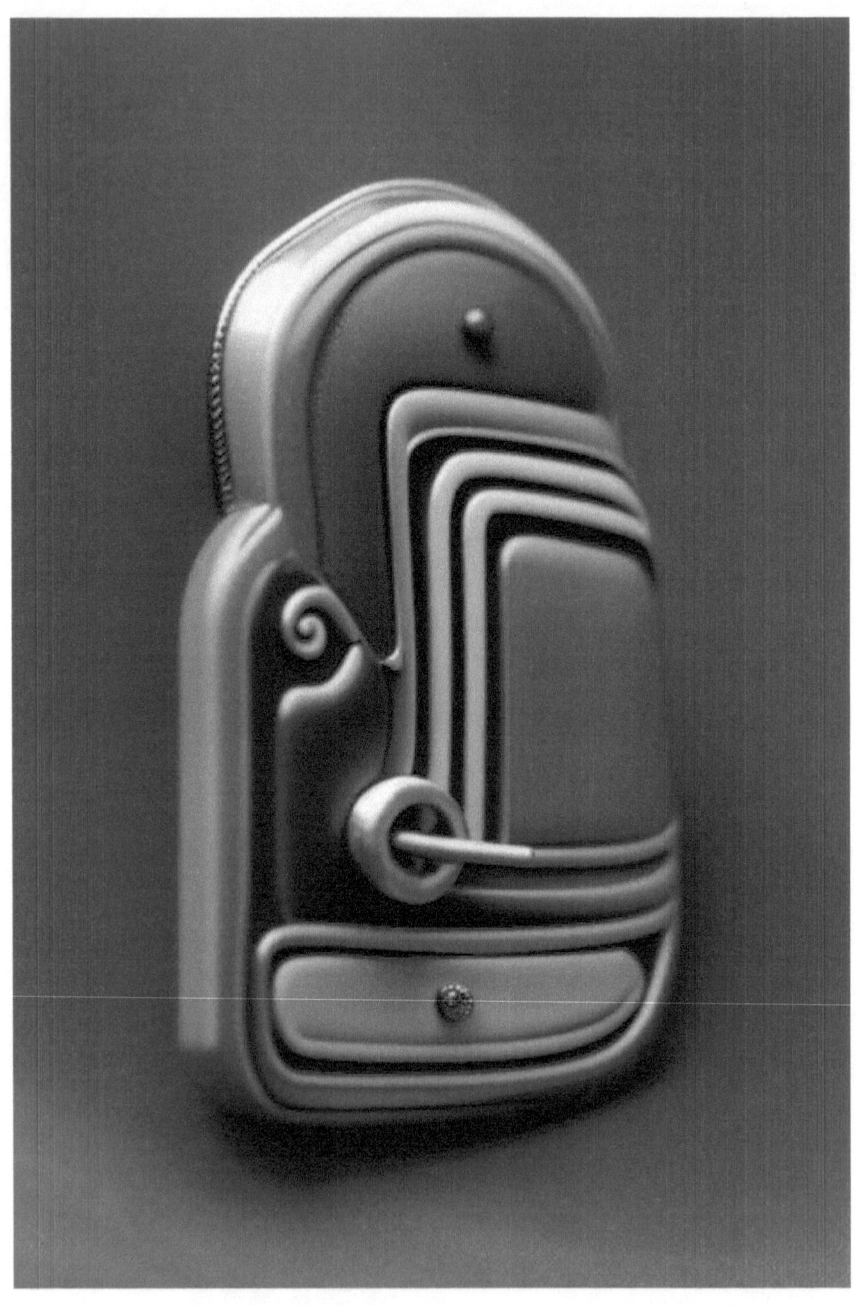

Hundertwasser's artistic vision, characterized by organic forms, vibrant colors, and a deep reverence for nature, continues to inspire and influence artists, architects, and jewelry designers worldwide.

Carl Fabergé: The Master Jeweler and Artist

Carl Fabergé was a renowned jeweler and artist who created some of the most exquisite and famous works of art in history. His creations, including jewelry and decorative objects, became iconic symbols of their era and continue to inspire jewelry designers today. In this article, we will explore the life and artistic contributions of Carl Fabergé, delve into the characteristics of his style, and discover how his legacy influences contemporary jewelry design.

The Style of Carl Fabergé:

Carl Fabergé's style can be described as historicism, a combination of methods, techniques, and aesthetic tastes from different eras. Although sometimes referred to with a dismissive term, "eclecticism," Fabergé's style showcased a refined craftsmanship and a deep appreciation for beauty. His works garnered admiration and interest from his aristocratic patrons. Some of the distinctive features of his style include:

1. Attention to Detail: Fabergé's creations were renowned for their meticulous attention to detail. He employed intricate techniques such as enameling, guilloché, and gem-setting to achieve exquisite craftsmanship and precision in his jewelry pieces and decorative objects.

2. Aesthetic Diversity: Fabergé drew inspiration from various artistic periods and cultures. His designs incorporated elements of Renaissance, Baroque, Rococo, and Art Nouveau styles, among others. This fusion of influences resulted in a unique and captivating aesthetic.

3. Imperial Easter Eggs: One of Fabergé's most famous achievements was the creation of the Imperial Easter Eggs, made for the Russian emperors Alexander III and Nicholas II. These intricately crafted eggs, adorned with precious metals, gemstones, and enamel, showcased Fabergé's mastery and creativity. Each egg contained a surprise or a hidden object within, adding an element of intrigue and delight.

4. Diversified Creations: In addition to the Imperial Easter Eggs, Fabergé crafted a wide range of other objects, including cigarette cases, picture frames, and jewelry. These pieces reflected his commitment to excellence in design and craftsmanship, and they served as examples for contemporary jewelers and artists.

Prompt: A faberge-style brooch with a blue enamel background and a gold floral pattern, the brooch has a large oval ruby in the center and four smaller diamonds around it, the brooch is made of 18-karat gold

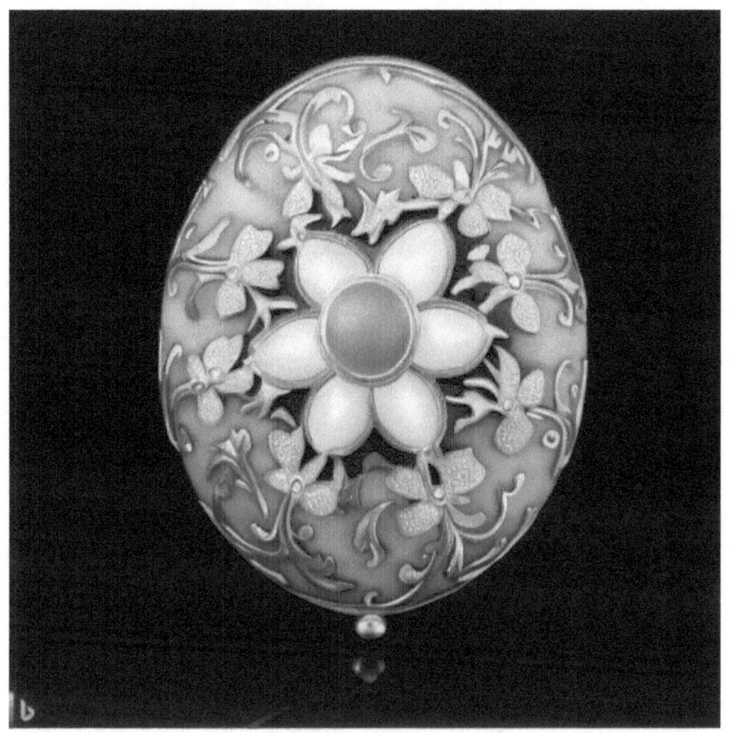

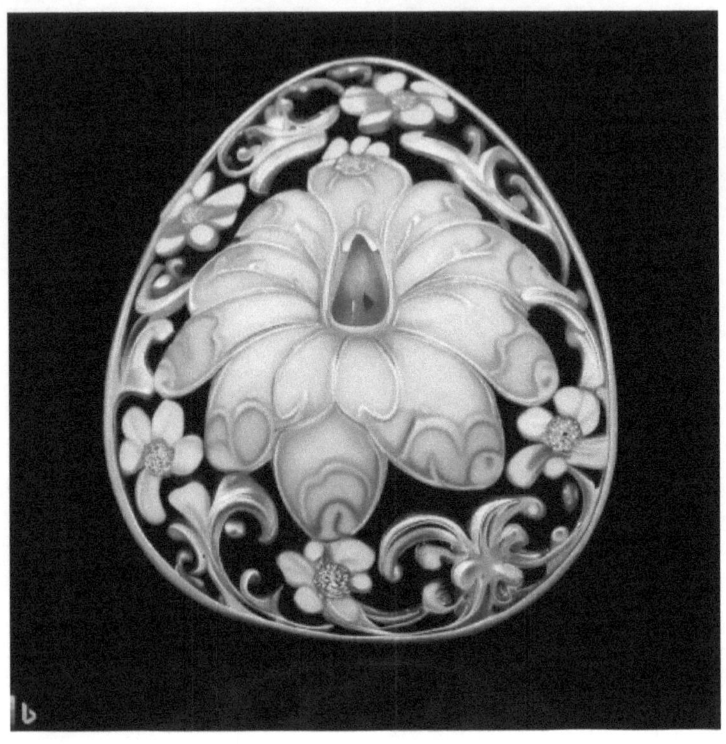

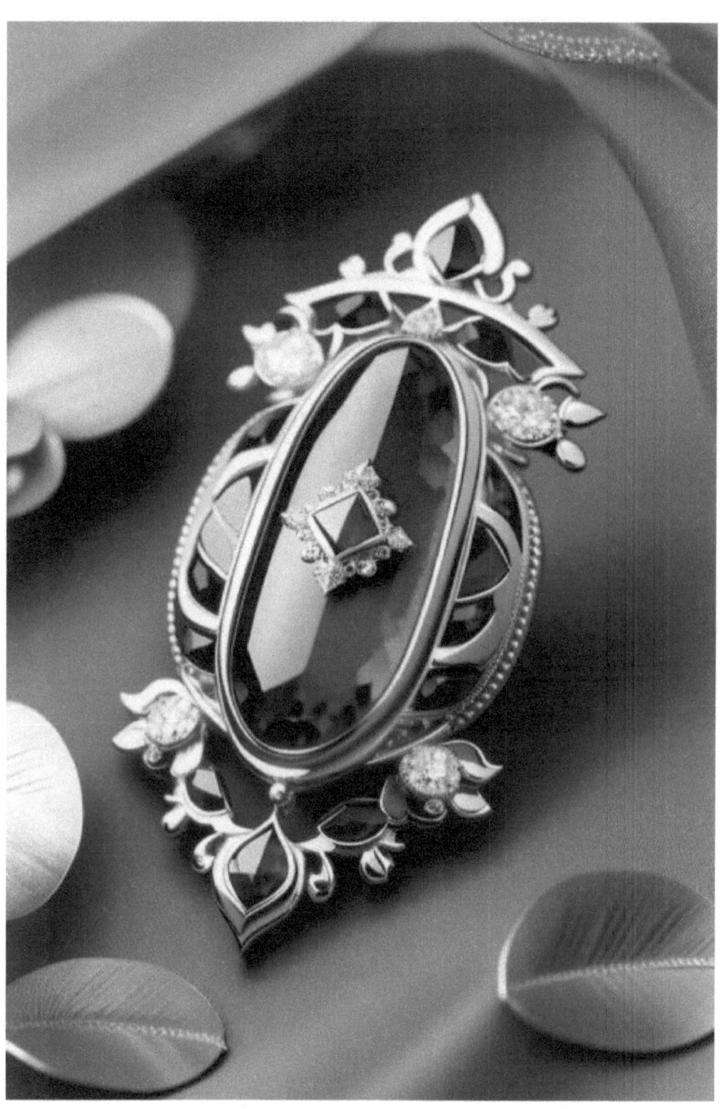

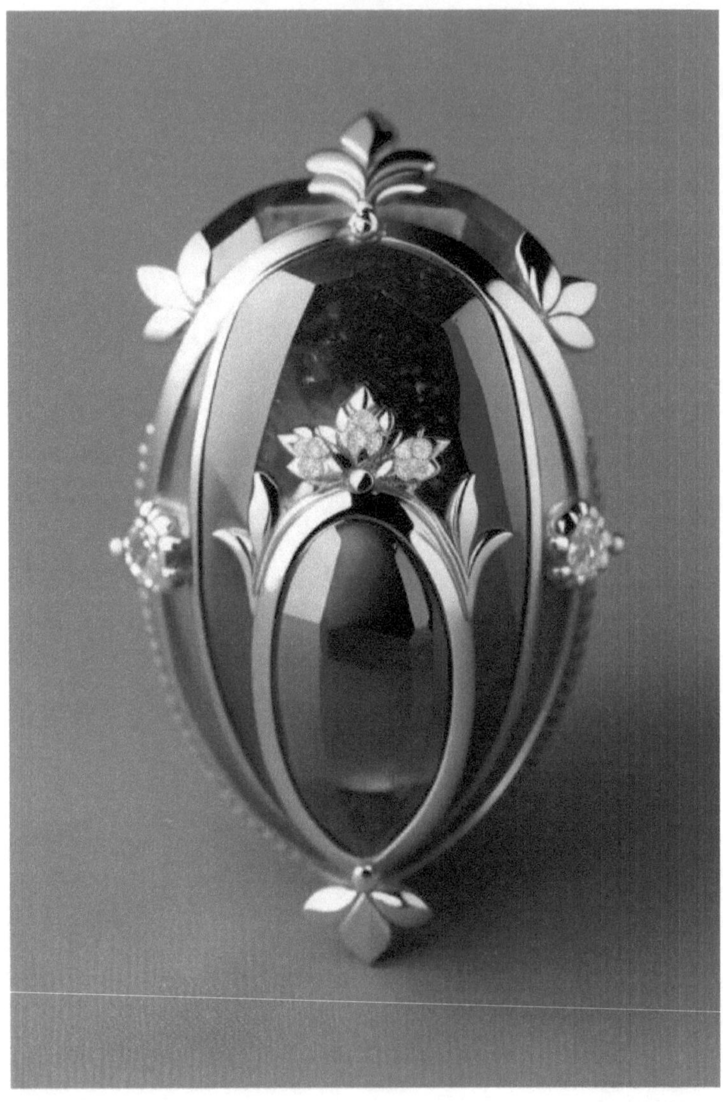

Fabergé's Influence on Contemporary Jewelry Design:
The legacy of Carl Fabergé continues to inspire and influence contemporary jewelry designers. His emphasis on fine craftsmanship, creativity, and beauty serves as a guiding principle for many artisans. Fabergé's creations are celebrated for their elegance, attention to detail,

and storytelling elements, which resonate with modern jewelry designers. Today, jewelers draw inspiration from Fabergé's style to create stunning jewelry pieces that capture the essence of his craftsmanship and evoke a sense of timeless luxury.

Prompt: faberge eggs, 3 d model, very coherent symmetrical artwork, 8 k,

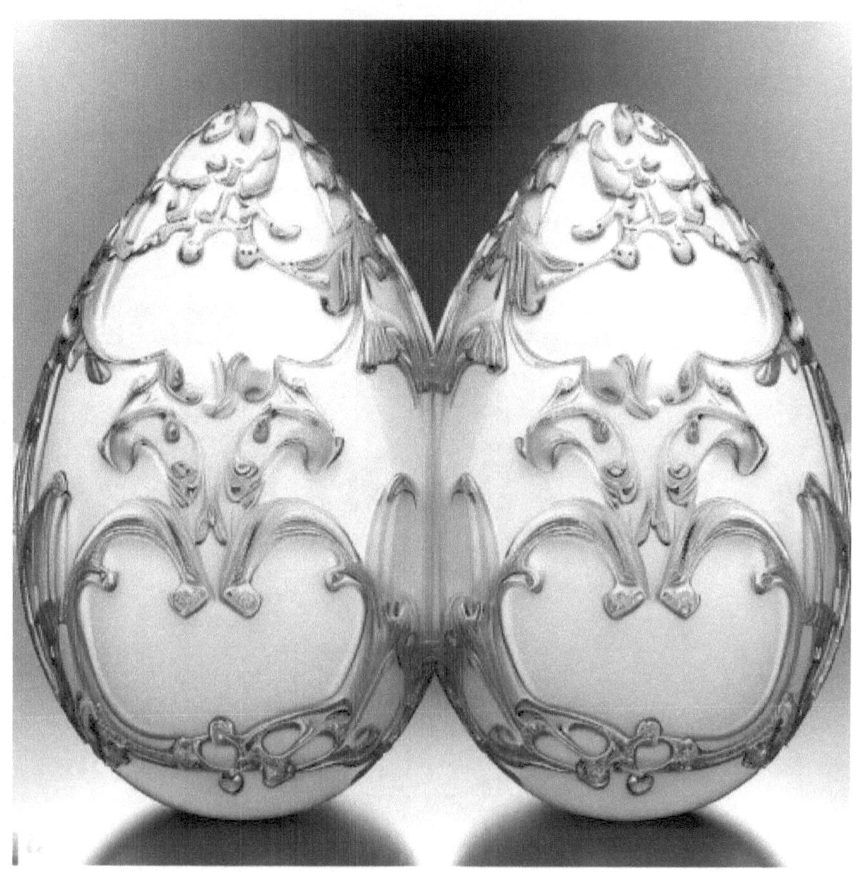

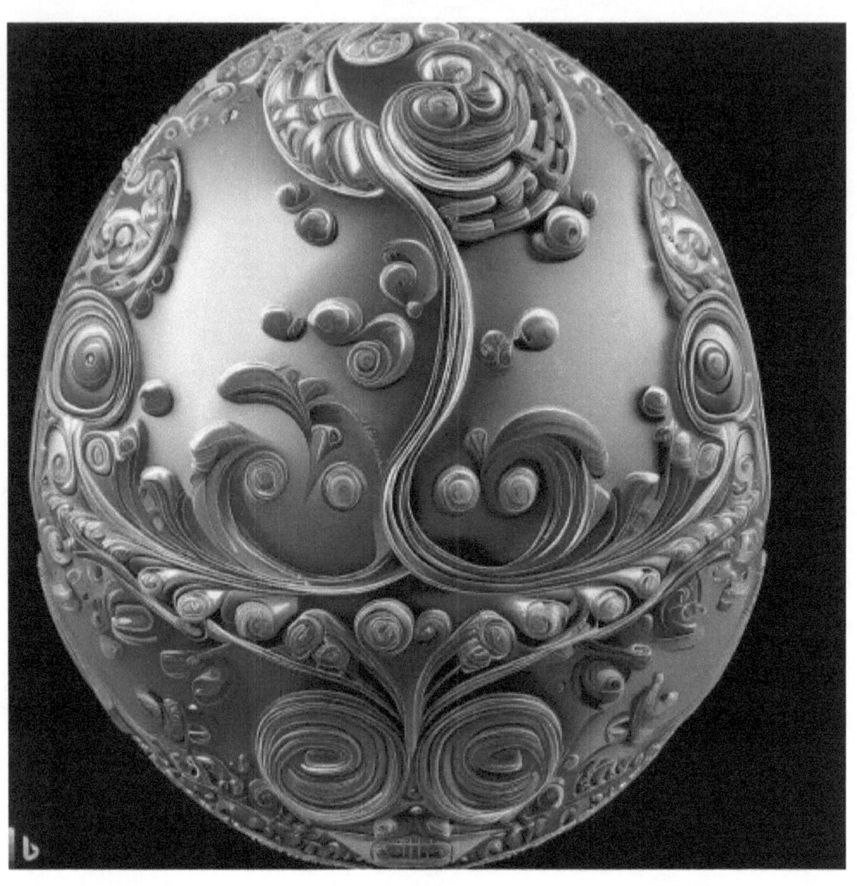

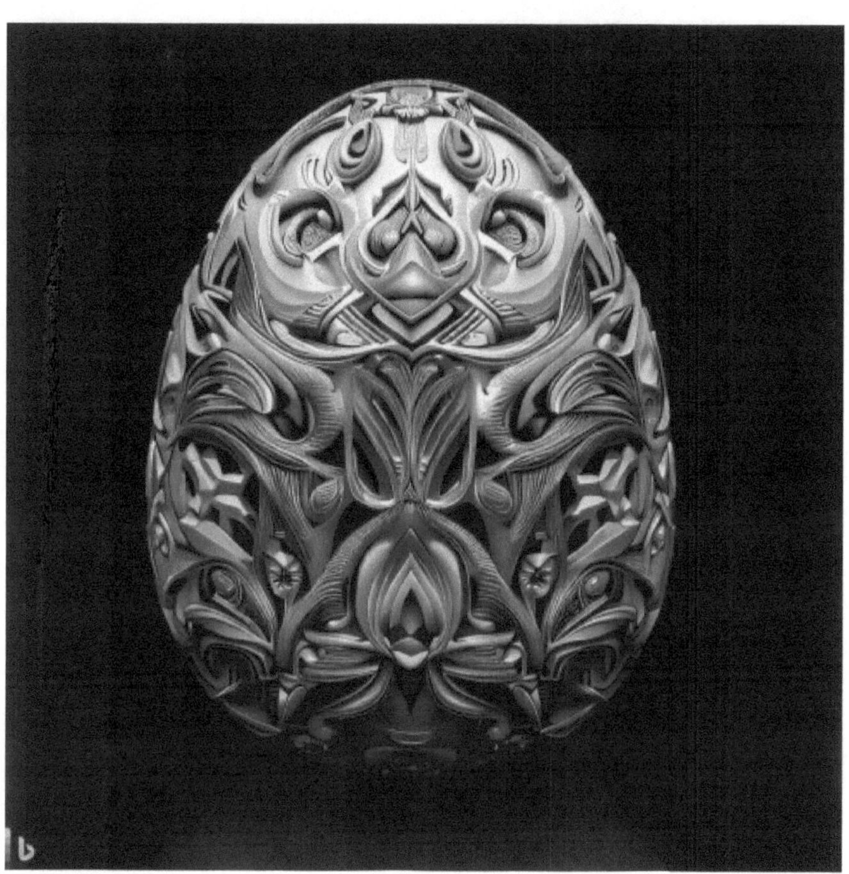

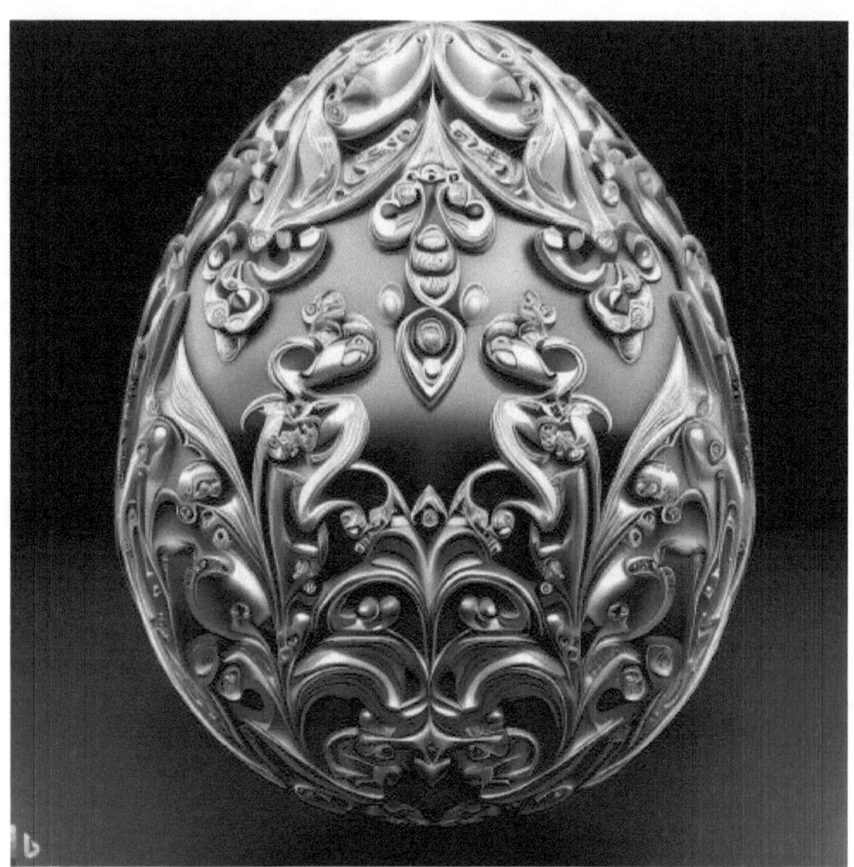

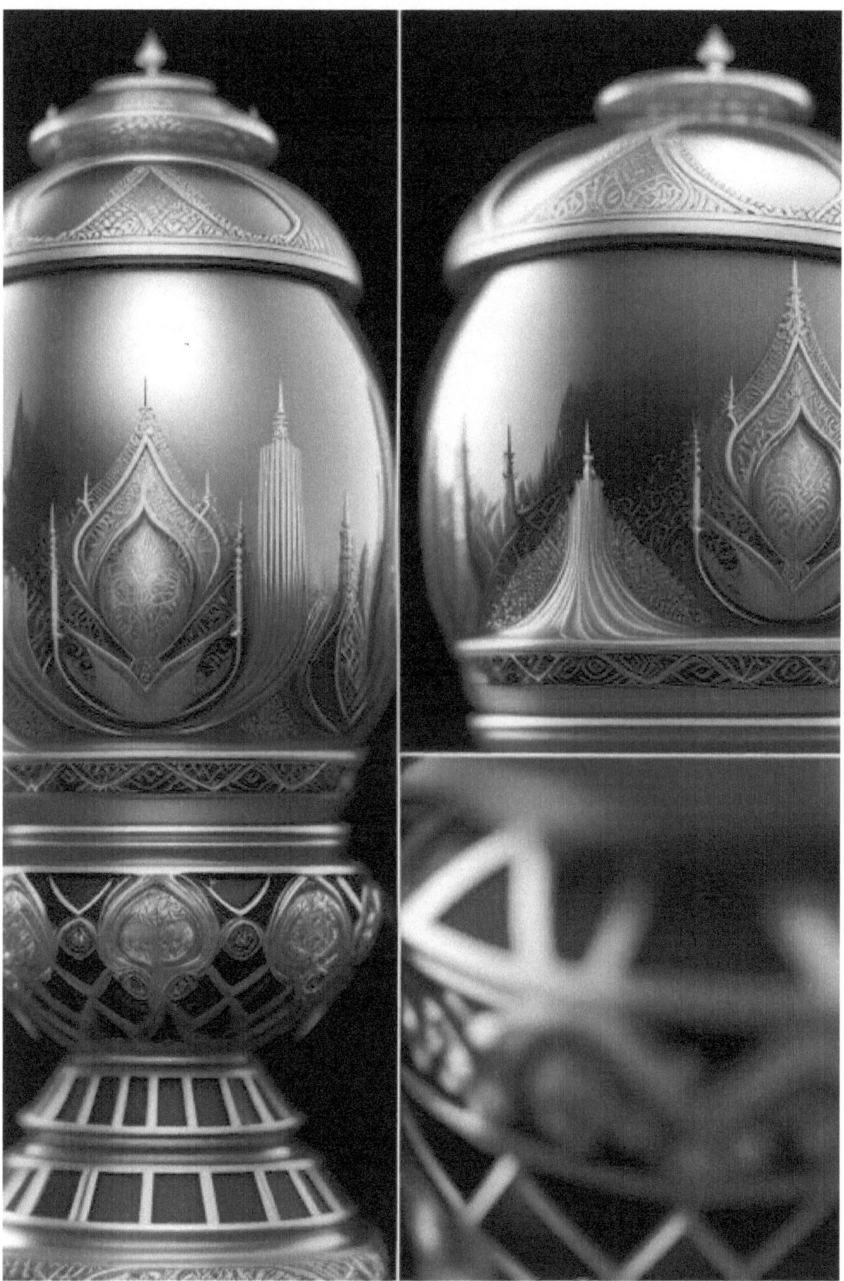

Carl Fabergé's contributions to the world of jewelry and art are immeasurable. His distinct style, characterized by attention to detail, aesthetic diversity, and his famous Imperial Easter Eggs, established him as a master jeweler and artist. Fabergé's creations have become symbols of opulence and refinement, inspiring contemporary jewelry designers to strive for excellence in craftsmanship and to push the boundaries of artistic expression. As his works continue to captivate audiences, Carl Fabergé remains an enduring icon in the world of jewelry design.

Alphonse Mucha: A Visionary Artist Inspiring Jewelry Design

Alphonse Mucha, a renowned artist, is celebrated for his unique style that seamlessly blends fantasy and natural motifs. He fearlessly challenged the established notions of jewelry design, leaving a lasting impact on the industry. In this article, we will explore the life and artistic contributions of Alphonse Mucha, delve into the distinctive features of his style, and discover how his works continue to inspire and influence contemporary jewelry creations.

The Style of Alphonse Mucha:

Alphonse Mucha's style can be characterized by the following key features:

> 1. Symbolism and Decorative Elegance: Mucha's artwork often incorporated symbolic elements, such as flowers, stars, and intricate ornamentation. He was renowned for his decorative elegance, employing flowing lines, intricate patterns, and richly adorned compositions in his illustrations. His designs exuded a sense of grace, mystique, and sensuality.

2. Naturalistic Motifs: Mucha drew inspiration from nature, incorporating elements such as flowing hair, floral patterns, and organic forms into his artwork. His portrayal of women, often depicted as ethereal and alluring figures, became synonymous with his style. Mucha's works celebrated the beauty and harmony of the natural world.

3. Harmonious Color Palettes: Mucha's use of colors was distinctively vibrant and harmonious. He employed a soft, pastel color palette, often incorporating jewel tones, which added depth and radiance to his illustrations. The delicate interplay of colors in his works enhanced their overall aesthetic appeal.

4. Asymmetry and Fluidity: Mucha embraced asymmetry in his compositions, deviating from traditional symmetrical designs. His artwork featured flowing lines and curves, creating a sense of movement and dynamism. This fluidity added a touch of enchantment to his pieces and reflected the artistic spirit of the Art Nouveau movement.

Prompt: pendant, Metal painting in the style of Alphonse Mucha,

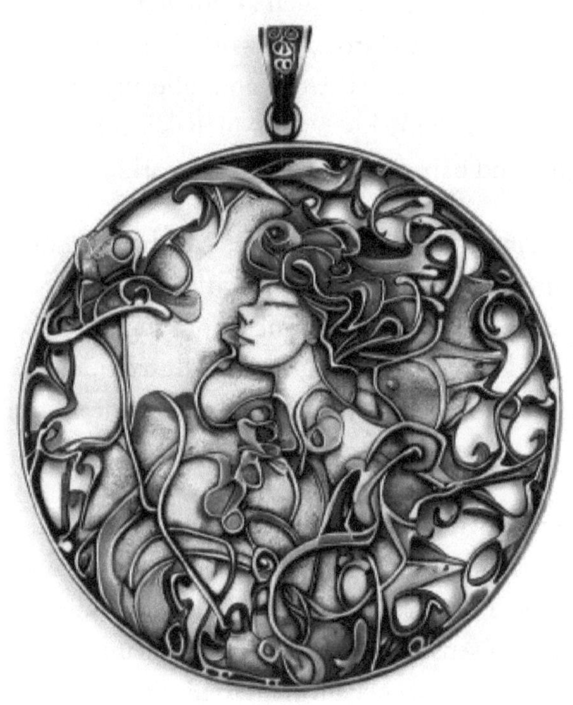

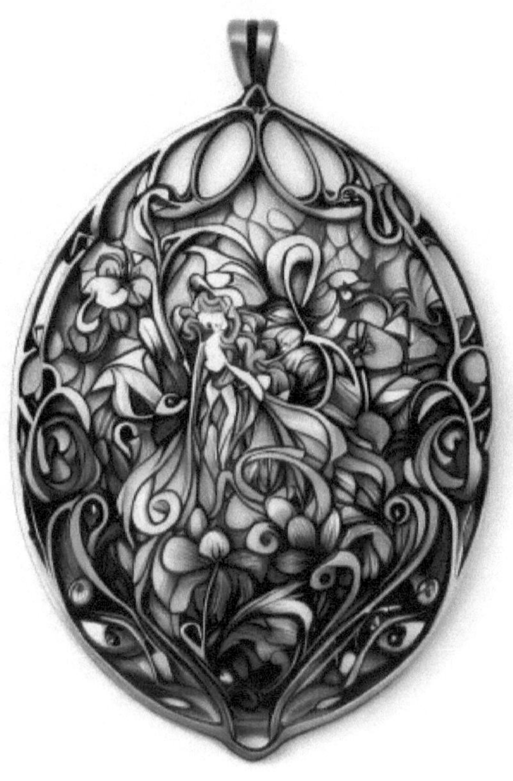

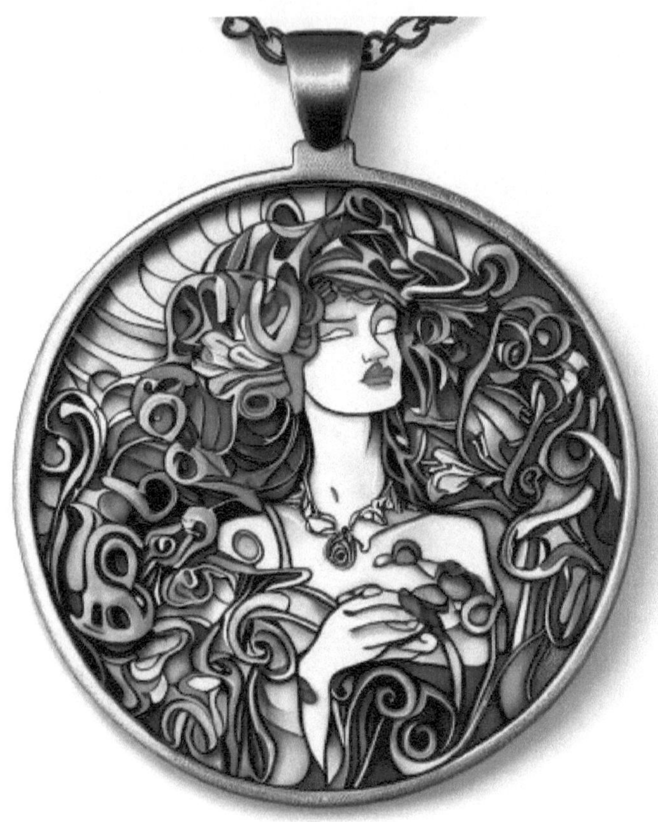

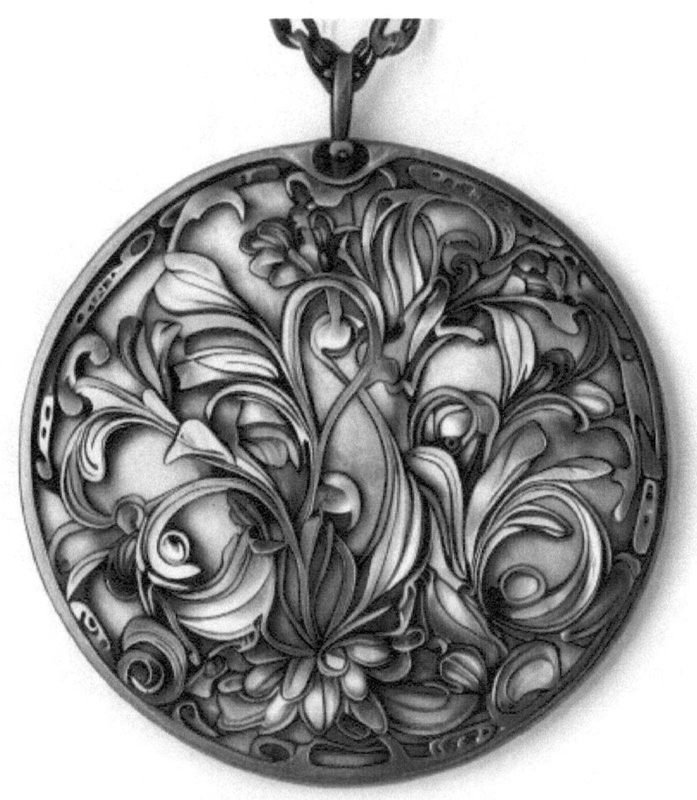

Influence on Contemporary Jewelry Design:

Alphonse Mucha's artistic legacy continues to inspire and influence contemporary jewelry designers. His imaginative motifs, harmonious color schemes, and organic forms provide a rich source of inspiration for creating unique and captivating jewelry pieces. Contemporary jewelers draw upon Mucha's style to infuse their designs with a sense of elegance, femininity, and artistic expression.

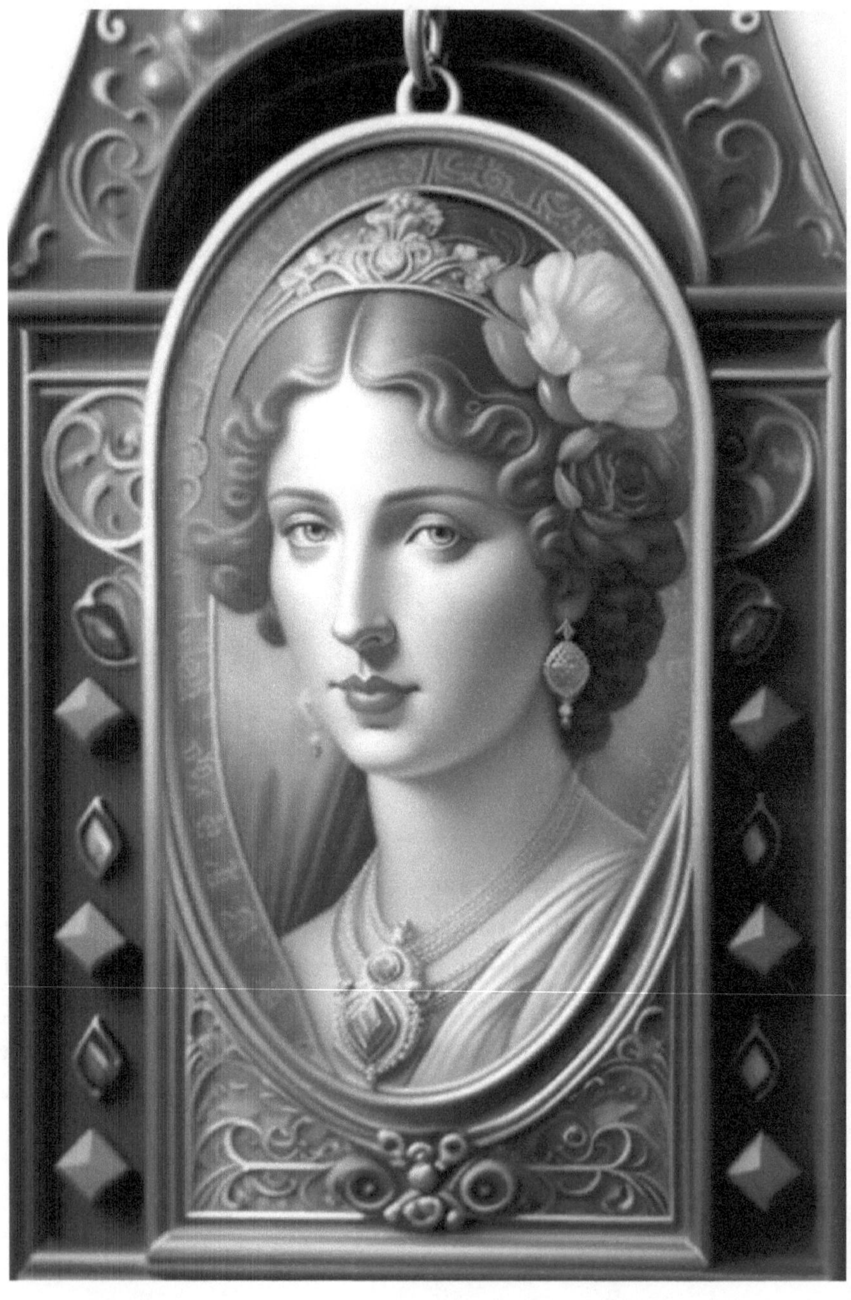

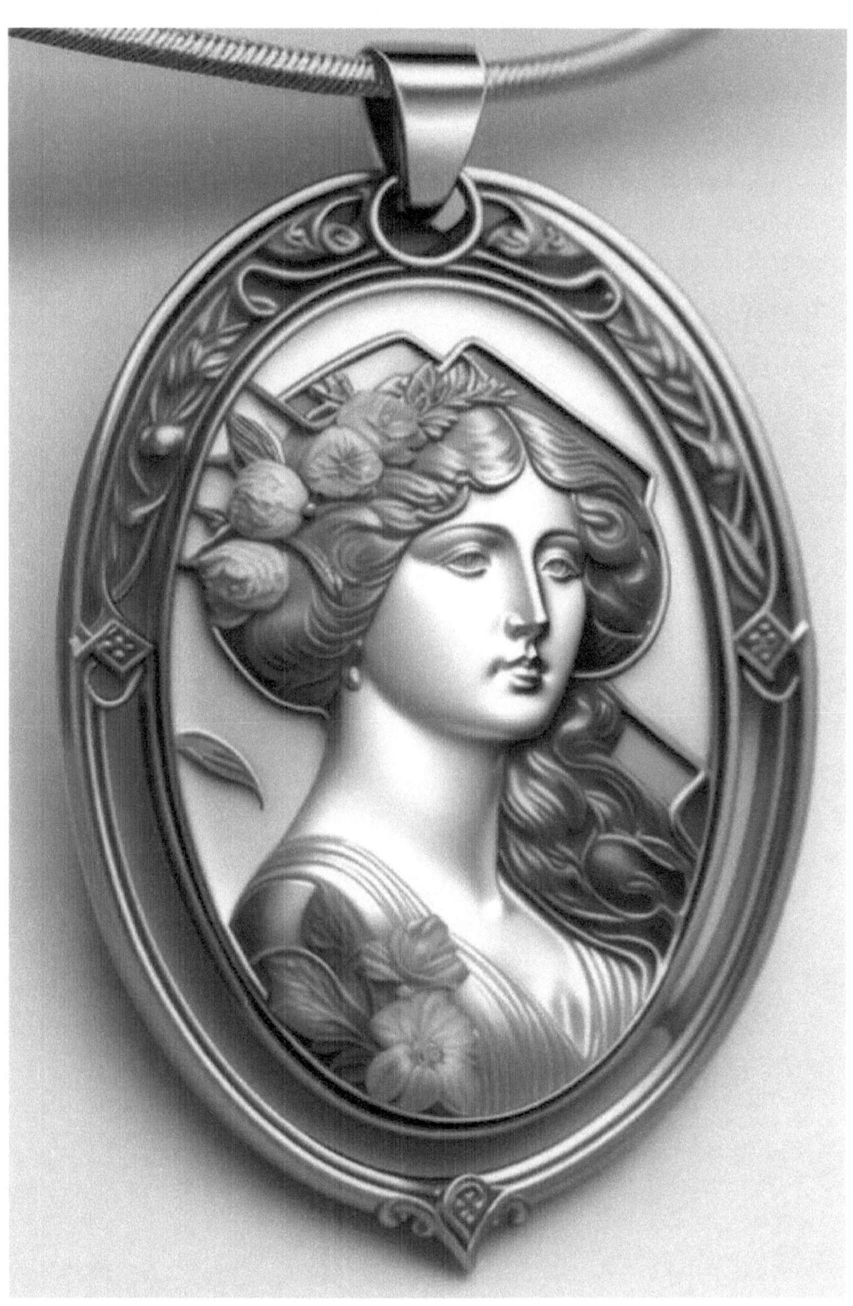

Jewelry pieces inspired by Mucha's style often incorporate elements such as intricately detailed filigree work, nature-inspired motifs, and the use of gemstones to enhance the overall aesthetic. Necklaces, earrings, and brooches echo the graceful lines and organic forms seen in Mucha's artwork, capturing the essence of his style and creating wearable pieces of art.

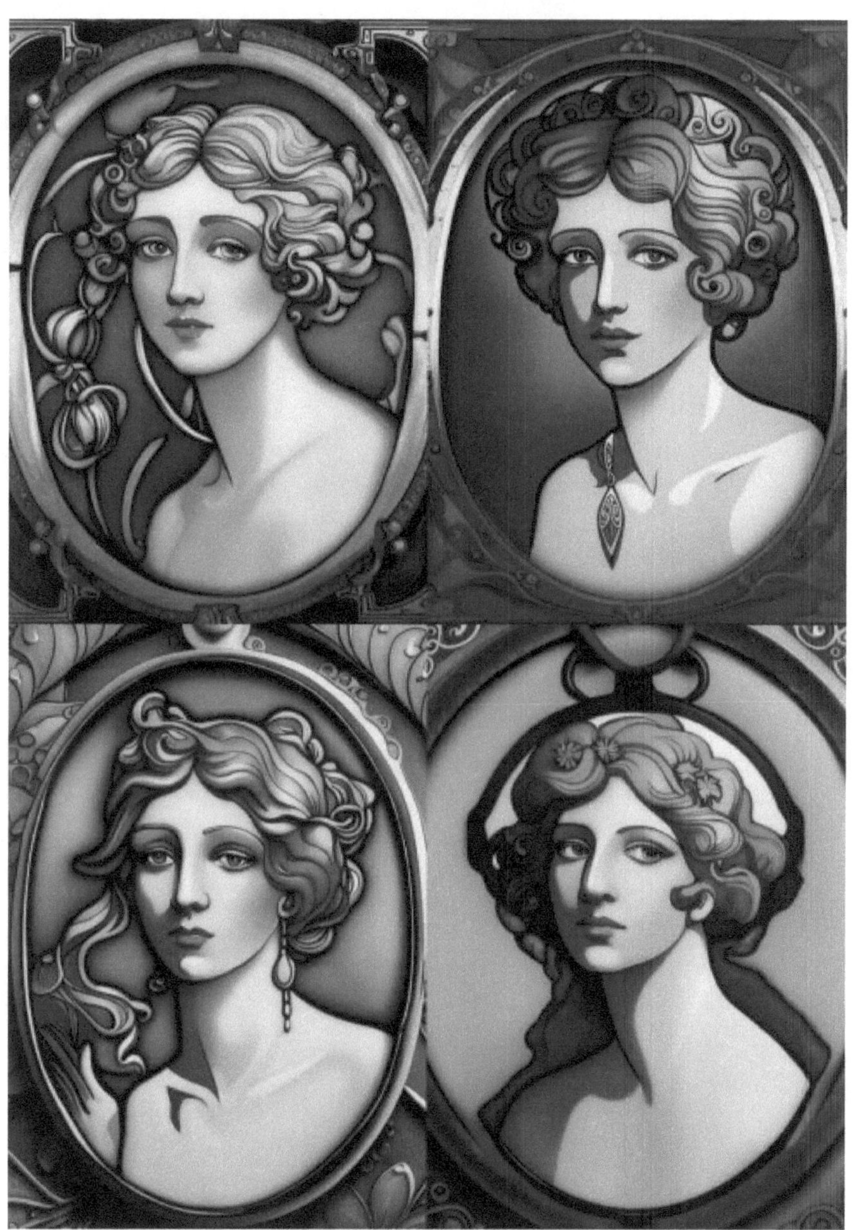

Alphonse Mucha's artistic vision and innovative approach to jewelry design have left an indelible mark on the industry. His unique style, characterized by symbolism, decorative elegance, naturalistic motifs, and harmonious color palettes, continues to inspire contemporary jewelry designers worldwide. Mucha's ability to seamlessly combine fantasy and nature in his works has created a timeless allure that transcends generations. As jewelers draw upon his techniques and motifs, Alphonse Mucha's influence remains a source of inspiration, ensuring that his artistic legacy lives on in the world of jewelry design.

Contemporary Handmade Techniques for Creating Jewelry Inspired by Famous Artists

Creating jewelry inspired by famous artists has become a popular trend in the world of handmade accessories. Artists' motifs and styles provide a rich source of inspiration for jewelry makers, allowing them to infuse their creations with artistic flair and uniqueness. In this article, we will explore a diverse range of contemporary handmade techniques used for making jewelry that draws inspiration from renowned artists. From working with wire and polymer clay to utilizing hot glue guns, 3D pens, wood burning, natural materials, sea glass, and more, we will delve into the exciting world of artistic jewelry craftsmanship.

Wire Wrapping:

1. Wire wrapping is a versatile technique that involves manipulating and weaving thin wires to create intricate designs. This technique is often used to mimic the flowing lines and organic forms found in the works of artists such as Gustav Klimt and Alphonse Mucha. Jewelry makers employ various wire wrapping techniques, including coiling, spiraling, and weaving, to add texture and dimension to their pieces.

Polymer Clay:

2. Polymer clay is a versatile material that can be shaped, molded, and cured to create unique jewelry designs. Artists inspired by the vibrant colors and abstract patterns of artists like Piet Mondrian and Wassily Kandinsky often use polymer clay to replicate their iconic styles. Polymer clay

jewelry can feature geometric shapes, bold color blocks, and intricate patterns, allowing for endless creative possibilities.

Hot Glue Gun:

3. The hot glue gun is not only a handy tool for everyday crafts but can also be utilized to create textured surfaces and abstract designs in jewelry making. Artists influenced by the unconventional styles of Salvador Dali and Joan Miró often employ the hot glue gun to add dimension and surrealistic elements to their jewelry pieces. By layering and manipulating molten glue, artists can achieve unique textures and shapes that resemble the artists' distinctive aesthetics.

3D Pen:

4. The advent of 3D printing technology has opened up exciting possibilities for jewelry makers. Using a 3D pen, artists can create intricate three-dimensional designs that mimic the sculptural qualities found in the works of renowned sculptors like Alexander Calder and Henry Moore. The 3D pen allows for precise control over the material, enabling the creation of detailed and complex jewelry pieces with ease.

Wood Burning:

5. Wood burning, also known as pyrography, involves using a heated metal tool to create burn marks on wood surfaces. Artists inspired by the natural motifs and earthy tones seen in the works of René Lalique and Georgia O'Keeffe incorporate wood burning techniques into their jewelry designs. By etching intricate patterns or designs onto

wooden pendants or beads, artists can infuse their jewelry with a rustic and organic appeal.

Natural Materials:

6. Artists often incorporate natural materials such as feathers, stones, shells, and dried flowers into their jewelry designs. Drawing inspiration from the motifs of tribal art or the ecological themes of Andy Goldsworthy, these artists create eco-friendly and nature-inspired jewelry. By combining different natural elements with traditional jewelry-making techniques, they craft pieces that evoke a sense of connection with the natural world.

Sea Glass:

7. Sea glass, with its smooth, frosted appearance, holds a unique appeal for jewelry makers. Inspired by the soothing colors and organic shapes found in the works of beach landscape painters like Winslow Homer, artists transform discarded glass fragments into beautiful jewelry pieces. By wire wrapping or bezel-setting sea glass, they create elegant and ethereal accessories that capture the essence of coastal beauty.

Contemporary jewelry makers are constantly exploring new techniques and materials to create unique pieces inspired by famous artists. From wire wrapping and polymer clay to hot glue guns, 3D pens, wood burning, natural materials, and sea

Creating a Wire-Wrapped Pendant Inspired by Gustav Klimt

Wire wrapping is a versatile and artistic technique that allows jewelry makers to manipulate and weave thin wires into intricate designs. In this article, we will explore the process of creating a wire-wrapped pendant inspired by the flowing lines and organic forms seen in the works of the renowned artist Gustav Klimt. To bring our vision to life, we will be using materials such as gold-plated aluminum wire and tools like round-nose pliers, wire cutters, a glue gun, epoxy resin, dyes, beads, and foil. Let's embark on this creative journey and learn how to craft a stunning pendant in the style of Gustav Klimt.

Materials and Tools:

- Gold-plated aluminum wire
- Round-nose pliers
- Wire cutters
- Glue gun
- Epoxy resin
- Dyes (optional)
- Beads
- Foil

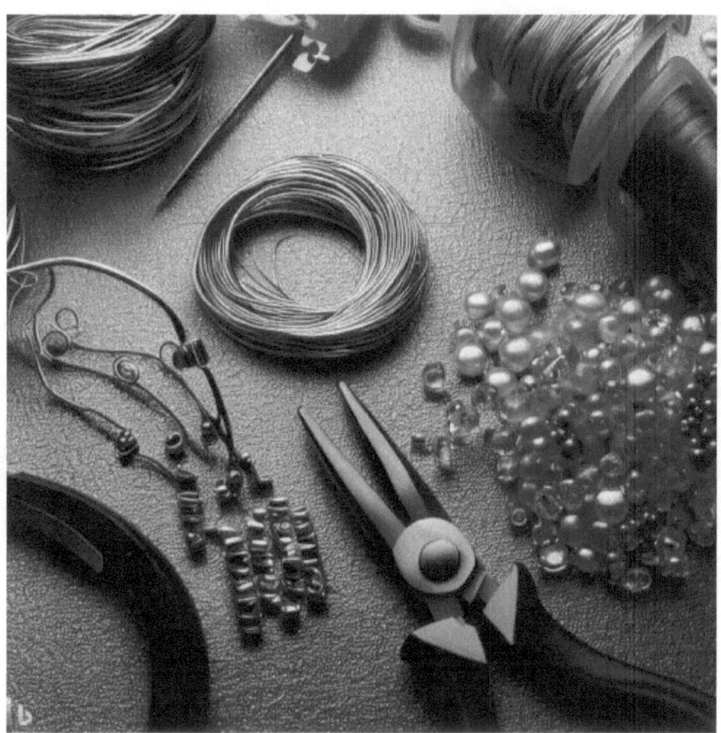

Step 1: Sketching the Design:

Begin by sketching your desired design on a piece of paper. Take inspiration from Gustav Klimt's signature motifs, such as swirling patterns, geometric shapes, or nature-inspired elements. This sketch will serve as your guide throughout the wire-wrapping process.

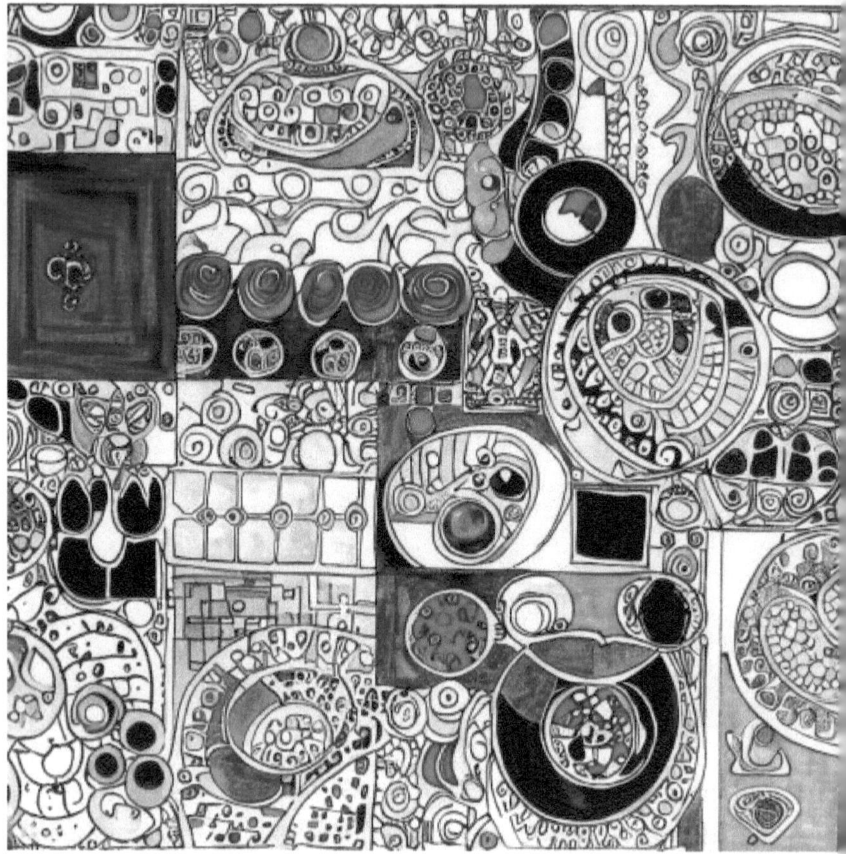

Step 2: Bending the Wire:

Using round-nose pliers, carefully manipulate the gold-plated aluminum wire to match the contours of your sketched design. Start by creating the basic outline, bending and shaping the wire according to your desired pattern. The pliers will help you achieve precise curves and angles.

Step 3: Securing the Wire:

Once you are satisfied with the wire's shape, use a glue gun to secure the overlapping sections of the wire. Apply a small amount of glue at the connection points to ensure stability and prevent the wire from moving or unraveling.

Step 4: Adding Decorative Elements:

To enhance the aesthetic appeal of your pendant, consider incorporating beads or small gemstones into the design. Carefully thread them onto the wire, positioning them strategically to complement the overall composition. You can also add foil accents by cutting small pieces of foil and wrapping them around certain wire sections, mimicking Gustav Klimt's use of gold leaf.

Step 5: Coating with Epoxy Resin:

To protect and preserve your wire-wrapped pendant, apply a coat of epoxy resin. Mix the epoxy resin according to the manufacturer's instructions, and carefully pour it over the pendant, ensuring that it covers all wire surfaces and decorative elements. Allow the resin to cure as per the recommended time.

Step 6: Optional Coloring:

If desired, you can add color to your pendant by incorporating dyes into the epoxy resin. Mix the dyes according to the desired shades, and apply them to specific areas of the pendant to enhance the overall aesthetic and capture the essence of Gustav Klimt's vibrant palette.

Step 7: Finishing Touches:

Once the epoxy resin has fully cured, inspect your wire-wrapped pendant for any rough edges or imperfections. Use wire cutters or sandpaper to smooth out any uneven areas and refine the final shape. Pay attention to details, ensuring that the pendant is visually appealing from all angles.

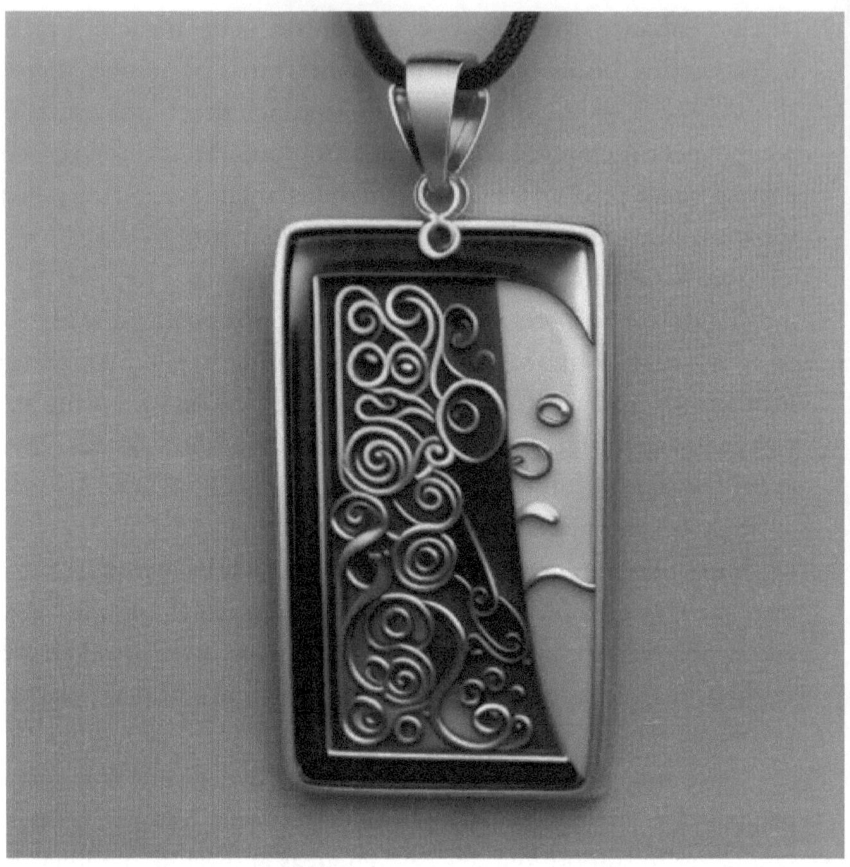

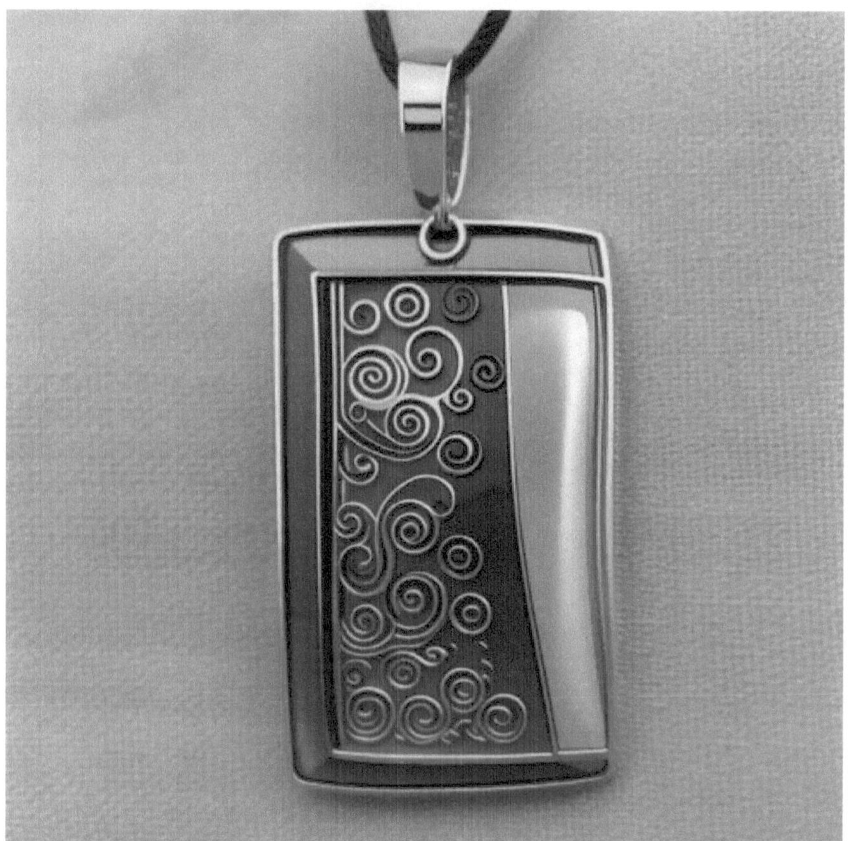

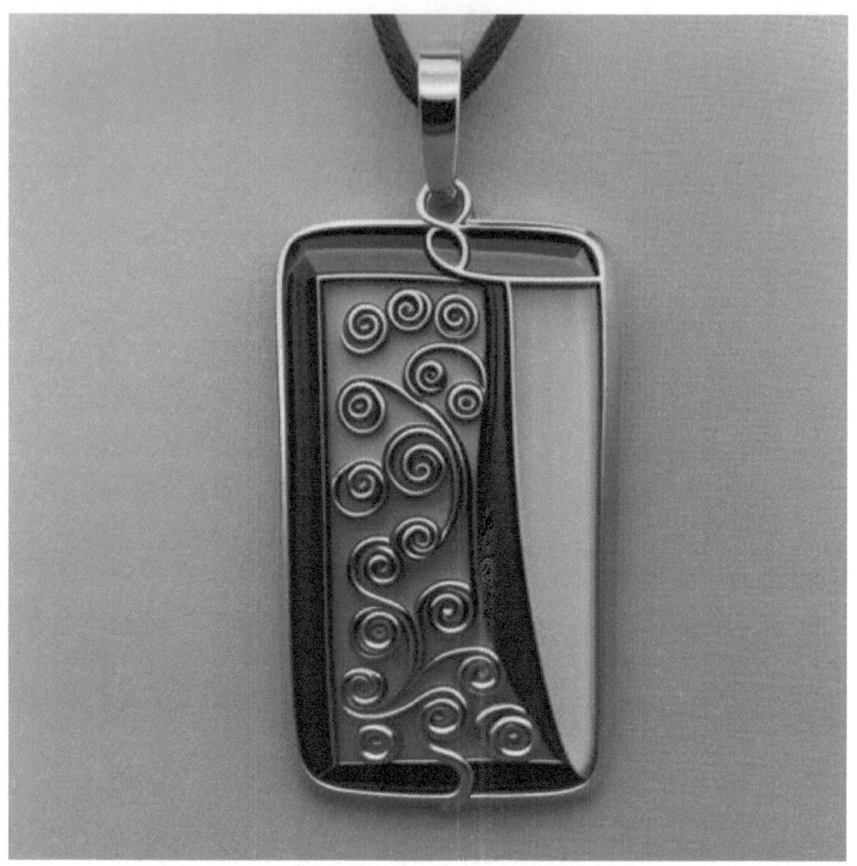

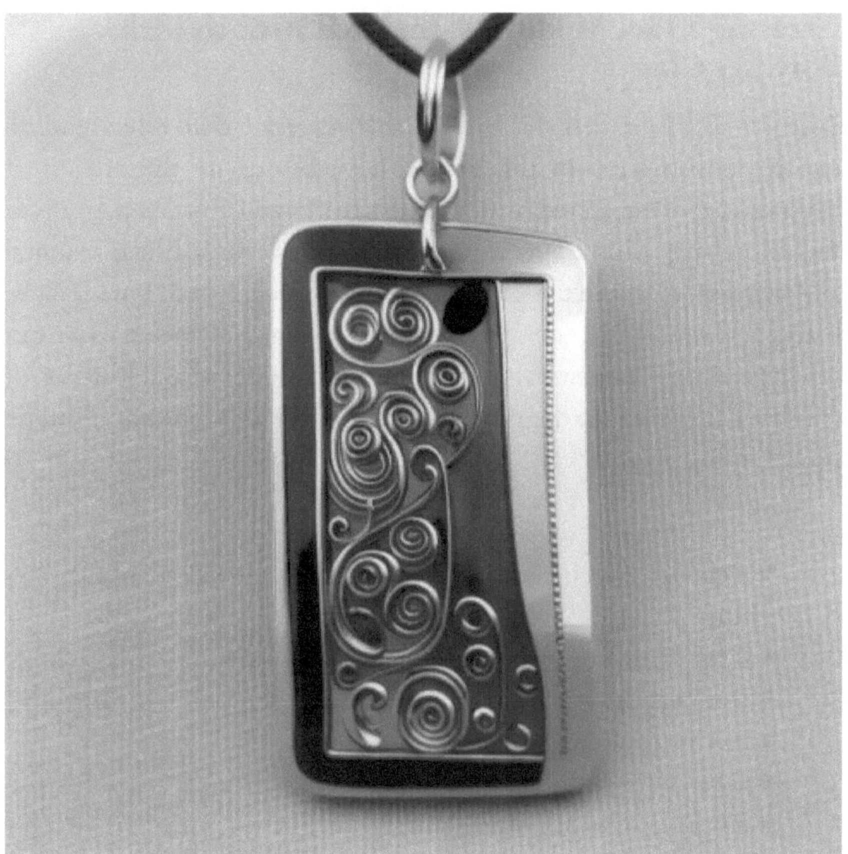

By combining the artistry of wire wrapping with the inspiration of Gustav Klimt's iconic style, you can create a stunning pendant that showcases the flowing lines, intricate patterns, and organic forms found in his artwork. The materials and tools mentioned in this article will guide you through the process of crafting your own wire-wrapped pendant, allowing you to express your creativity and pay homage to the legendary artist. Let your imagination soar as you explore the possibilities of wire wrapping and immerse yourself in the artistic world of Gustav Klim

Creating a Piet Mondrian-Inspired Brooch with Polymer Clay

Polymer clay is a versatile and pliable material that offers endless creative possibilities. In this article, we will explore the process of making a brooch inspired by the vibrant colors and abstract patterns of Piet Mondrian. Mondrian's iconic style features contrasting horizontal and vertical lines, the use of primary colors such as red, blue, yellow, black, and white, and geometric shapes. By using polymer clay, we can replicate these elements and create a unique and wearable piece of jewelry. Let's dive into the process of crafting a Piet Mondrian-inspired brooch using polymer clay.

Materials:

- Polymer clay in vibrant colors (red, blue, yellow, black, white)
- Craft knife or clay cutting tool
- Rolling pin
- Baking tray and parchment paper
- Oven with temperature indicator
- Jewelry findings (brooch pin)
- Polymer clay gloss or varnish

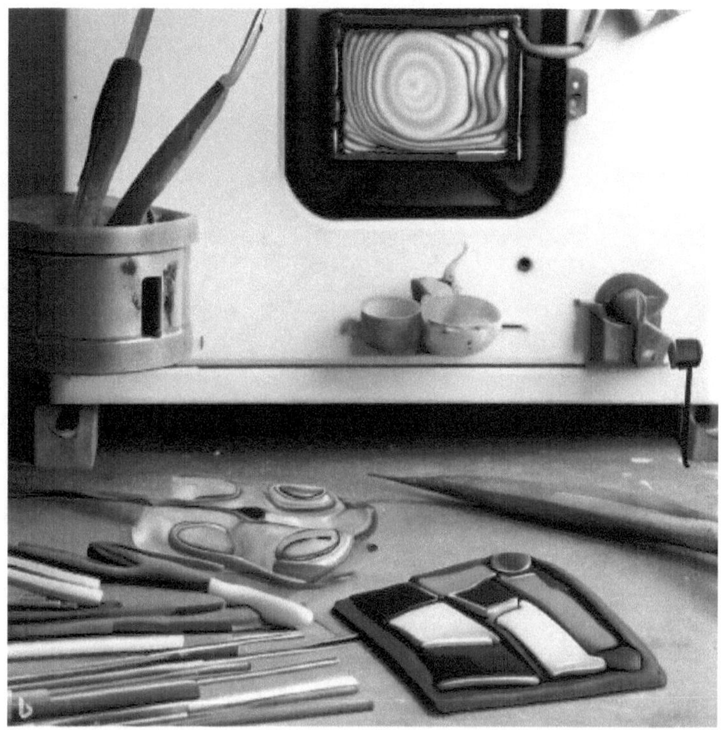

Step 1: Design Planning:

Begin by studying Piet Mondrian's artwork to understand his characteristic style. Note the arrangement of bold lines, color blocks, and geometric shapes. Use this as a reference to plan your brooch design. Decide on the size and shape of your brooch, keeping in mind the wearable aspect.

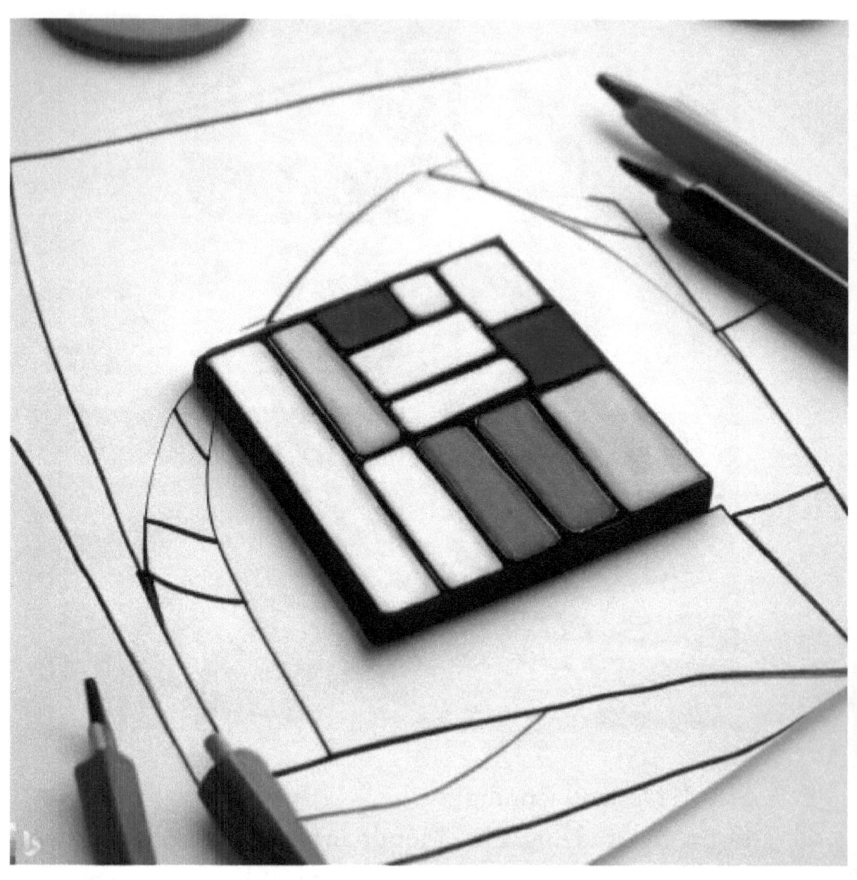

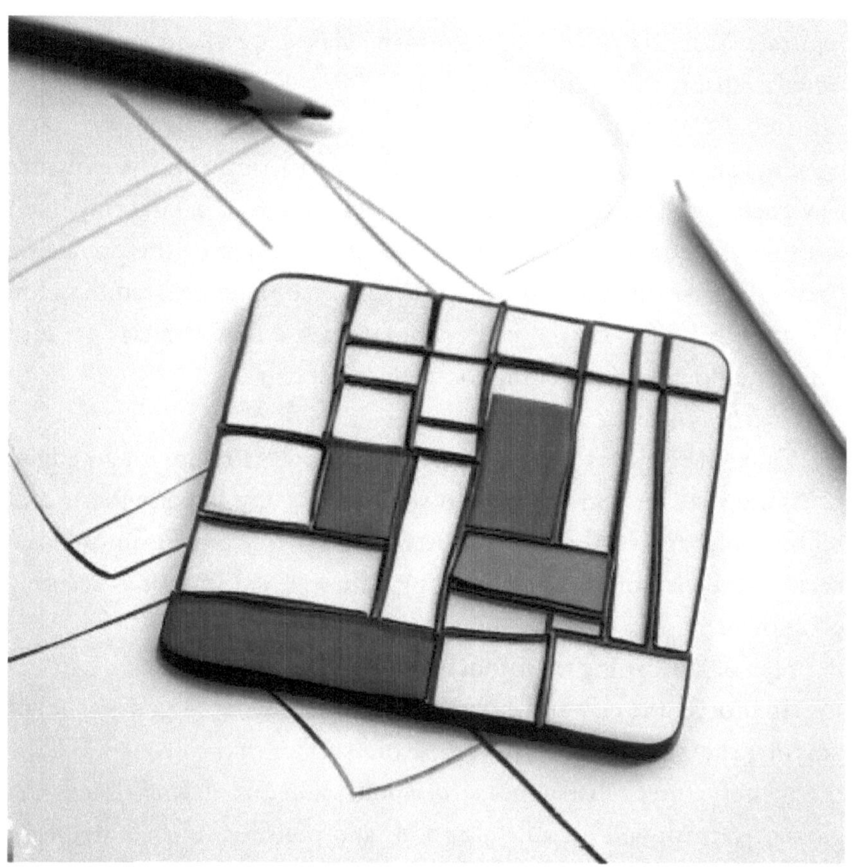

Step 2: Working with Polymer Clay:

Condition the polymer clay by kneading it until it becomes soft and pliable. Roll out each color of clay separately into thin sheets using a rolling pin. Cut the sheets into various geometric shapes, such as squares and rectangles, representing Mondrian's signature style. Experiment with different sizes and arrangements to achieve a visually appealing composition.

Step 3: Assembling the Design:

Arrange the clay shapes on a flat surface, following the planned design. Create a contrast between the primary colors (red, blue, yellow) and the neutral colors (black, white). Position the shapes to form the desired composition, incorporating horizontal and vertical lines to replicate Mondrian's aesthetic. Press the clay shapes lightly onto each other to ensure they adhere together.

Step 4: Baking the Clay:

Preheat your oven according to the instructions on the polymer clay package. Place the assembled clay design onto a baking tray lined with parchment paper. Carefully transfer the tray into the preheated oven and bake the clay according to the recommended temperature and time specified by the clay manufacturer. Allow the clay to cool completely before proceeding to the next step.

Step 5: Finishing Touches:

Once the clay has cooled, inspect the brooch for any rough edges. Use sandpaper or a craft knife to smooth out any imperfections and refine the shape of the brooch. Attach a brooch pin finding to the back of the clay piece using a strong adhesive, ensuring it is securely positioned.

Step 6: Varnishing the Brooch:

To protect the clay and enhance its appearance, apply a thin coat of polymer clay gloss or varnish to the front surface of the brooch. Follow the manufacturer's instructions for application and drying times. The gloss or varnish will provide a smooth and polished finish, enhancing the vibrancy of the colors.

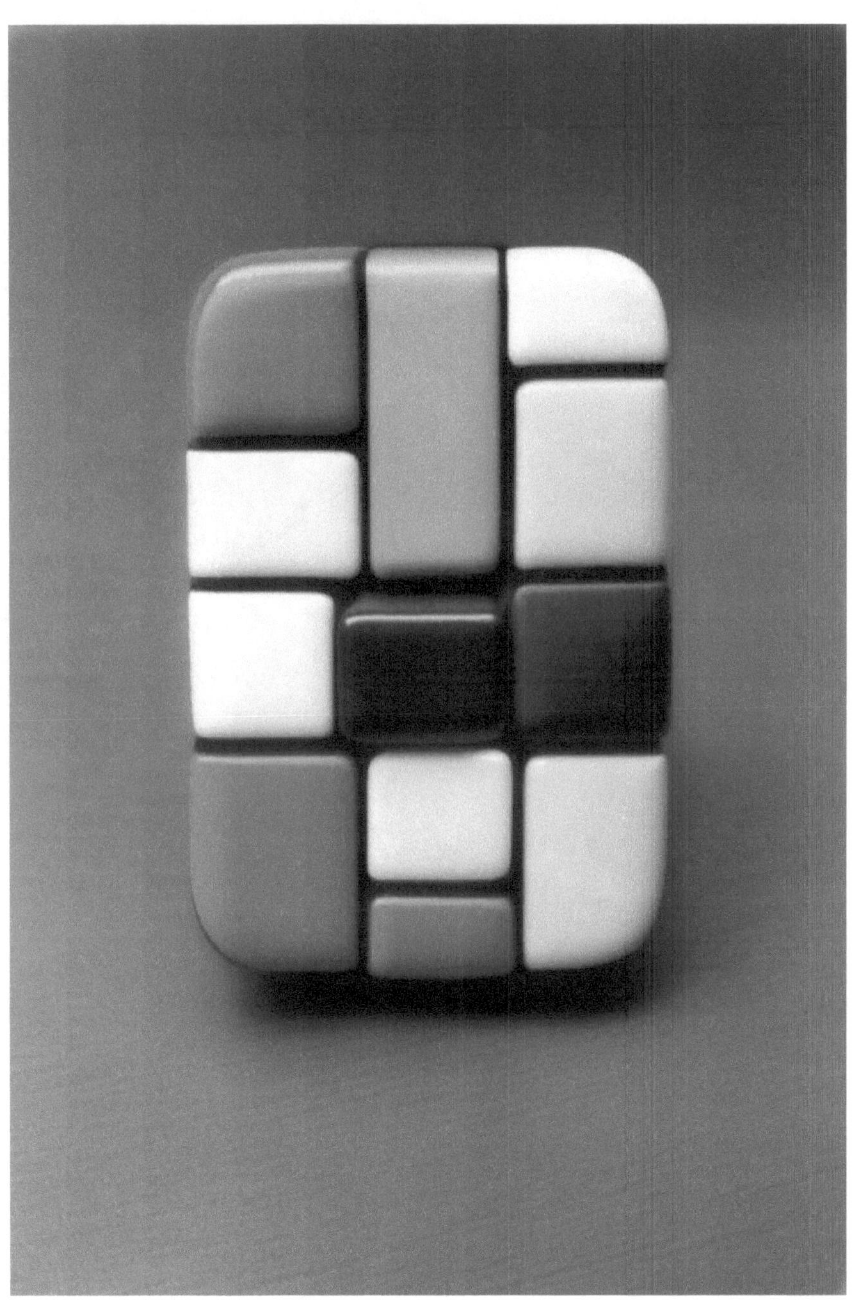

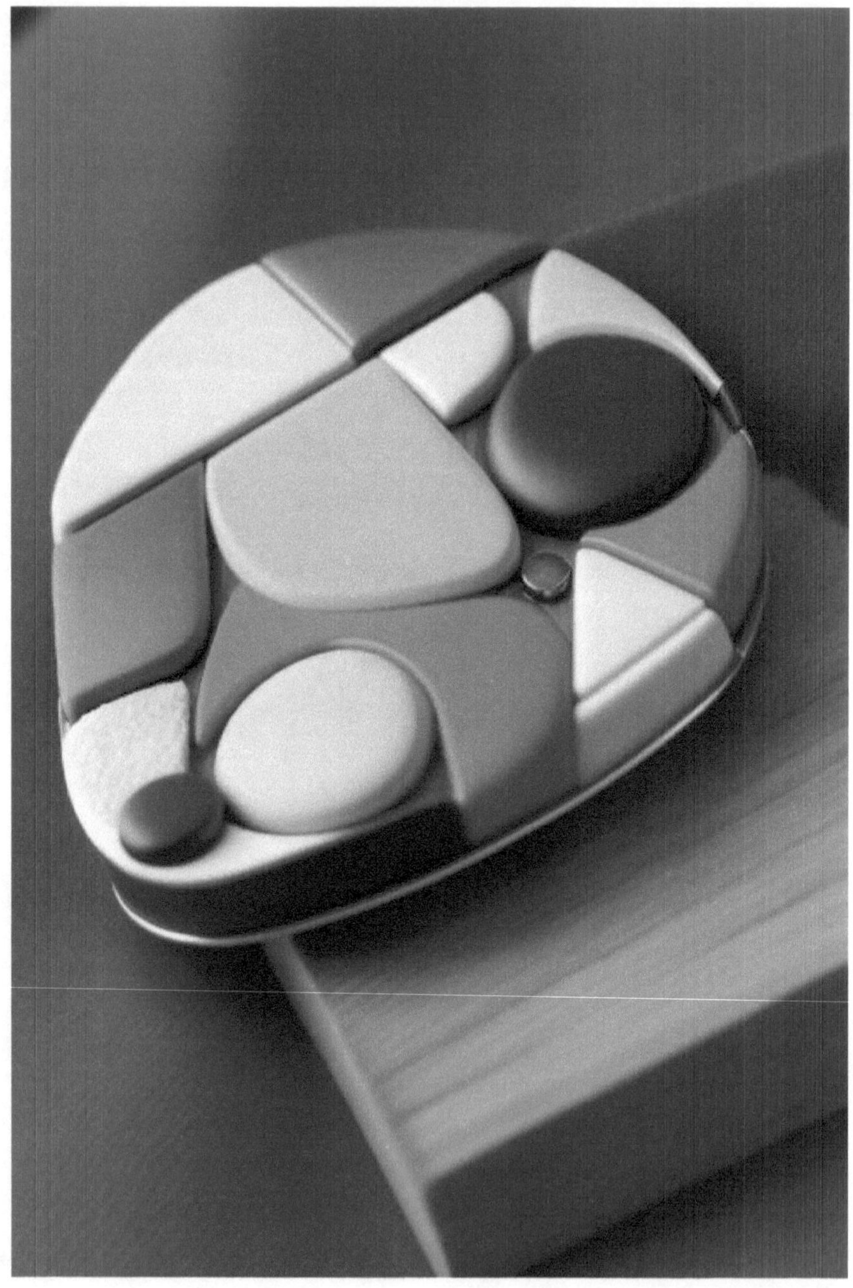

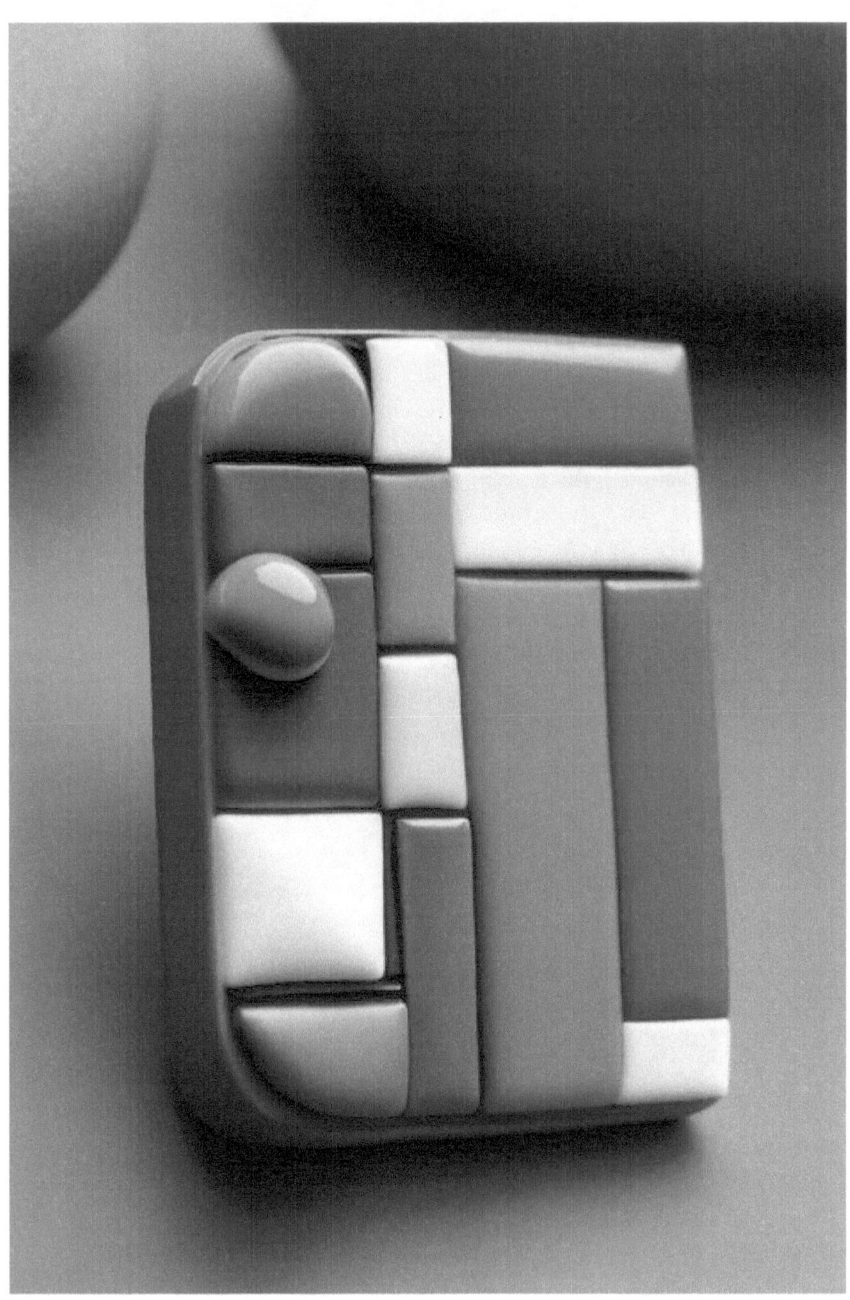

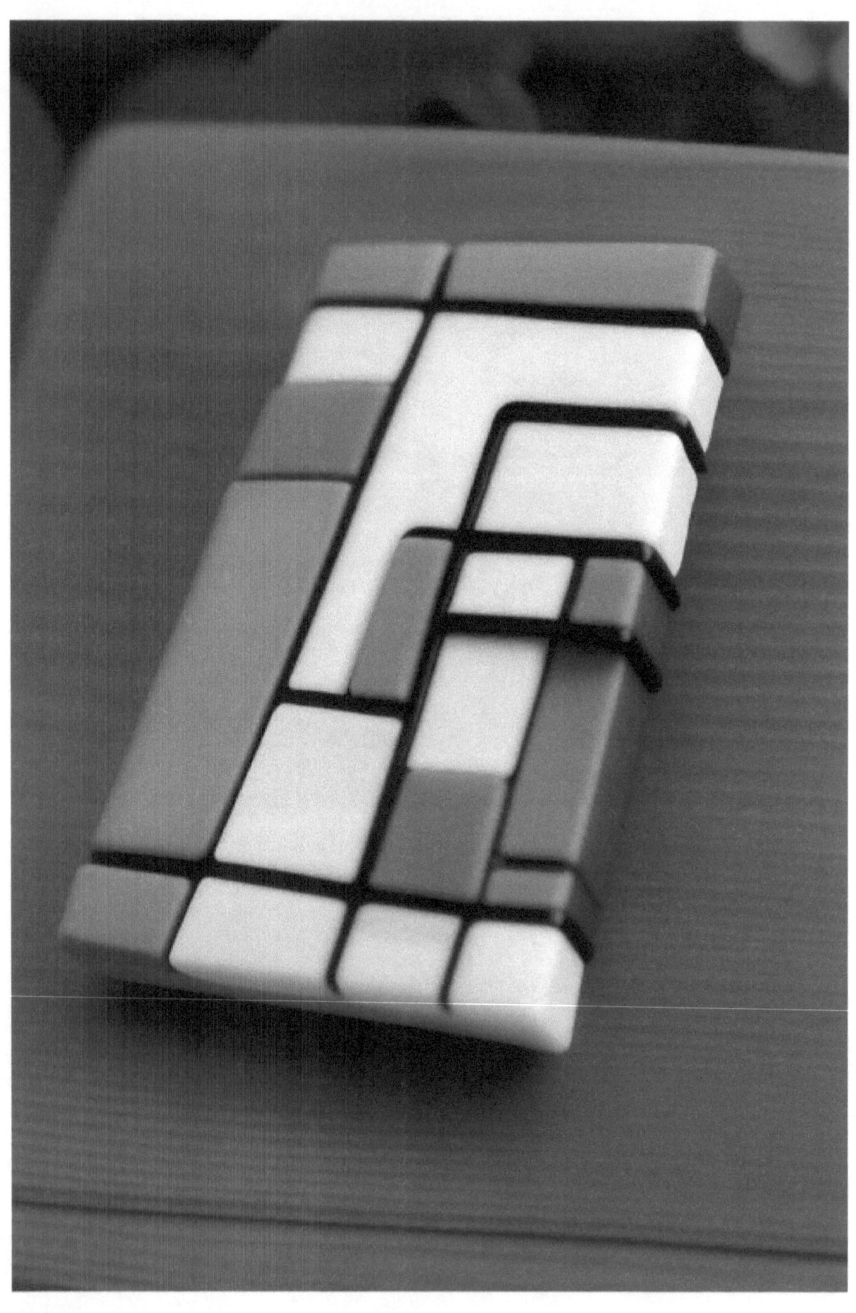

By working with polymer clay and drawing inspiration from Piet Mondrian's iconic style, you can create a striking and wearable brooch that reflects his signature aesthetic. The use of vibrant colors, geometric shapes, and contrasting lines will capture the essence of Mondrian's artwork. Polymer clay allows for flexibility and artistic expression, making it an ideal medium for replicating Mondrian's abstract patterns and bold color blocks. Wear your Piet Mondrian-inspired brooch with pride, showcasing your creativity and appreciation for this influential artist.

Creating a Joan Miró-Inspired Bracelet with a Glue Gun and Beads

Joan Miró, the renowned artist, was known for his experimental approach to form and color in his artworks. He seamlessly combined naturalism with abstraction, frequently incorporating bright colors and geometric shapes in his paintings. Throughout his career, Miró's style evolved, but he always remained true to his experimental approach to art. In this article, we will explore the process of creating a bracelet inspired by Joan Miró using a glue gun and embellished with beads. This project allows us to capture the essence of Miró's vibrant and expressive art in a wearable piece of jewelry. Let's dive into the steps of making a Joan Miró-inspired bracelet.

Materials:

- Metal, wood, or plastic bracelet base
- Glue gun and glue sticks
- Half beads or cabochons in various colors
- Colored glue sticks (optional)
- Foil sheets (optional)
- Scissors
- Protective gloves (optional)

Step 1: Selecting the Bracelet Base:

Choose a bracelet base made of metal, wood, or plastic. Consider the width and style of the bracelet, ensuring it provides a suitable canvas for your Joan Miró-inspired design. The base can be solid or open, depending on your preference.

Step 2: Preparing the Glue Gun:

Plug in the glue gun and allow it to heat up according to the manufacturer's instructions. Ensure you work in a well-ventilated area and take necessary precautions to protect your hands, such as wearing protective gloves.

Step 3: Applying Beads with the Glue Gun:

Carefully place a bead or half bead onto the bracelet base in the desired position. Apply a small amount of hot glue directly onto the back of the bead using the glue gun. Press the bead firmly onto the base, ensuring it adheres securely. Repeat this process with additional beads, creating your design inspired by Joan Miró's vibrant and geometric style. Allow the glue to cool and set before proceeding.

Step 4: Adding Colored Glue (Optional):

For an extra touch of color and texture, consider using colored glue sticks with the glue gun. Insert a colored glue stick into the glue gun and allow it to melt. Apply the colored glue directly onto the bracelet base or around the beads, following your desired design. The colored glue can mimic Miró's use of bold and expressive brushstrokes. Allow the glue to cool and solidify.

Step 5: Using Foil Sheets (Optional):

To further enhance the visual appeal of your bracelet, consider incorporating foil sheets. Cut small pieces of foil using scissors. While the glue from the glue gun is still hot, gently press the foil onto the surface, creating a metallic and textured effect. Experiment with different colors of foil to add depth and dimension to your design. Allow the glue to cool completely.

Step 6: Finishing Touches:

Inspect the bracelet to ensure all beads, colored glue, and foil are securely attached. Make any necessary adjustments or additions to achieve the desired look. Trim any excess glue or foil for a clean finish.

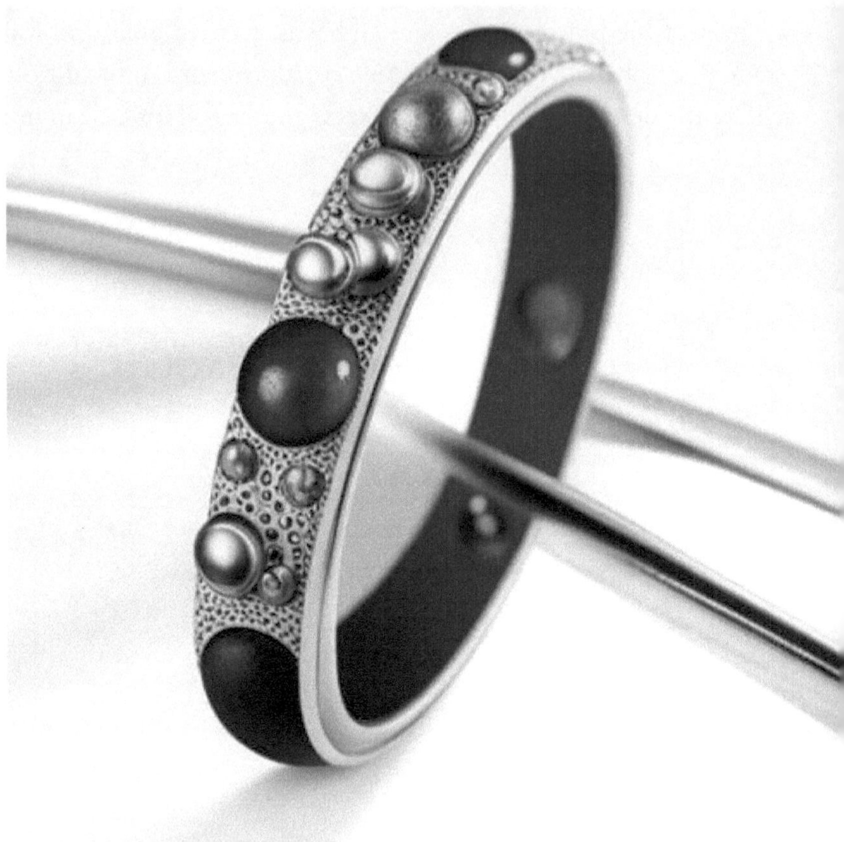

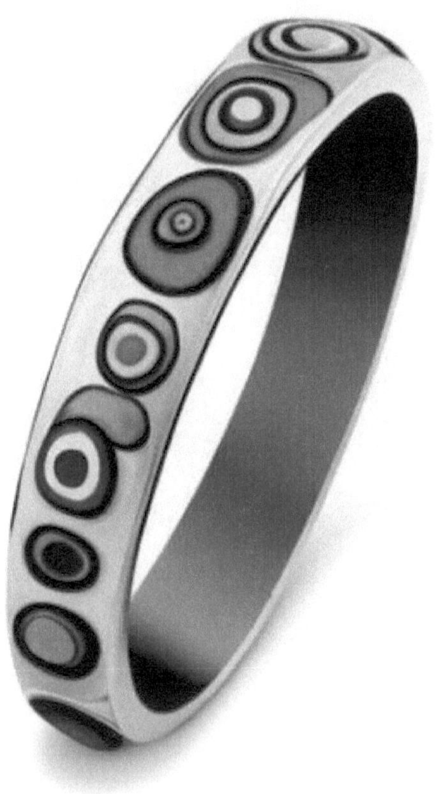

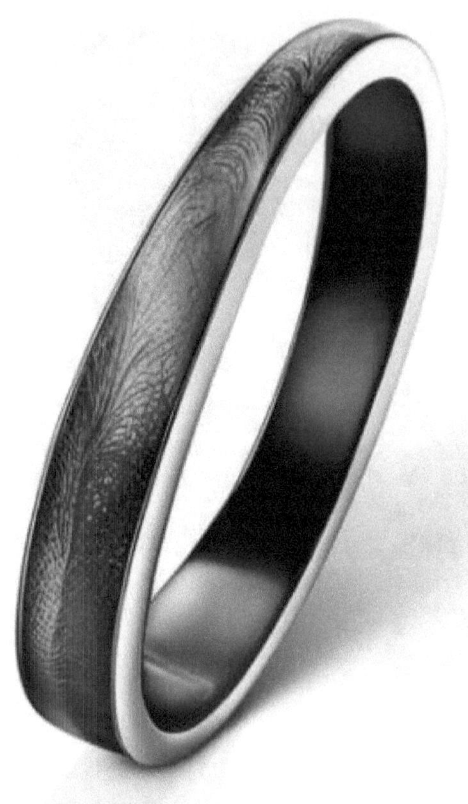

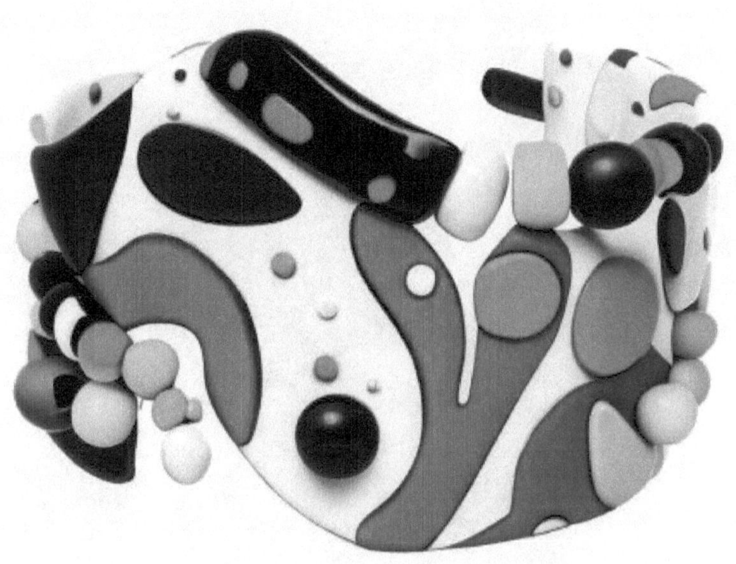

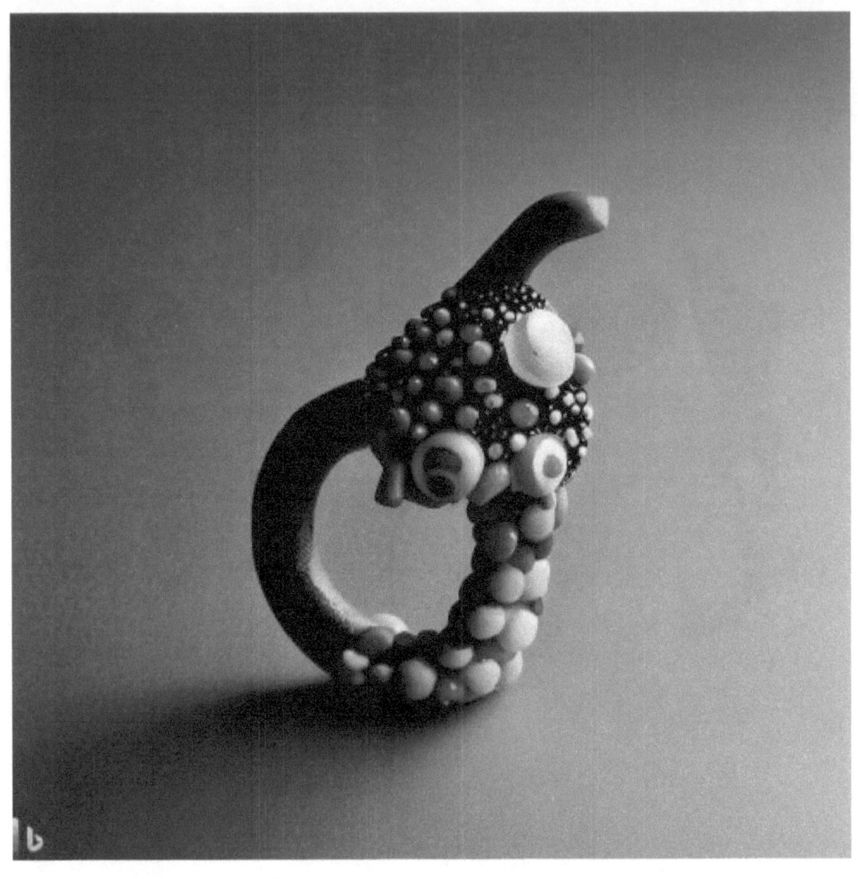

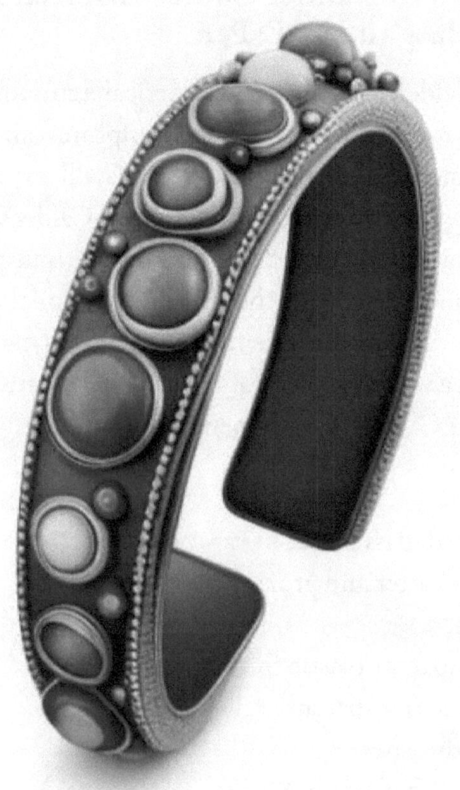

By utilizing a glue gun and embellishing with beads, colored glue, and foil, you can create a unique bracelet inspired by the artistic style of Joan Miró. Miró's vibrant colors, geometric shapes, and experimental approach to art come to life in this wearable piece of jewelry. Wear your Joan Miró-inspired bracelet with pride, showcasing your creativity and appreciation for this influential artist. This project allows you to carry a piece of Miró's expressive and abstract art wherever you go, making a stylish statement that reflects your artistic sensibilities.

Creating an Alexander Calder-Inspired Pendant Using Stained Glass and a 3D Pen

Alexander Calder, the renowned American sculptor, gained worldwide recognition for his intricate wire sculptures and kinetic artworks known as "mobiles." In this article, we will explore the process of creating a pendant inspired by Alexander Calder's unique style using stained glass and a 3D pen. By combining the transparency and vibrant colors of stained glass with the three-dimensional capabilities of a 3D pen, we can capture the essence of Calder's dynamic and whimsical sculptures in a wearable piece of art. Let's delve into the steps of making an Alexander Calder-inspired pendant.

Materials:

- Stained glass pieces in various colors
- Glass cutter and grozing pliers
- 3D pen
- Transparent plastic from beverage bottles
- Acrylic transparent and opaque paints
- Paintbrushes
- Jewelry bail or jump ring
- Chain or cord for the pendant
- Glue (optional)

Step 1: Designing the Pendant:

Begin by sketching a design inspired by Alexander Calder's whimsical sculptures. Consider incorporating dynamic shapes, abstract forms, and playful elements into your design. Keep in mind that Calder's art often features balanced compositions and a sense of movement.

Step 2: Cutting Stained Glass Pieces:

Using a glass cutter, carefully cut the stained glass pieces according to your design. Use grozing pliers to refine the edges and ensure a precise fit for each piece. Remember to handle the glass with care and wear appropriate safety equipment.

Step 3: Preparing the 3D Pen:

Load the 3D pen with black plastic filament. Allow the pen to heat up according to the manufacturer's instructions. Ensure you work in a well-ventilated area and take necessary precautions to protect your hands.

Step 4: Assembling the Pendant:

Using the 3D pen, start by creating a framework or base for your pendant. Build three-dimensional elements that will serve as the support structure for the stained glass pieces. Calder's sculptures often feature abstract and curved shapes, so feel free to experiment with different forms and contours.

Step 5: Attaching the Stained Glass:

Carefully place the cut stained glass pieces onto the 3D pen framework. Use the heated 3D pen to create small adhesive points that will secure the glass to the structure. Take your time to ensure each piece is firmly attached.

Step 6: Adding Color and Details:

Once the stained glass pieces are securely attached, use acrylic paints to enhance the design and add depth. Apply transparent and opaque paints to the glass, creating a play of colors and textures inspired by Calder's vibrant artworks. Experiment with different brush techniques to achieve the desired effect.

Step 7: Finishing Touches:

Inspect the pendant to ensure all elements are securely attached and the colors are vibrant. Make any necessary adjustments or additions to achieve the desired look. Attach a jewelry bail or jump ring to the top of the pendant for easy attachment to a chain or cord.

Step 8: Optional Step - Sealing the Pendant:

To protect the painted surface and add durability, you may choose to seal the pendant with a clear varnish or resin. Follow the manufacturer's instructions for the chosen sealing product and allow it to cure completely before wearing the pendant.

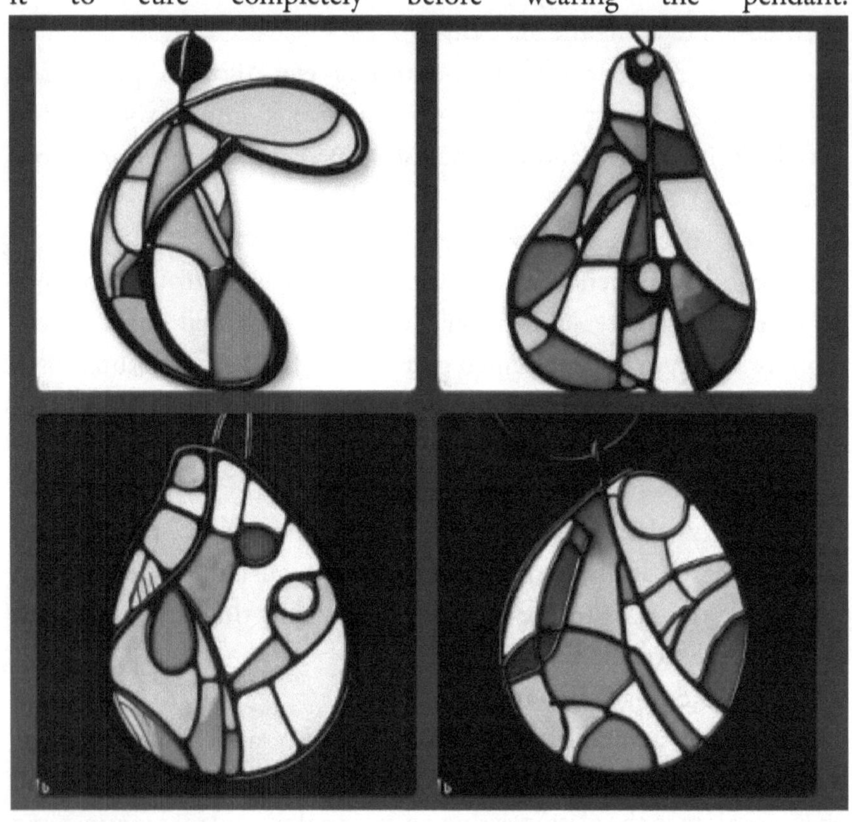

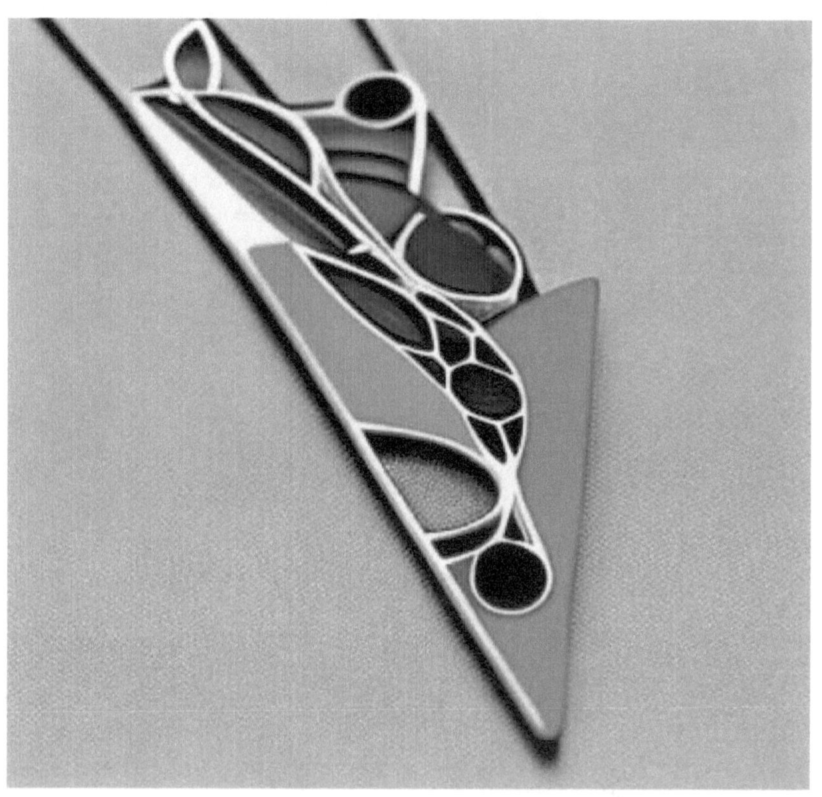

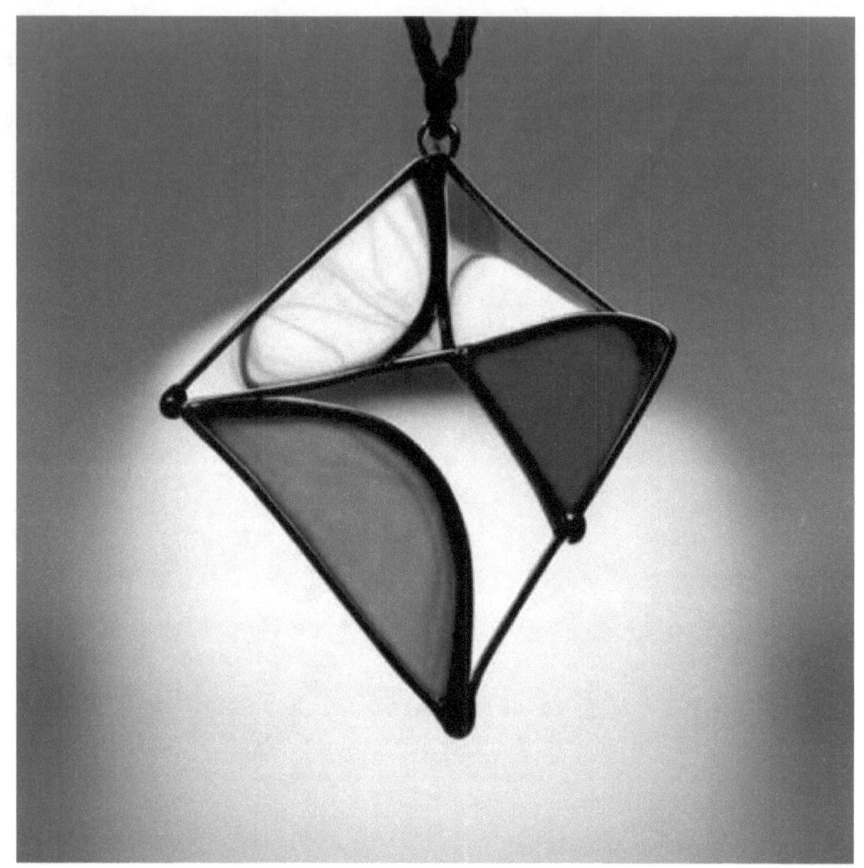

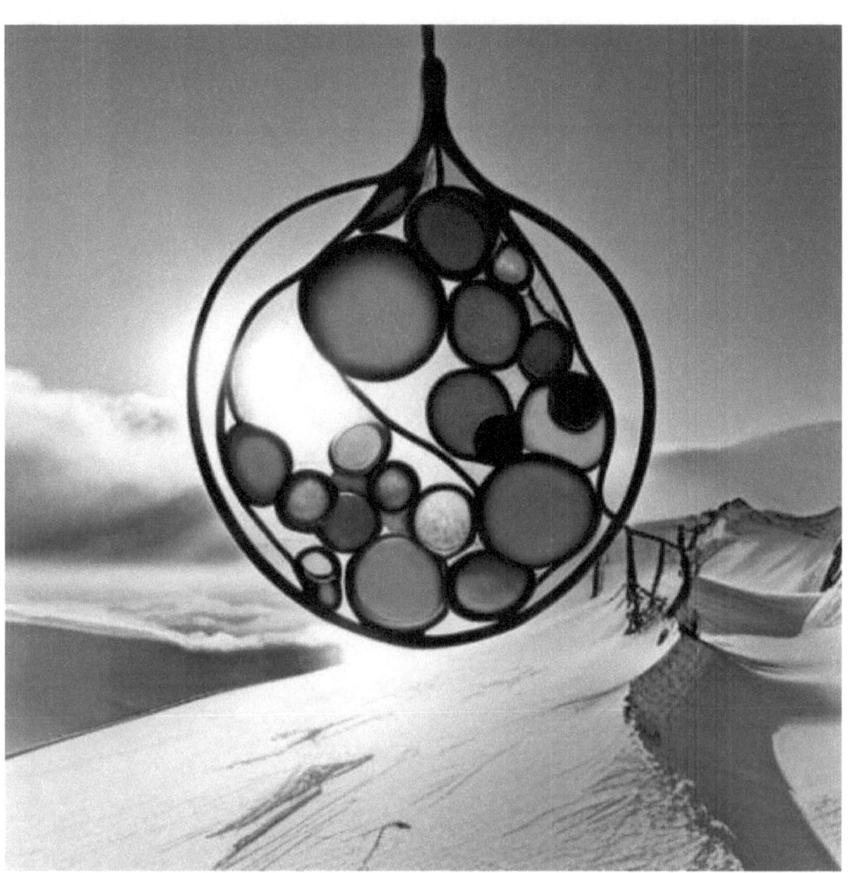

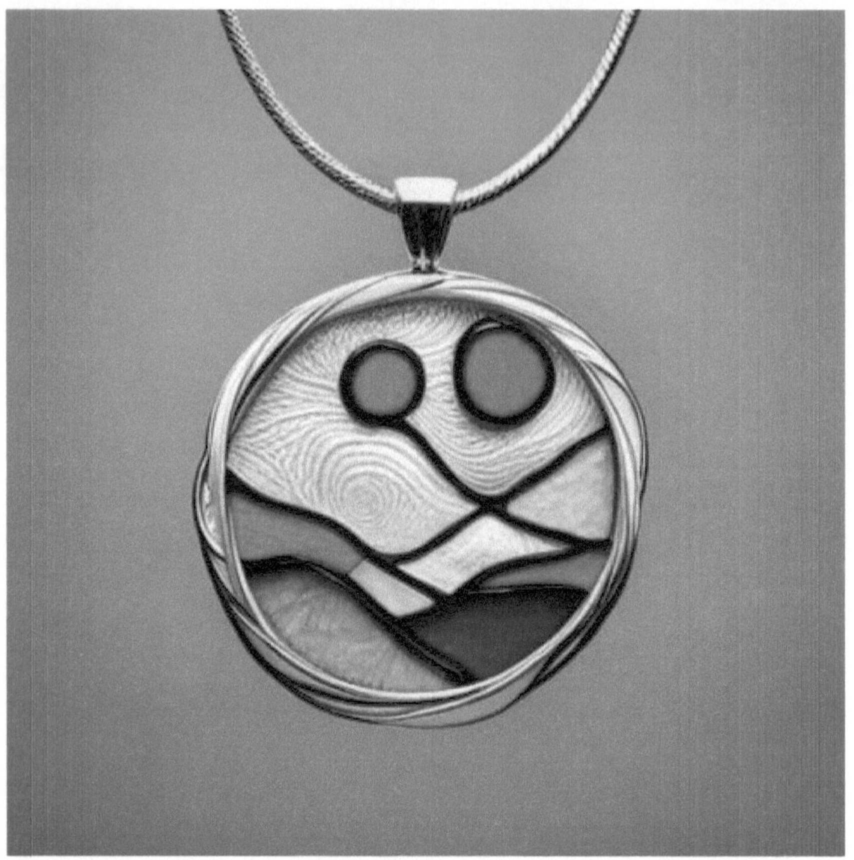

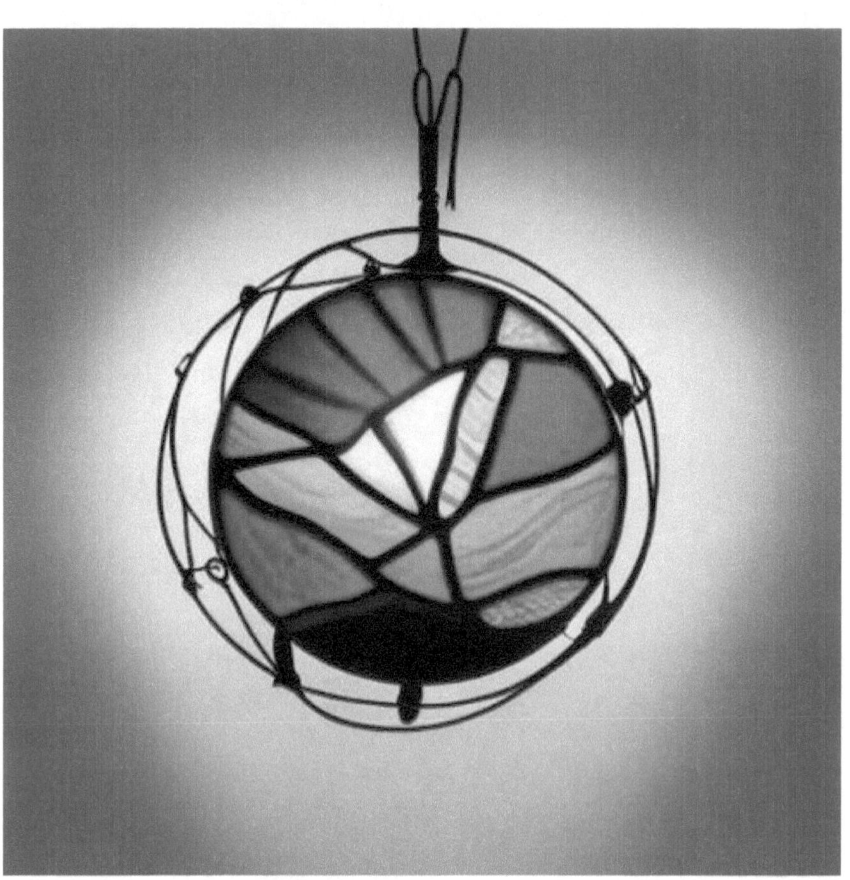

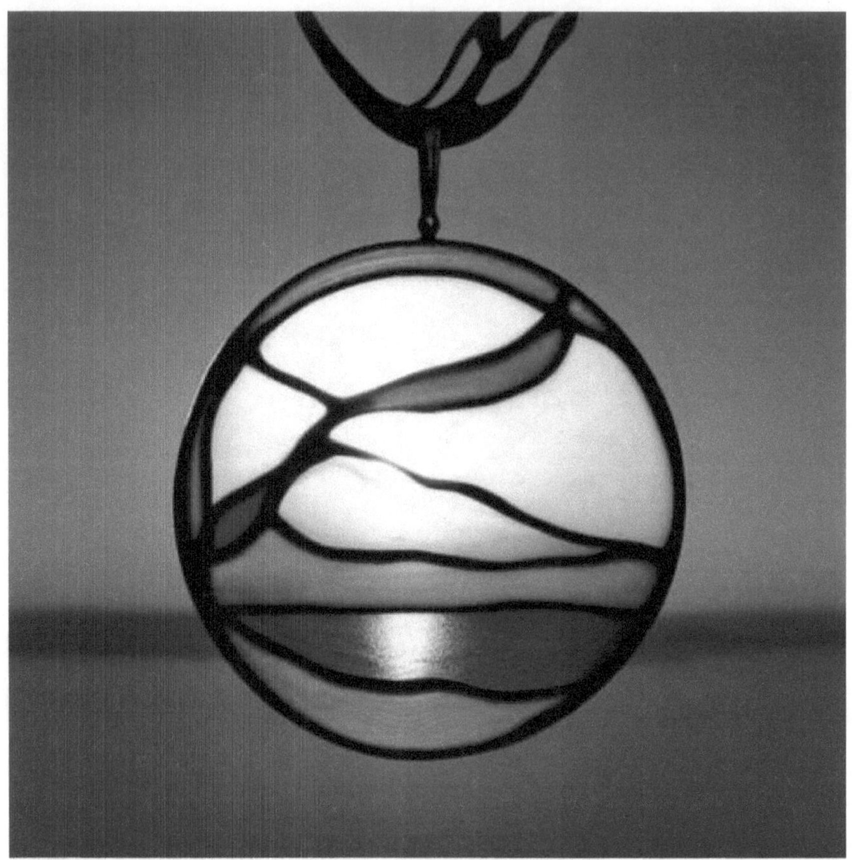

By combining the translucent beauty of stained glass with the versatility of a 3D pen, you can create a unique pendant inspired by the whimsical style of Alexander Calder. Calder's dynamic sculptures and playful use of form and color come to life in this wearable piece of art. Wear your Calder-inspired pendant with pride, showcasing your creativity and appreciation for this influential artist. This project allows you to carry a piece of Calder's imaginative and kinetic art wherever you go,

Creating a René Lalique-Inspired Pendant Using Pyrography

René Lalique, a renowned French jeweler and glass designer, made significant contributions to the Art Nouveau and Art Deco movements during the early 20th century. His distinct style, characterized by natural motifs and exquisite craftsmanship, continues to inspire artists today. In this article, we will explore how to create a pendant inspired by René Lalique using the art of pyrography, also known as wood burning. By incorporating intricate burn marks onto wooden surfaces, we can infuse our jewelry designs with Lalique's organic and artistic aesthetic. Let's delve into the process of creating a René Lalique-inspired pendant using pyrography.

Materials:

- Wood or plywood of various wood species
- Saw
- Drill
- Pyrography tool
- Sandpaper
- Varnish or lacquer
- Design template (optional)
- Pencil

Step 1: Selecting the Wood and Preparing the Surface:

Choose a piece of wood or plywood that suits your design and desired pendant size. Cut the wood into the desired shape using a saw. Use sandpaper to smooth the surface, ensuring it is clean and free from any rough edges.

Step 2: Designing the Pendant:

Consider Lalique's signature motifs, such as flowing lines, natural forms, and intricate patterns, as you plan your design. You can draw your own design directly onto the wood using a pencil or use a template for guidance.

Step 3: Transferring the Design:

If using a template, place it on the wood surface and secure it with tape. Trace the design onto the wood using a pencil, applying gentle pressure to transfer the image. Remove the template and ensure that the design is clearly visible on the wood.

Step 4: Wood Burning:

Using a pyrography tool with a fine-pointed tip, carefully trace the design lines on the wood. Adjust the temperature of the pyrography tool according to the wood's hardness and your desired burn intensity. Take your time and maintain a steady hand as you create the intricate burn marks that emulate Lalique's artistry.

Step 5: Adding Details:

Once the main design lines are burned, you can enhance the pendant by adding additional details or shading. Experiment with different techniques, such as varying the pressure or angle of the pyrography tool, to achieve desired effects and depth in your design.

Step 6: Finishing Touches:

After completing the wood burning, use sandpaper to smooth any rough areas or uneven edges. Wipe away any wood debris. Apply a coat of varnish or lacquer to protect the pendant and enhance the natural beauty of the wood. Allow the finish to dry completely before proceeding.

Step 7: Attachments and Assembly:

To transform the wood pendant into a wearable piece of jewelry, attach a jump ring or bail to the top of the pendant using pliers. Thread a chain or cord through the jump ring to complete the necklace. Alternatively, you can incorporate the wood pendant into a more elaborate jewelry design, such as combining it with beads or metal components.

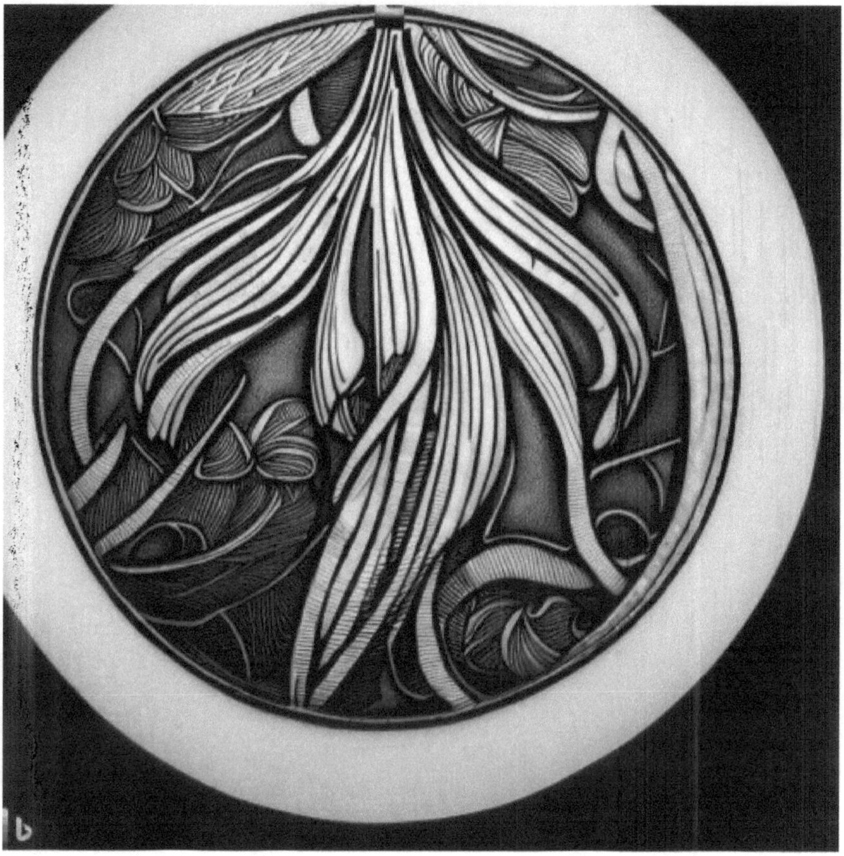

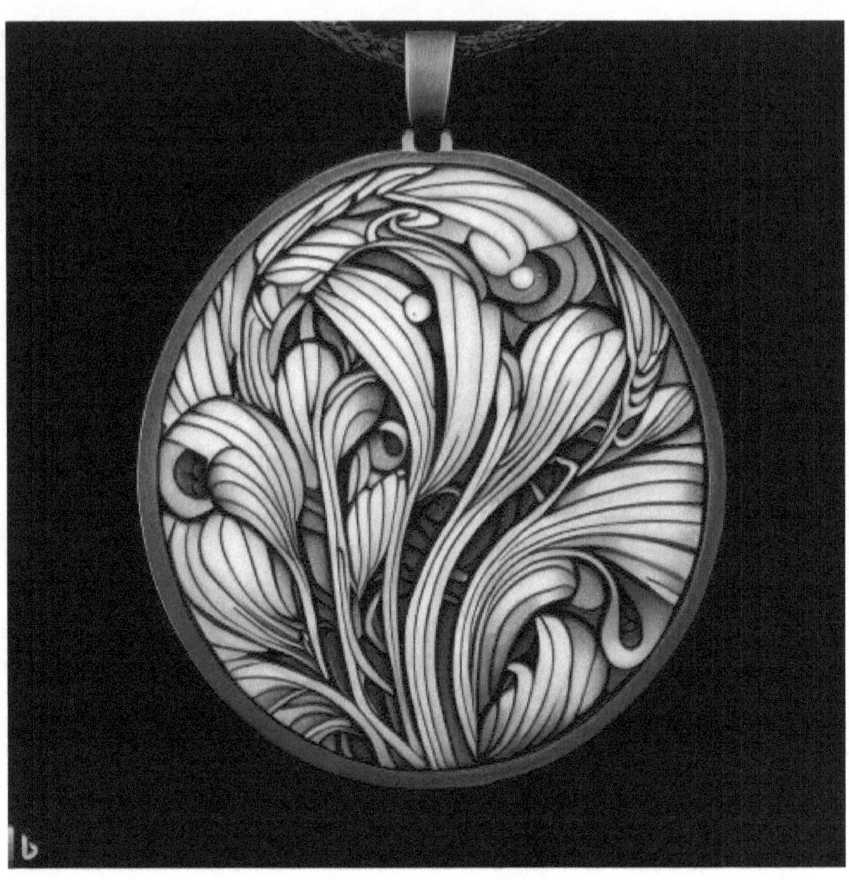

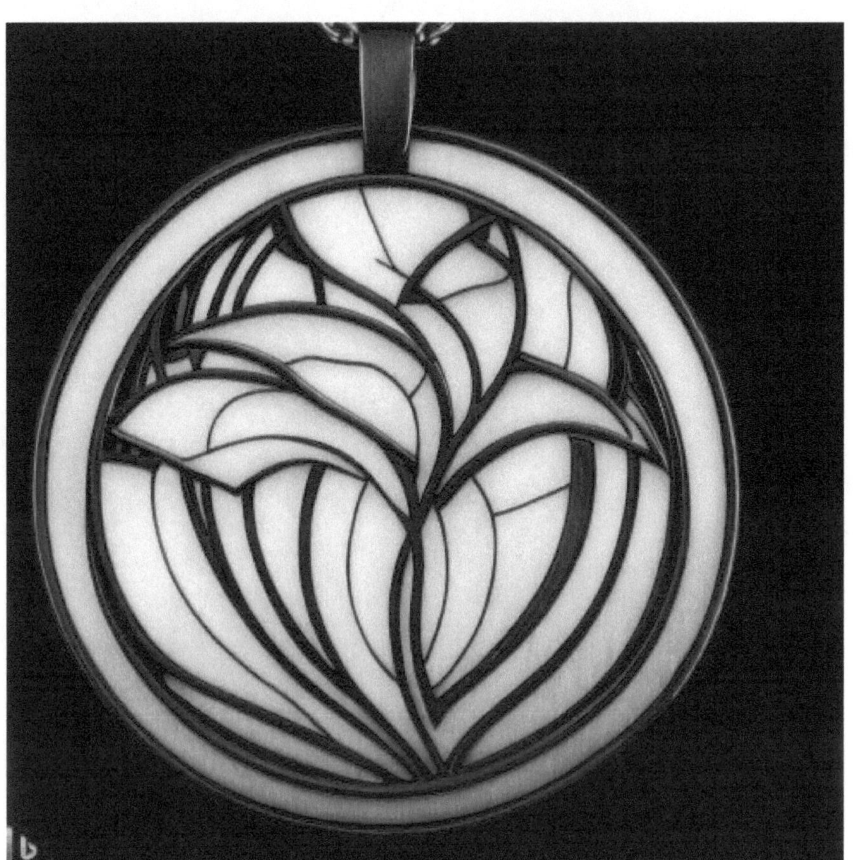

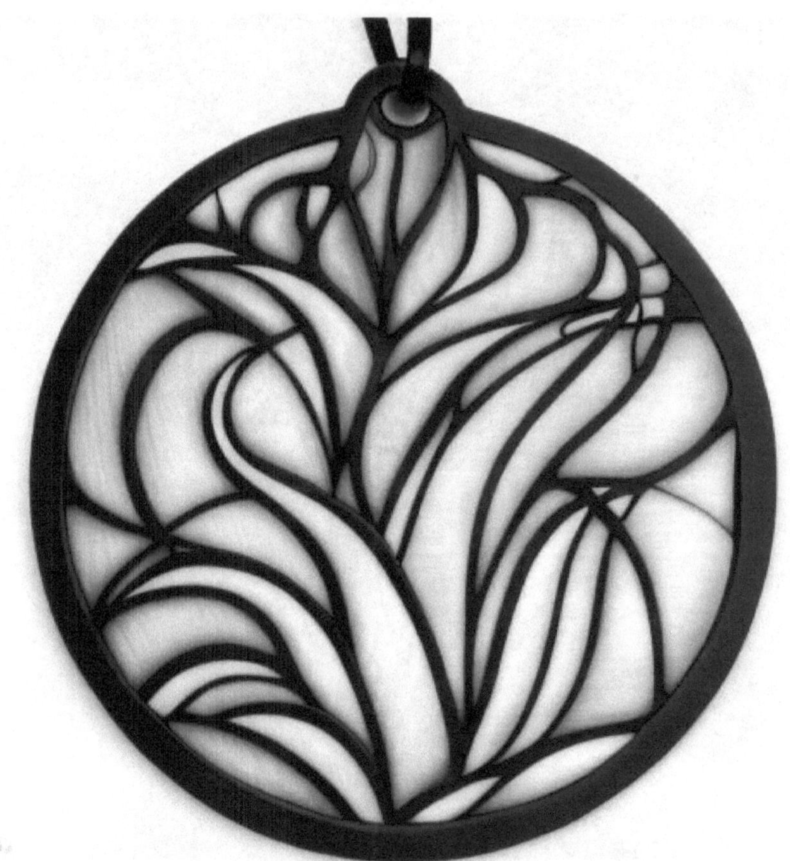

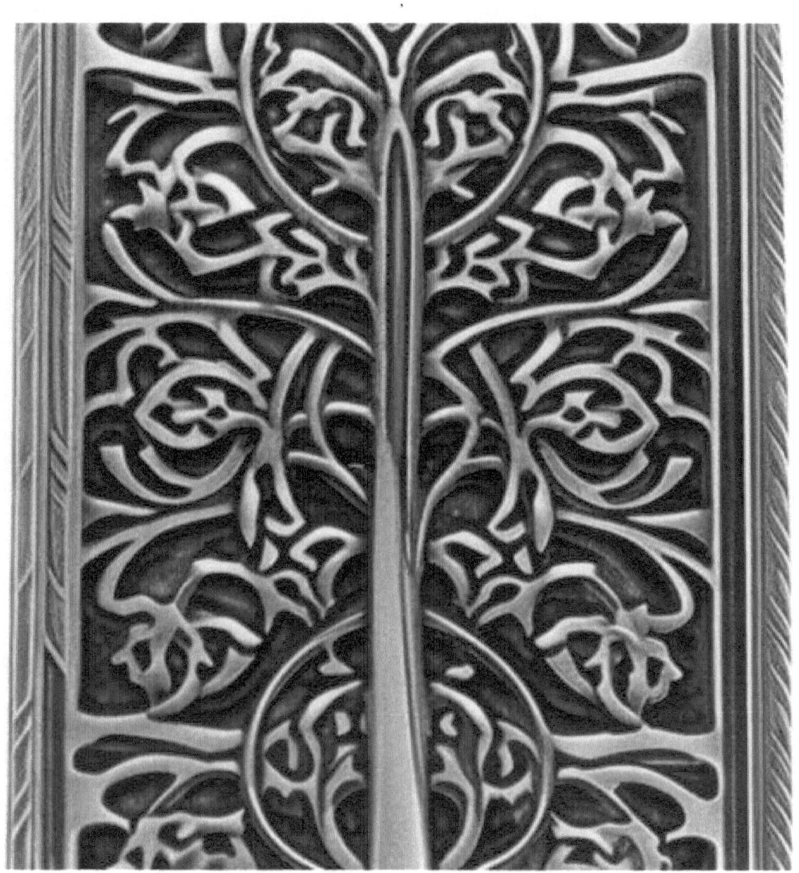

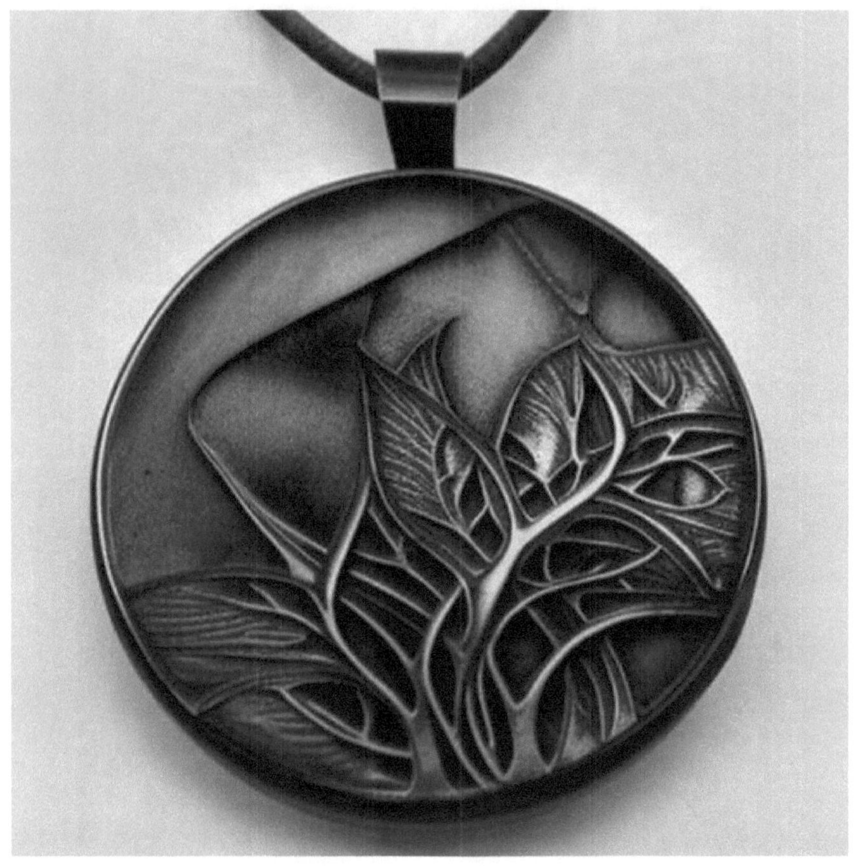

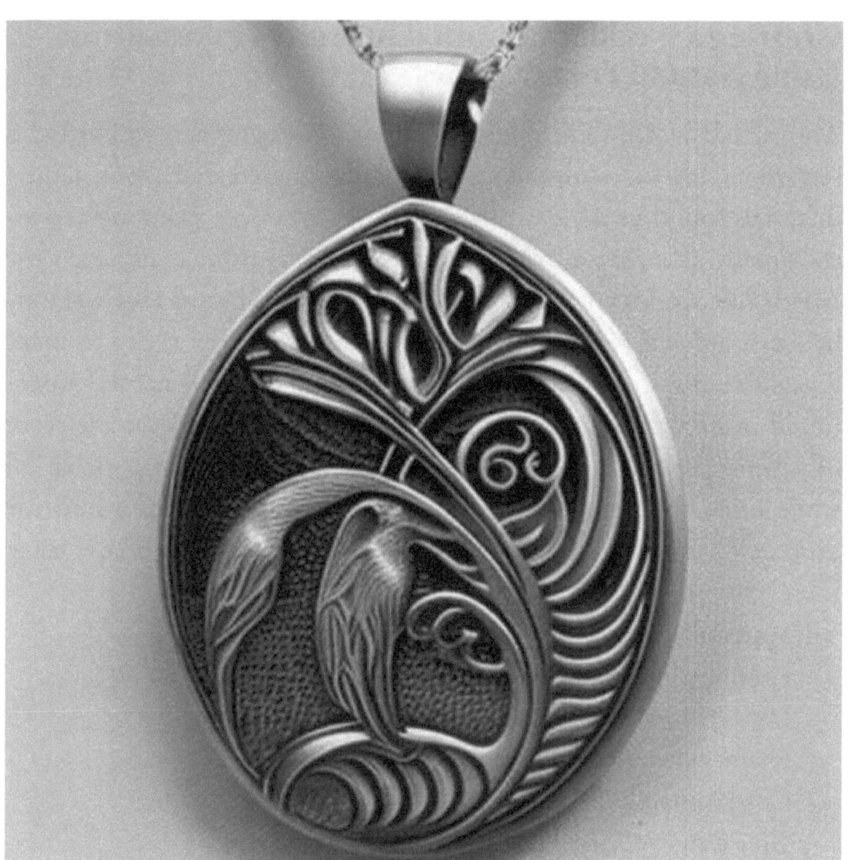

By employing the art of pyrography, we can create a pendant inspired by René Lalique's distinctive style and motifs. The careful application of burn marks onto wood surfaces allows us to emulate Lalique's organic and artistic aesthetic, infusing our jewelry designs with timeless elegance. Whether worn as a standalone pendant or incorporated into a more intricate jewelry piece, a René Lalique-inspired pendant created through pyrography showcases the beauty of natural materials and pays homage to the masterful craftsmanship of this influential artist.

Creating a Necklace Inspired by Andy Goldsworthy, Using Natural Found Stones

Andy Goldsworthy, an English sculptor, photographer, and artist, is renowned for his sculptures and installations created from natural materials found in the environment. With artworks spanning various continents, from Japan to the United States, Australia, and even the North Pole, Goldsworthy's creations showcase the beauty and harmony between art and nature. In this article, we will explore how to make a necklace inspired by Andy Goldsworthy's style using natural stones found in nature. By incorporating these stones into a wearable piece of jewelry, we can capture the essence of Goldsworthy's artistic vision while celebrating the organic beauty of nature. Let's delve into the process of creating an Andy Goldsworthy-inspired necklace using found stones.

Materials:

Found stones of various shapes, sizes, and colors

Drill

Diamond-coated drill bit

Cord or string

Glue gun (optional)

Varnish or lacquer (optional)

Step 1: Collecting and Preparing the Stones:

Embark on a nature walk to collect an assortment of stones that catch your eye. Look for stones of different shapes, sizes, and colors to add visual interest to your necklace. Once collected, clean the stones thoroughly using water and a brush to remove any dirt or debris. Allow the stones to dry completely before proceeding.

Step 2: Drilling Holes in the Stones:

Using a drill fitted with a diamond-coated drill bit, carefully drill holes into the stones. Start with a low drill speed and apply gentle pressure to avoid cracking or damaging the stones. Take your time and ensure the holes are clean and smooth. The number of stones and holes will depend on your desired necklace design.

Step 3: Stringing the Stones:

Choose a durable and aesthetically pleasing cord or string to thread the stones. Consider the color and thickness of the cord, keeping in mind that it should complement the stones while providing sufficient strength to support the necklace. Thread the stones through the holes, arranging them in a pattern or layout that appeals to you.

Step 4: Securing the Stones (Optional):

For added durability, you can use a glue gun to secure the stones in place on the cord. Apply a small amount of hot glue around the hole on each stone and press firmly onto the cord. Be cautious not to use excessive glue that may detract from the natural beauty of the stones.

Step 5: Finishing Touches (Optional):

To protect the stones and enhance their natural beauty, consider applying a coat of varnish or lacquer. This step is particularly beneficial if the stones have porous surfaces or if you desire a polished finish. Apply the varnish or lacquer according to the manufacturer's instructions and allow it to dry completely before wearing the necklace.

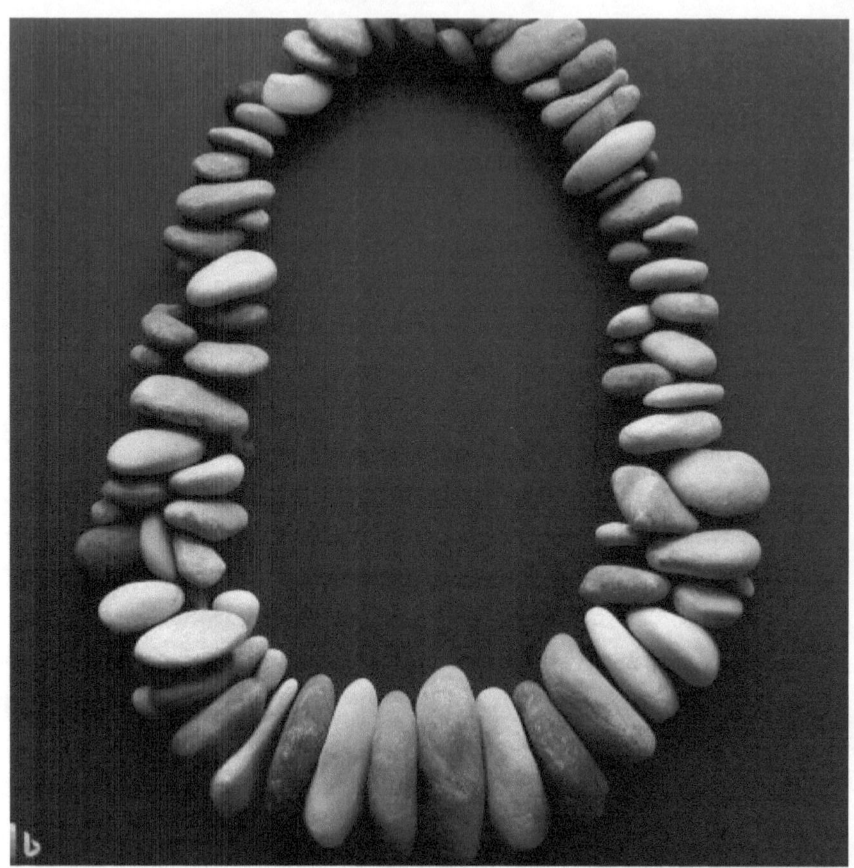

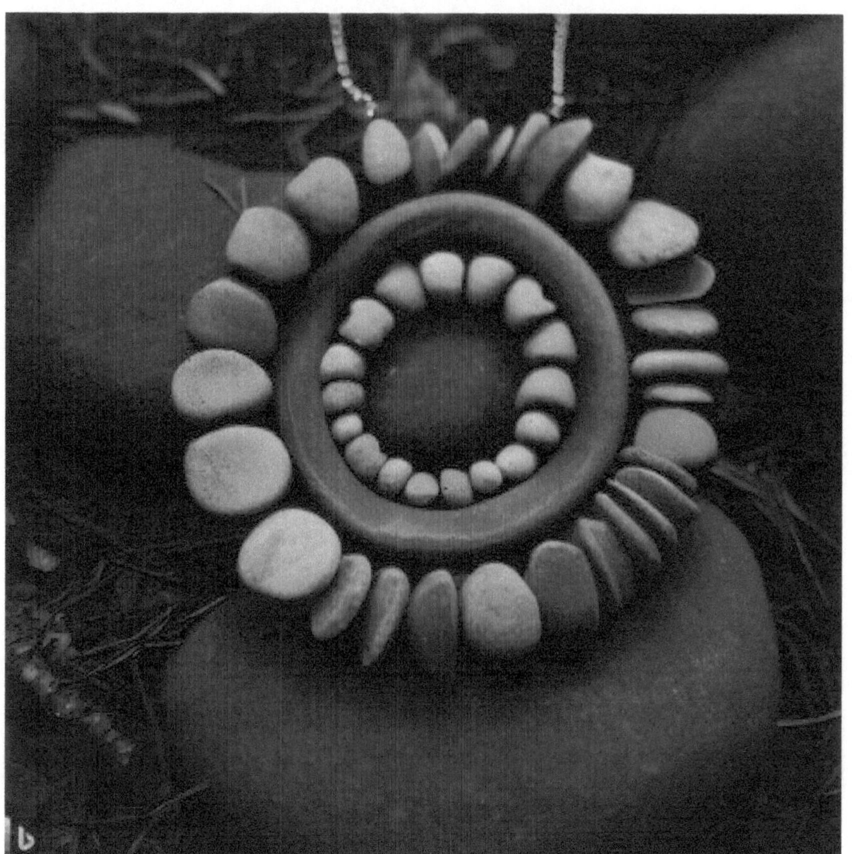

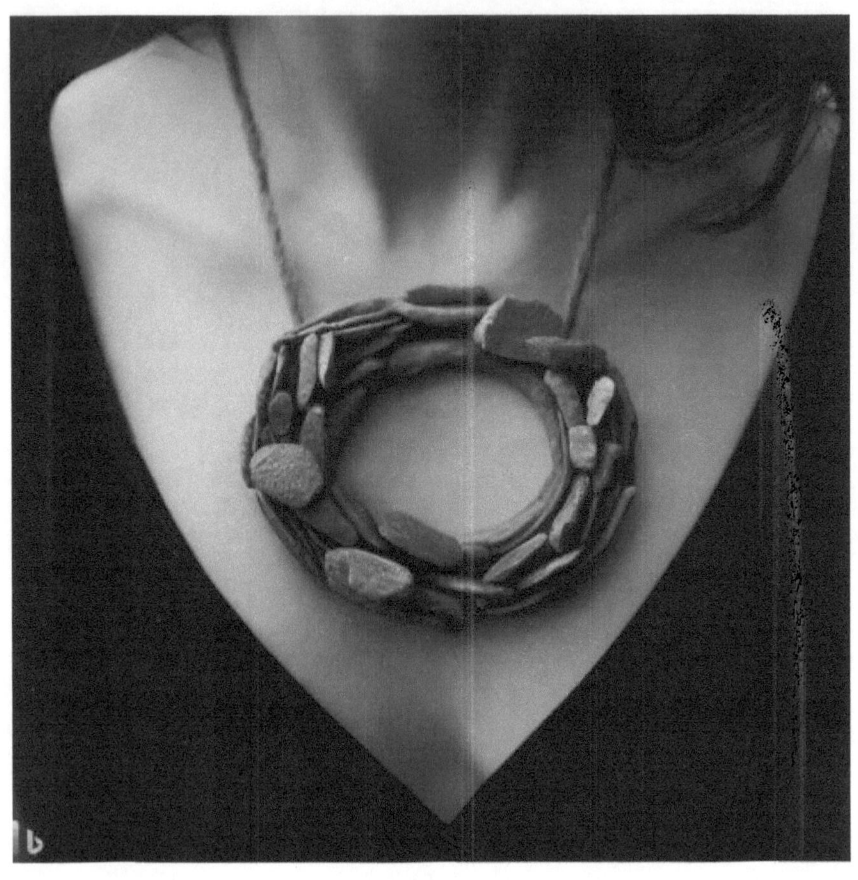

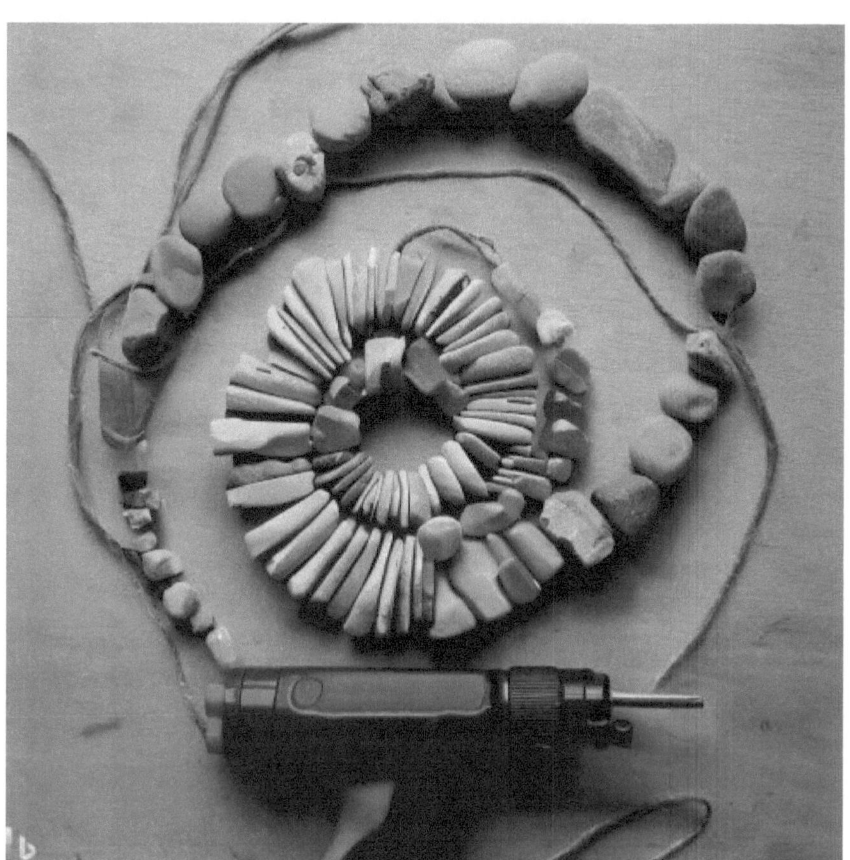

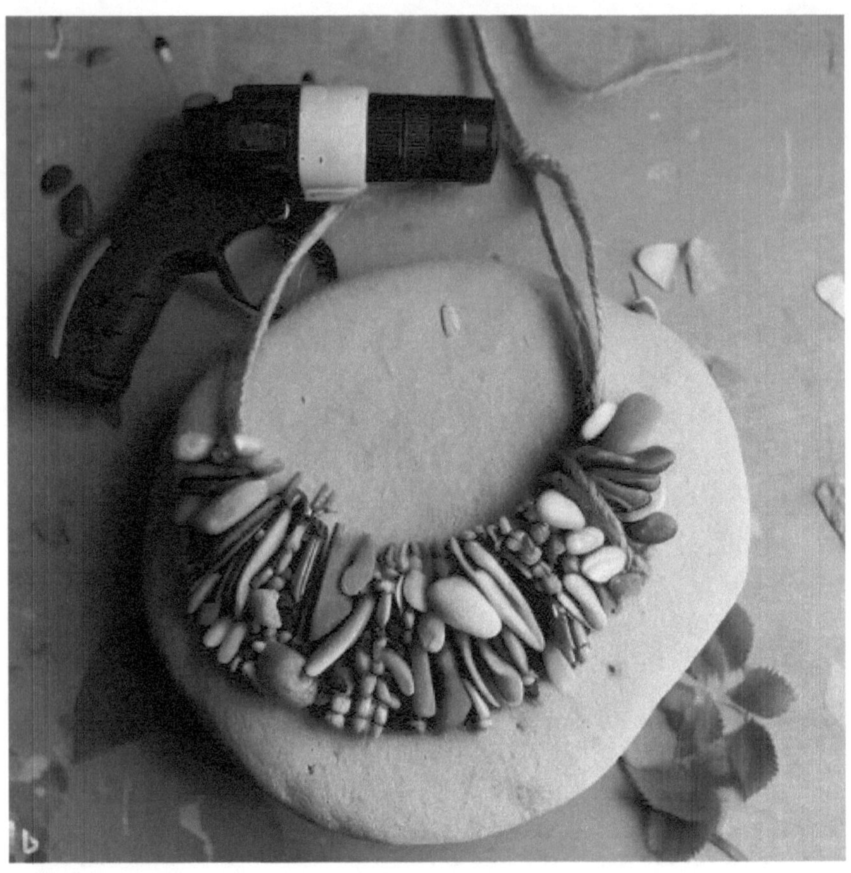

Creating a necklace inspired by Andy Goldsworthy allows us to embrace the beauty and simplicity found in nature. By collecting and incorporating natural stones into a wearable piece of art, we pay homage to Goldsworthy's philosophy of using found materials to create harmonious and organic creations. Through drilling holes, stringing the stones, and optionally securing them with glue, we can transform these found stones into a unique necklace that encapsulates the essence of Goldsworthy's artistic style. Whether worn as a statement piece or a subtle accent, an Andy Goldsworthy-inspired necklace made from natural

found stones serves as a reminder of the profound connection between art and the natural world.

Creating a Pendant in the Style of Winslow Homer Using Sea Glass

Winslow Homer, an American painter renowned for his marine subjects, created some of the most expressive and captivating artworks of late 19th-century American art. His vibrant and diverse range of styles and subjects showcased his mastery and vitality as an artist. In this article, we will explore how to make a pendant inspired by Winslow Homer's style using sea glass. Sea glass, with its smooth and frosted appearance, holds a unique charm that resonates with jewelry makers. Drawing inspiration from the soothing colors and organic shapes depicted in coastal landscapes, artists can transform discarded glass fragments into exquisite jewelry pieces. By bezel-setting sea glass, we can create elegant and ethereal pendants that capture the essence of coastal beauty. Let's dive into the process of creating a Winslow Homer-inspired pendant using sea glass.

Materials:

- Sea glass in suitable sizes and colors

- Acrylic paints in various colors

- Bezel setting materials such as a glue gun with black sticks or wire for creating a frame

Step 1: Selecting and Preparing Sea Glass:
Gather a collection of sea glass pieces in colors and sizes that resonate with Winslow Homer's coastal palette. Look for glass fragments with smooth, frosted surfaces that resemble the sea-tumbled appearance. Clean the sea glass thoroughly to remove any dirt or residue, ensuring they are ready for the next steps.

Step 2: Painting Sea Glass (Optional):

To enhance the colors and create unique effects, you can paint the sea glass using acrylic paints. Winslow Homer's paintings often feature vibrant and harmonious hues, so consider using colors inspired by his artwork. Apply thin layers of acrylic paint to the smooth side of the sea glass, allowing each layer to dry before adding another. Experiment with blending colors and creating subtle gradients to achieve the desired effect.

Step 3: Creating the Bezel Setting:

To showcase the sea glass and give the pendant structure, you can create a bezel setting using a glue gun with black sticks or wire. If using a glue gun, carefully apply hot glue around the edges of the sea glass, forming a frame-like structure. Alternatively, shape wire to fit the contours of the sea glass, creating a secure and decorative frame. Ensure the bezel setting securely holds the sea glass while allowing its beauty to shine through.

Step 4: Assembling the Pendant:

Once the sea glass is painted (if desired) and the bezel setting is ready, carefully insert the sea glass into the setting. Ensure a snug fit, adjusting the bezel or wire frame as necessary. Pay attention to the pendant's balance and aesthetics, ensuring it reflects the artistic harmony found in Winslow Homer's works.

Step 5: Finishing Touches:

Inspect the pendant to ensure all elements are securely in place. If using a glue gun, allow the glue to cool and harden fully before handling. Consider adding additional decorative elements such as small seashells, tiny beach stones, or even miniature paintings inspired by Winslow Homer's seascapes. These details can further enhance the pendant's coastal charm.

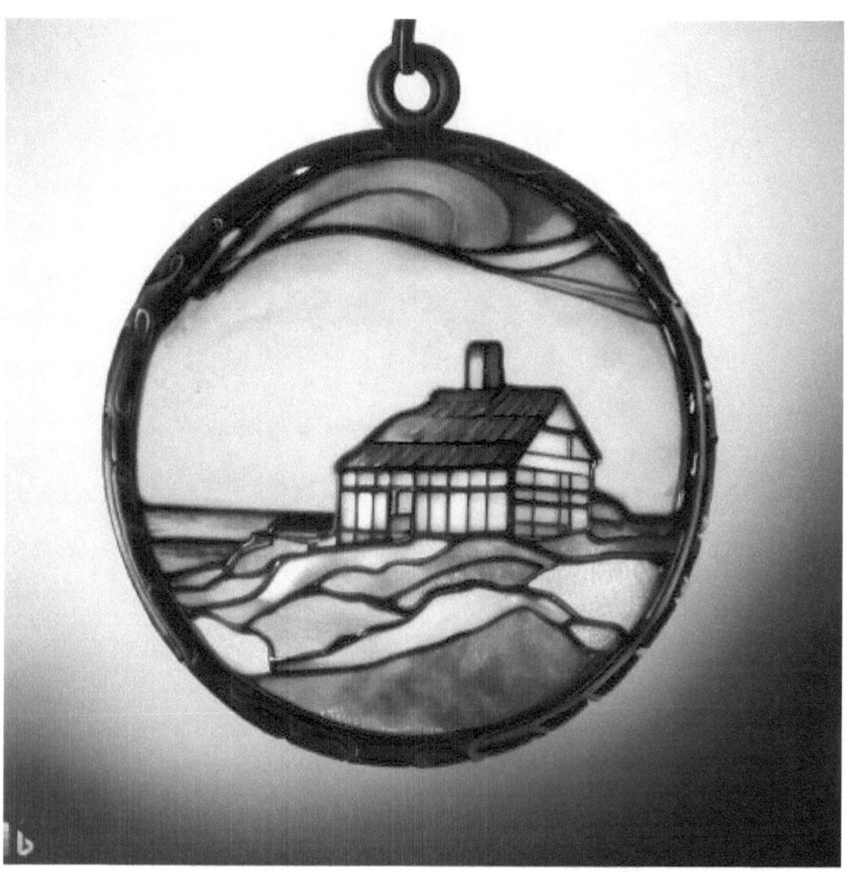

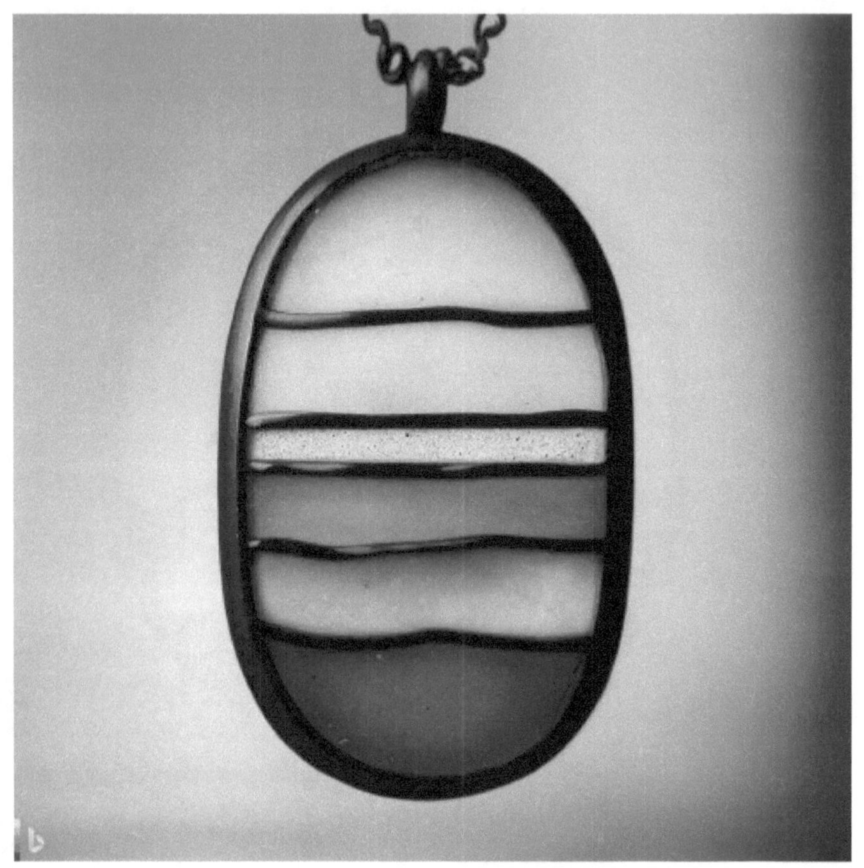

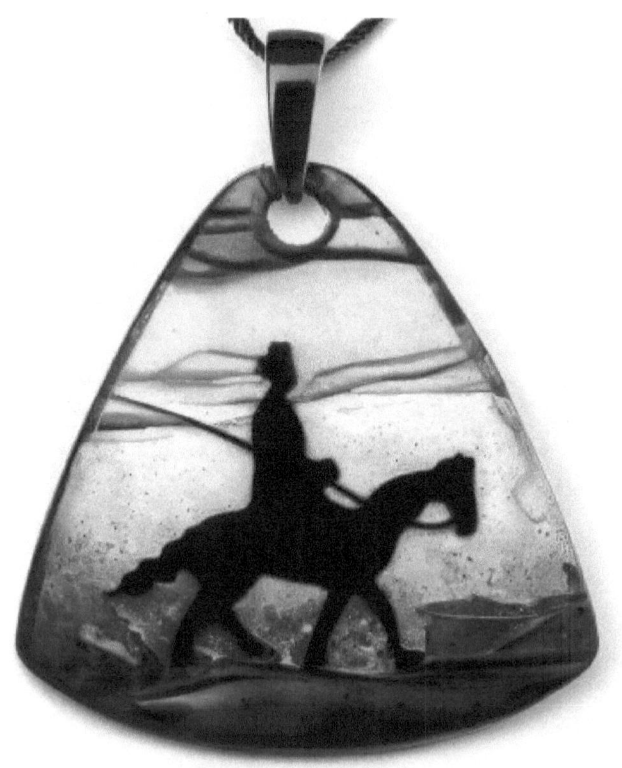

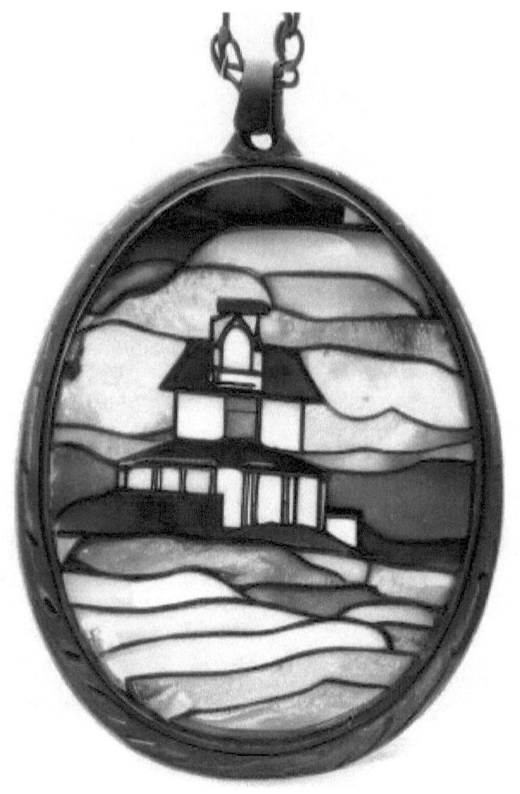

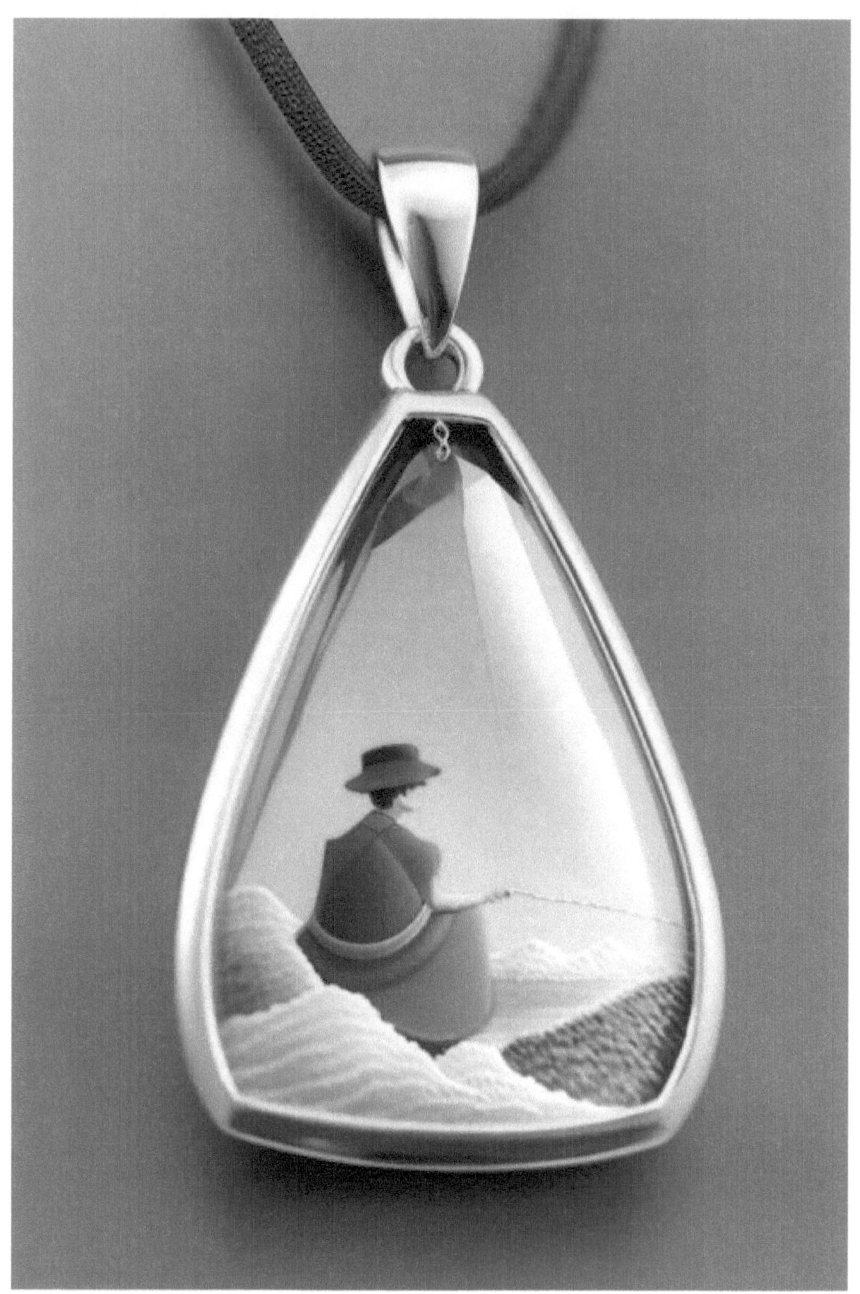

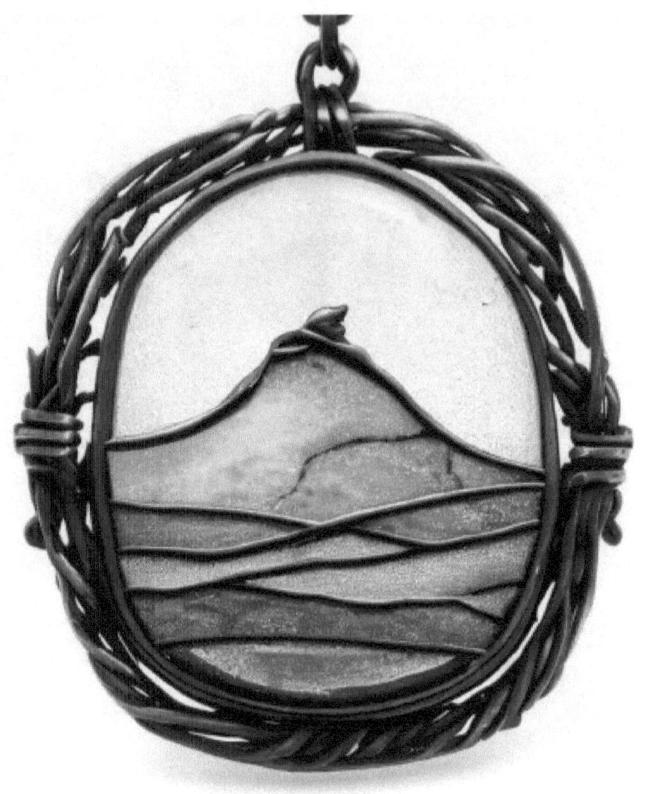

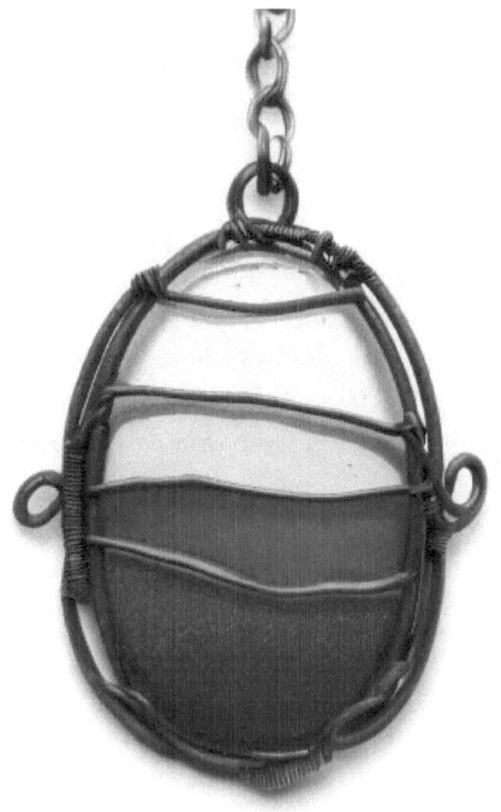

Creating a pendant inspired by Winslow Homer's style using sea glass allows us to encapsulate the beauty and serenity of coastal landscapes within wearable art. By selecting sea glass in hues reminiscent of Homer's palette and employing a bezel setting, we can transform discarded glass fragments into elegant and ethereal jewelry pieces. Whether painted or left in their natural state, the sea glass pendants pay homage to Winslow Homer's mastery of capturing the marine environment's essence. Wearing a Winslow Homer-inspired pendant not only celebrates the beauty of the sea but also serves as a personal connection to the artistry and inspiration of one of America's most revered painters.

Inspiring Jewelry: Transforming Art into Wearable Masterpieces

As we reach the conclusion of this book, I would like to offer you a collection of pages featuring images of jewelry inspired by famous artists. These small images can serve as a starting point for creating your own brooch, pendant, or keychain. By framing them and covering them with clear epoxy resin, you can showcase their beauty while also protecting the artwork. Alternatively, you may discover other creative ways to incorporate these images into your designs. They can serve as a source of inspiration, guiding you to create your unique jewelry pieces. In the world of contemporary jewelry making, artisans are constantly exploring new techniques and materials to bring wearable art to life, drawing inspiration from the works of renowned artists. Let's explore the possibilities of transforming art into stunning jewelry.

Exploring Artistic Inspirations:

Art has long been a wellspring of inspiration for jewelry makers. The mesmerizing brushstrokes, vibrant colors, and captivating motifs found in the works of famous artists provide endless possibilities for creating unique and expressive jewelry pieces. By studying the masterpieces of renowned artists, we can identify elements that resonate with us and translate them into wearable art.

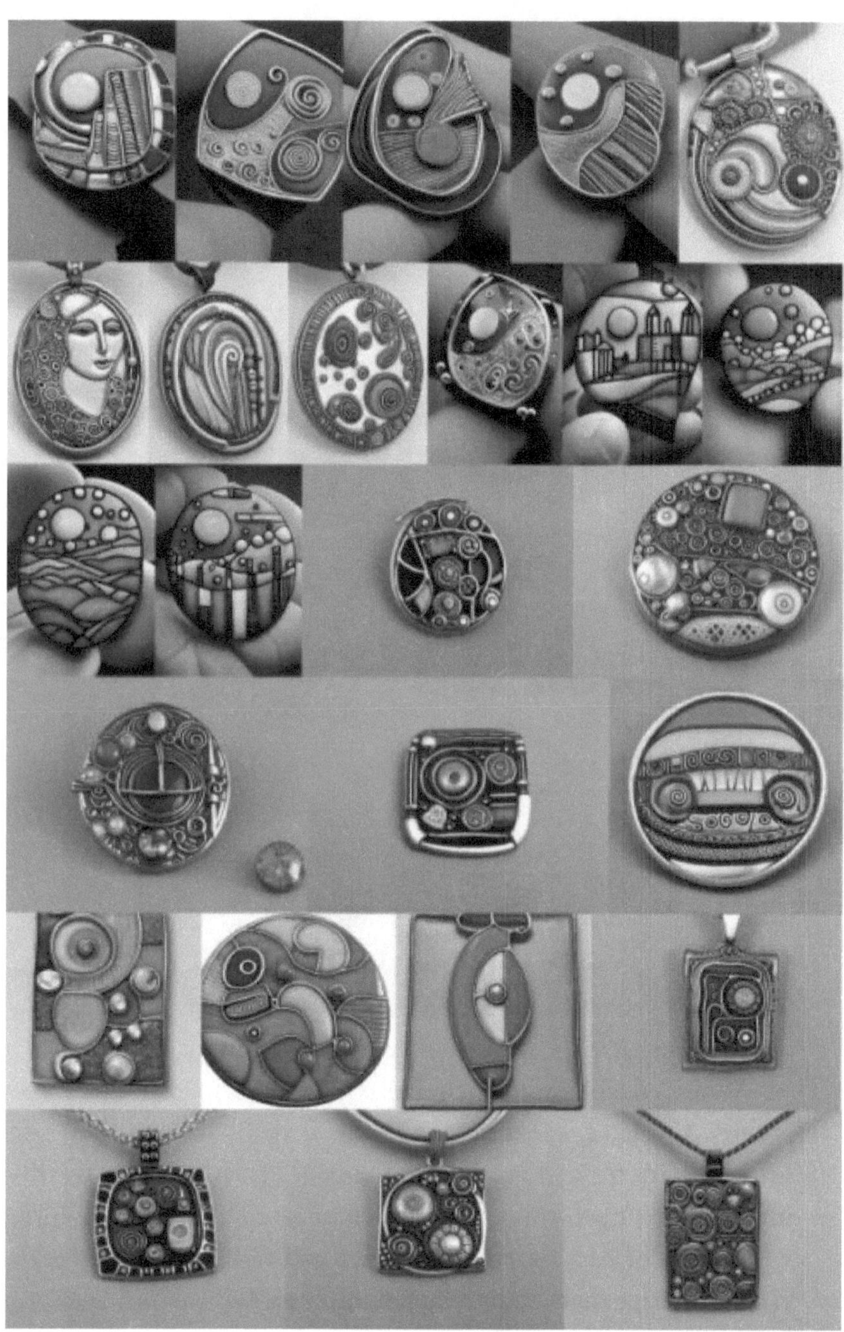

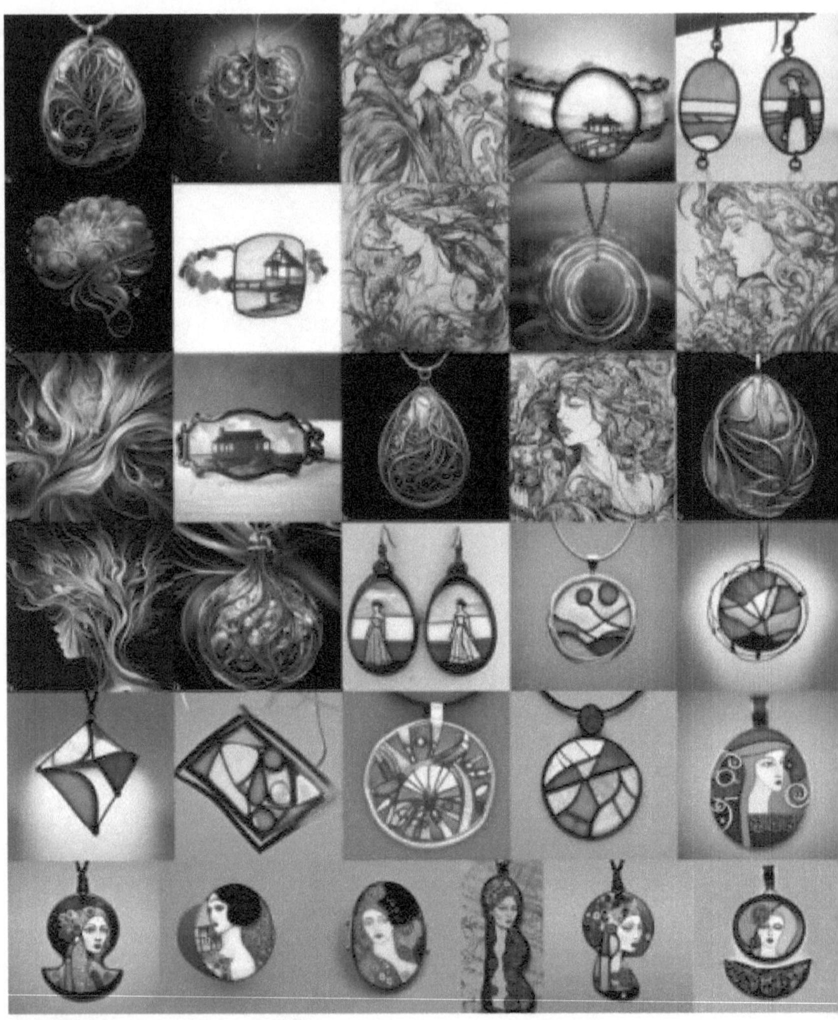

Selecting Artistic Motifs:

When considering which artists' motifs to incorporate into your jewelry, you have a wealth of options. Perhaps you are drawn to the intricate patterns and geometric shapes of Piet Mondrian, the flowing lines and organic forms of Gustav Klimt, or the kinetic sculptures and wire figures of Alexander Calder. Each artist offers a distinct style and visual language that can be adapted into wearable masterpieces.

Materials and Techniques:

To bring these artistic visions to life, jewelry makers employ various techniques and materials. For instance, wire wrapping can be used to mimic the flowing lines seen in Klimt's works. Polymer clay provides versatility for replicating Mondrian's vibrant color blocks and geometric shapes. Wood burning, or pyrography, allows for intricate etchings inspired by René Lalique's natural motifs. Sea glass and bezel settings can capture the essence of coastal beauty reminiscent of Winslow Homer's marine landscapes. The possibilities are limited only by your imagination and the materials at your disposal.

Crafting Unique Jewelry Pieces:

Once you have chosen your artistic inspiration and gathered the necessary materials, it's time to unleash your creativity. Consider how you can adapt the artistic motifs into wearable forms. Experiment with different techniques, such as wirework, clay molding, resin casting, or bead embroidery, to bring the essence of the artwork into your jewelry.

Preserving and Showcasing the Artwork:

To transform the small images into wearable masterpieces, protect them by encasing them in a frame and covering them with clear epoxy resin. This will not only preserve the artwork but also create a glossy and durable finish. The resin will enhance the colors and details, giving your jewelry a professional and polished look.

Inspiration for Personal Expression:

The images provided serve as a starting point for your creative journey, but they are not the endpoint. Let them ignite your imagination and inspire you to develop your unique designs. Use them as a springboard to experiment with different materials, techniques, and styles, allowing your personal expression to shine through in each piece of jewelry you create.

Conclusion:

As we conclude this book, I hope the collection of images featuring jewelry inspired by famous artists has sparked your creativity and imagination. The world of contemporary jewelry making offers endless possibilities for transforming art into wearable masterpieces. Whether you choose to recreate the depicted designs or use them as a catalyst for your unique creations, the fusion of art and jewelry allows for self-expression and individuality. Embrace the artistic inspiration, explore new techniques, and let your imagination soar as you embark on your jewelry-making journey.